Modern Data Architecture in AI

Optimize AI data storage, versioning, and partitioning with lakehouse

Abhik Choudhury

Praneeth Puchakayala

Aishwarya Badlani

bpb

www.bpbonline.com

First Edition 2025

To View Complete
BPB Publications Catalogue
Scan the QR Code:

Dedicated to

My wife, daughter, son and parents
                                    - Abhik Choudhury

*This book is dedicated to my family, friends, mentors, and,
above all, those teachers and lecturers who shaped my path*
                                    - Praneeth Puchakayala

Dedicated this book to my mom
                                    - Aishwarya Badlani

About the Authors

- **Abhik Choudhury**, based in Exton, PA, USA, is an analytics managing consultant and data scientist with more than 13 years of experience in scalable data solutions. He specializes in AI/ML, cloud computing, database management, and big data technologies. Abhik excels in leading teams and collaborating with stakeholders to drive data-driven decisions in pharmacy, medical claims, and drug distribution. His technical skills include cloud solutions, business intelligence, data visualization, machine learning, and data warehousing. Proficient in Python, R, SQL, and various cloud data platforms like Databricks, Google Cloud, and AWS, he holds an MS in analytics from Georgia Institute of Technology. At IBM, Abhik designs data architecture solutions for healthcare and pharma clients, focusing on legal and compliance platforms. His previous roles include senior data scientist, lead business intelligence engineer, and business intelligence analyst at IBM, where he implemented data models, ETL pipelines, machine learning models, and analytical reports.

- **Praneeth Reddy Amudala Puchakayala** is an accomplished data scientist and designer of scalable, innovative solutions using machine learning, AI, and advanced analytics. He is experienced in several industry verticals, including financial services and healthcare, and he helps his clients achieve high impact with data-driven and results-oriented strategies. With a strong foundation in applied research and real-world problem-solving, Praneeth provides a thoughtful combination of technical depth along with practical implementation. He is an active contributor to the AI community as a speaker, reviewer, and mentor.

- **Aishwarya Badlani** is a passionate data scientist and analytics leader specializing in transforming complex data into strategic business insights. With a background spanning marketing analytics, customer behavior modeling, and AI-powered decision systems, she brings a unique blend of technical expertise and business acumen to every project.Aishwarya has made significant contributions across the retail and e-commerce industries, where she has helped drive customer-centric growth through data innovation. Her work integrates advanced analytics, experimentation, and AI to solve real-world challenges at scale. An advocate for continuous learning and mentorship, Aishwarya actively engages with the data and AI community as a speaker, collaborator, and lifelong learner.

About the Reviewer

Srik Gorthy is a senior data scientist at TikTok, leveraging over 11 years of expertise in machine learning, artificial intelligence, and data-driven innovation. Throughout his career, he has worked at renowned organizations like Google and AMD and co-founded his own music and social media startup, showcasing his entrepreneurial spirit and technical acumen.

Srik is a certified expert coach, deeply passionate about mentoring and guiding professionals in their data science careers, having supported over 25 individuals in achieving their goals. He is a frequent speaker at major technical conferences and workshops, where he shares insights on AI, data science, trust and safety, and automation. As a peer reviewer, he has contributed to books and publications on AI and data science, helping to shape the future of the field. Srik's dedication to fostering learning and innovation has made him a respected leader in the global AI and data science community.

Acknowledgements

This book would not have been possible without the invaluable support and contributions of many individuals and organizations. We are deeply grateful to the vibrant AI and data engineering community whose shared knowledge, open-source contributions, and thought leadership have shaped the foundations of this work.

We would like to extend special thanks to our technical reviewers who provided critical insights and helped refine complex concepts into practical guidance. We extend our appreciation to the teams at leading technology companies and class-leading platforms, including Databricks, AWS, Google Cloud, and Microsoft Azure, whose class-leading innovations continue to push the boundaries of what is possible in AI data architecture.

We owe sincere gratitude to our family and colleagues for their patience and encouragement throughout this journey, and to the countless practitioners who shared their real-world experiences and challenges.

Finally, we are immensely grateful to BPB Publications for their guidance and expertise in bringing this book to fruition. Their support and assistance were invaluable in navigating the complexities of the publishing process.

Preface

In the burgeoning world of artificial intelligence, modern data architecture designed specifically to facilitate AI and ML is crucial to support building scalable and intelligent systems. The aim of this book is to provide a deep exploration of the tools, technologies, strategies, and best practices that necessitate the design, implementation, and management of data architectures tailored to AI.

The book starts by introducing basic concepts of modern data architecture for AI, laying the groundwork for understanding its importance. It then digs deep into the aspects of data ingestion and collection strategies. Subsequently, it discusses data storage and management techniques that cater specifically to AI workloads. Readers will understand the concepts of data processing, transformation, and building scalable and efficient data pipelines and how to orchestrate interconnected processes. There are chapters dedicated to data governance, security, and compliance aspects, as well as the impact of AI algorithms on data architecture. The book further unravels the topics of scalable machine learning infrastructure and stream processing, concluding with insights into visualization, explainable AI, and future trends.

By the end of this book, the readers will have a comprehensive understanding and skills to develop and manage scalable and efficient AI systems. They will have firm grasp on collection, storage, processing and transformation of data, ensuring data governance and security. This book empowers readers to build cutting-edge AI solutions and spearhead in the dynamic field of AI data architecture.

Chapter 1: Introduction to Modern Data Architecture for AI

This chapter introduces the fundamental concepts of modern data architecture for AI systems, covering the evolution from traditional databases to distributed and cloud-native solutions. It explores the unique challenges of AI data management, including scalability, real-time processing, and handling unstructured data. The chapter discusses key technologies like data lakes, data warehouses, and emerging paradigms such as data mesh. It also introduces essential tools and platforms for AI data architecture, setting the foundation for the rest of the book.

Chapter 2: Data Collection and Ingestion Strategies

This chapter explores various strategies and technologies for efficient data collection and ingestion in AI systems. It covers both batch and real-time data ingestion methods, emphasizing scalable architectures and tools. The chapter discusses data quality and validation techniques essential for maintaining the integrity of AI datasets. It also addresses security and compliance considerations in data ingestion. The focus is on practical approaches using modern tools and platforms, with special attention to cloud-native and distributed processing solutions.

Chapter 3: Data Storage and Management for AI Workloads

This chapter examines modern data storage and management solutions optimized for AI workloads. It compares traditional, NoSQL, and NewSQL databases, focusing on their suitability for different AI applications. The chapter explores distributed storage systems and cloud-based solutions, emphasizing scalability and performance. It discusses data versioning, lineage, and metadata management crucial for AI development. The chapter also covers strategies for efficient data organization, including partitioning and indexing, tailored for AI-specific access patterns.

Chapter 4: Data Processing and Transformation for AI

This chapter focuses on essential data processing and transformation techniques for AI applications. It explores both batch and stream processing paradigms, emphasizing scalable solutions for large datasets. The chapter covers feature engineering at scale, data normalization, and strategies for handling imbalanced datasets. It discusses GPU-accelerated data processing and automated preprocessing pipelines. The chapter also addresses data augmentation techniques and the integration of data processing with machine learning workflows.

Chapter 5: Modern Data Pipeline Management

This chapter explores the design and implementation of robust data pipelines for AI systems. It covers workflow management and orchestration tools, emphasizing scalability and reliability. The chapter discusses monitoring, error handling, and performance optimization in data pipelines. It addresses CI/CD practices for data workflows and explores serverless architectures for data processing. The chapter also covers testing and validation strategies for ensuring data pipeline integrity and examines how modern cloud platforms facilitate end-to-end pipeline management.

Chapter 6: Data Governance, Security, and Compliance in AI

This chapter addresses critical aspects of data governance, security, and compliance in AI systems. It explores frameworks for ethical AI data management and privacy-preserving techniques. The chapter covers regulatory compliance requirements and their impact on AI data architectures. It discusses data encryption, access control, and audit trail mechanisms. The chapter also addresses bias detection and mitigation in AI datasets, emphasizing responsible AI practices. It examines how modern data platforms integrate these governance and security features into the AI development lifecycle.

Chapter 7: AI Algorithms and Their Impact on Data Architecture

This chapter examines various AI algorithms and their influence on data architecture design. It covers the spectrum from traditional machine learning to deep learning and reinforcement learning, focusing on their unique data requirements. The chapter explores large language models and generative AI, discussing their massive data needs and architectural implications. It addresses federated learning and edge AI, highlighting their impact on distributed data architectures. The chapter also covers AutoML and neural architecture search, examining how these technologies shape data management strategies.

Chapter 8: Scalable Machine Learning Infrastructure

This chapter focuses on building and managing scalable infrastructure for machine learning workflows. It explores distributed training architectures and efficient model serving strategies for large-scale AI applications. The chapter covers AutoML and hyperparameter optimization techniques, emphasizing their role in streamlining ML pipelines. It discusses containerization and orchestration for ML workloads, as well as MLOps practices for managing the entire ML lifecycle. The chapter also addresses edge AI and federated learning infrastructures, highlighting their unique scaling challenges and solutions.

Chapter 9: Real-time AI Systems and Stream Processing

This chapter explores the architecture and implementation of real-time AI systems, focusing on stream processing technologies and their integration with AI models. It covers online learning and adaptive models for continuously evolving data streams. The chapter addresses real-time feature engineering and low-latency data processing techniques essential for responsive AI applications. It discusses scalability challenges specific to real-time AI and strategies to overcome them. The chapter also examines use cases and best practices for deploying real-time AI in production environments.

Chapter 10: Data Visualization and Explainable AI

This chapter explores techniques for visualizing AI insights and making AI systems more interpretable. It covers advanced data visualization methods tailored for complex AI outputs and high-dimensional data. The chapter examines various **explainable AI (XAI)** approaches, focusing on their integration with modern machine learning pipelines. It addresses the visualization of model predictions, uncertainties, and decision boundaries. The chapter also discusses the creation of interactive dashboards for AI systems and explores emerging trends in AI-driven data storytelling and augmented analytics.

Chapter 11: Emerging Trends in AI Data Architecture

This chapter looks into the future of AI data architecture, exploring groundbreaking technologies and their integration with existing platforms like Databricks. We examine quantum computing, neuromorphic computing, and AI-driven optimization for enhanced data processing and management. Additionally, we discuss decentralized AI, Green AI, natural language interfaces, data synthesis, and AI-powered self-optimization, showcasing their potential to revolutionize data architectures.

Coloured Images

Please follow the link to download the
Coloured Images of the book:

https://rebrand.ly/811565

We have code bundles from our rich catalogue of books and videos available at https://github.com/bpbpublications. Check them out!

Errata

We take immense pride in our work at BPB Publications and follow best practices to ensure the accuracy of our content to provide with an indulging reading experience to our subscribers. Our readers are our mirrors, and we use their inputs to reflect and improve upon human errors, if any, that may have occurred during the publishing processes involved. To let us maintain the quality and help us reach out to any readers who might be having difficulties due to any unforeseen errors, please write to us at :

errata@bpbonline.com

Your support, suggestions and feedbacks are highly appreciated by the BPB Publications' Family.

Piracy

If you come across any illegal copies of our works in any form on the internet, we would be grateful if you would provide us with the location address or website name. Please contact us at business@bpbonline.com with a link to the material.

If you are interested in becoming an author

If there is a topic that you have expertise in, and you are interested in either writing or contributing to a book, please visit www.bpbonline.com. We have worked with thousands of developers and tech professionals, just like you, to help them share their insights with the global tech community. You can make a general application, apply for a specific hot topic that we are recruiting an author for, or submit your own idea.

Reviews

Please leave a review. Once you have read and used this book, why not leave a review on the site that you purchased it from? Potential readers can then see and use your unbiased opinion to make purchase decisions. We at BPB can understand what you think about our products, and our authors can see your feedback on their book. Thank you!

For more information about BPB, please visit www.bpbonline.com.

Join our Discord space

Join our Discord workspace for latest updates, offers, tech happenings around the world, new releases, and sessions with the authors:

https://discord.bpbonline.com

Table of Contents

CHAPTER 1
Introduction to Modern Data Architecture for AI

Introduction

This chapter introduces the fundamental concepts of modern data architecture for **artificial intelligence (AI)** systems, covering the evolution from traditional databases to distributed and cloud-native solutions. We will explore the unique challenges of AI data management, including scalability, real-time processing, and handling unstructured data. We will further discuss key technologies like data lakes, data warehouses, and emerging paradigms such as data mesh. We will additionally touch upon essential tools and platforms for AI data architecture, setting the foundation for the rest of the book.

Structure

The chapter covers the following topics:

- Importance of architecture specific to AI
- Evolution of data architecture for AI
- Challenges in AI data management
- Data lakes and data warehouses
- Distributed computing frameworks
- Cloud-native data solutions

- Containerization and orchestration
- Data formats and serialization
- Emerging trends

Objectives

The objective of this chapter is to familiarize readers with the fundamental concepts and frameworks that underpin modern data architecture for AI. We aim to provide insights into key components such as data storage, processing, and management while also highlighting emerging trends like federated learning and quantum computing. Additionally, we will explore cloud-native solutions, focusing on the comprehensive suites of data and AI/ML tools and touching upon the concepts of containerization and orchestration. By the end of this chapter, readers will have a foundational understanding necessary to explore more technical details and practical applications in the subsequent chapters.

Importance of architecture specific to AI

The architecture of data systems plays a crucial role in the success of AI initiatives. Efficient data architectures ensure that data is accessible, scalable, and reliable, which is vital for training accurate and resilient AI models. A well-designed architecture can accommodate large volumes of data and handle the complex calculations required for AI, enabling faster processing and real-time analytics. This efficiency is particularly important in scenarios where quick decision-making is essential, such as in predictive maintenance, fraud detection, or personalized customer experiences. Additionally, a robust architecture supports the seamless integration and deployment of AI models, ensuring that insights can be rapidly transformed into actionable outcomes, driving tangible business results.

Investing in the right architecture is crucial for leveraging AI to drive innovation and maintain a competitive edge. A well-structured AI-specific architecture not only enhances computational efficiency but also strengthens data governance and security, safeguarding sensitive information while ensuring compliance with regulatory requirements. Furthermore, it allows for flexibility and scalability, enabling organizations to incorporate emerging technologies and adapt to the ever-evolving AI landscape. The integration of cloud-based solutions and distributed computing frameworks can significantly improve resource utilization and operational agility.

Moreover, a thoughtful architecture promotes collaboration across various departments, ensuring that AI initiatives are aligned with broader business goals. By establishing a strong architectural foundation, organizations can unlock the full potential of AI, leading to improved decision-making, enhanced operational efficiency, and sustainable growth. Ultimately, prioritizing AI-specific architecture is a strategic investment that empowers businesses to innovate, stay competitive, and thrive in the digital age.

Evolution of data architecture in AI

The evolution of data architecture has been a fascinating journey, shaped by technological advancements and the changing needs of businesses and researchers. As AI has grown from a niche domain into a mainstream technology, its data architecture requirements have undergone significant transformations. This section explores the historical context and the progression of data architecture, focusing on its adaptation to meet the demands of AI systems.

Early days of traditional databases

In the early days of computing, data management was primarily handled by traditional relational databases (RDBMS) such as *Oracle*, *MySQL*, and *SQL Server*. These databases were designed to store structured data in tables, leveraging the **structured query language (SQL)** for data manipulation and retrieval. The architecture was centralized, with a single database server handling all queries.

This approach was suitable for transactional systems where data consistency, integrity, and relational operations were paramount. However, as the volume of data grew and the complexity of queries increased, traditional databases' limitations became evident. They struggled to scale horizontally, and their rigid schema design made them less adaptable to the unstructured and semi-structured data often used in AI applications.

Rise of NoSQL databases

The limitations of RDBMS led to the emergence of NoSQL databases in the late 2000s. NoSQL databases, such as MongoDB, Cassandra, and Couchbase, were designed to handle large-scale, distributed data storage and retrieval. They offered flexibility in data modeling, allowing for the storage of unstructured and semi-structured data without the constraints of a fixed schema.

NoSQL databases support various data models, including document, key-value, column-family, and graph, making them suitable for a wide range of AI applications. They also provided horizontal scalability, enabling the distribution of data across multiple servers to handle large datasets and high query loads. This shift was crucial for AI systems, which require the ingestion and processing of vast amounts of diverse data.

Advent of distributed computing frameworks

As data volumes continued to grow, the need for more robust and scalable data processing frameworks became apparent. The advent of distributed computing frameworks like Apache Hadoop and Apache Spark marked a significant milestone in the evolution of data architecture.

Apache Hadoop

In 2006, Hadoop introduced the **Hadoop Distributed File System** (**HDFS**) and the MapReduce programming model. HDFS allowed for the storage of large datasets across a cluster of commodity hardware, while MapReduce enabled the parallel processing of data. Hadoop became a cornerstone for big data analytics, providing the scalability and fault tolerance needed for large-scale AI applications.

Apache Spark

Introduced in 2014, Spark built upon Hadoop's foundation but offered significant improvements in performance and usability. Spark's in-memory processing capabilities and support for a wide range of data processing tasks, including batch processing, streaming, **machine learning** (**ML**), and graph processing, make it a versatile tool for AI data workflows. Its ability to integrate with various data sources and execute complex transformations efficiently further cemented its role in modern data architecture.

Cloud-native data solutions

The shift to cloud computing has been another transformative phase in the evolution of data architecture. Cloud platforms like **Amazon Web Services** (**AWS**), Microsoft Azure, and **Google Cloud Platform** (**GCP**) provide scalable, on-demand infrastructure and a suite of services tailored for AI data management.

Data lakes and warehouses

Cloud-native data lakes (for example, AWS S3) and data warehouses (for example, Google BigQuery, Snowflake) offer flexible and scalable storage solutions. Data lakes allow for the storage of raw, unstructured data, while data warehouses provide optimized storage for structured data, supporting complex analytical queries. These solutions enable organizations to manage their data more efficiently and cost-effectively, facilitating AI-driven insights.

Containerization and orchestration

Technologies like Docker and Kubernetes have revolutionized the deployment and management of AI applications. Containerization allows for the encapsulation of applications and their dependencies into portable containers, ensuring consistency across different environments. Kubernetes provides orchestration capabilities, automating the deployment, scaling, and management of containerized applications. These tools enhance the agility and scalability of AI data architecture, enabling seamless integration and deployment of AI models.

Data mesh and lakehouse architecture

The evolution of data architecture continues with emerging paradigms like data mesh and lakehouse architecture, which address the complexities of modern AI data workflows.

Data mesh

Proposed by *Zhamak Dehghani*, data mesh is a decentralized approach to data management. It treats data as a product and assigns ownership to domain-specific teams, promoting a federated and self-serve data infrastructure. This paradigm aims to overcome the bottlenecks of centralized data platforms, enabling scalable and agile AI data management.

Lakehouse architecture

The lakehouse architecture combines the best of data lakes and data warehouses, providing a unified platform for data storage, processing, and analytics. Solutions like Delta Lake and Apache Iceberg offer **Atomicity, Consistency, Isolation, Durability** (**ACID**) transactions, schema enforcement, and performant querying capabilities on top of data lakes. This approach simplifies data management, ensuring consistency and reliability for AI applications.

Challenges in AI data management

As AI systems become more pervasive and sophisticated, managing the data that fuels these systems presents numerous challenges. Effective data management is critical for ensuring the accuracy, scalability, and ethical deployment of AI applications. This section looks at the key challenges in AI data management, highlighting the complexities and considerations that data architects and engineers must navigate. The challenges are as follows:

- **Scalability**: One of the foremost challenges in AI data management is scalability. AI applications often require massive datasets for training, validation, and testing. Managing such large volumes of data necessitates a robust infrastructure that can scale horizontally and vertically.

- **Data volume**: The sheer volume of data generated and consumed by AI systems can be overwhelming. Traditional storage solutions often fall short, requiring distributed storage systems like HDFS, cloud-based object storage, or data lakes to handle petabytes of data efficiently.

- **Processing power**: Scalable data processing frameworks such as Apache Spark and distributed databases like Cassandra are essential for handling the computational demands of AI workloads. These tools need to support parallel processing and real-time analytics to meet the performance requirements of modern AI applications.

- **Real-time processing**: Real-time data processing is critical for AI applications that require immediate insights and rapid decision-making, such as autonomous vehicles, fraud detection systems, and recommendation engines.

- **Low latency**: Achieving low-latency data processing is challenging, especially when dealing with high throughput data streams. Stream processing frameworks like Apache Kafka and Apache Flink are designed to handle real-time data ingestion and transformation, but ensuring consistent performance under varying loads remains complex.

- **Data freshness**: Ensuring the freshness of data is crucial for real-time AI systems. This involves maintaining up-to-date data pipelines and minimizing delays in data propagation from source to destination.

- **Handling unstructured data**: AI systems increasingly rely on unstructured data, such as text, images, video, and audio, which do not fit neatly into traditional relational database schemas. Managing diverse data types requires flexible storage solutions that can accommodate different formats and structures. NoSQL databases and data lakes are commonly used to store unstructured data, but indexing and querying this data efficiently can be challenging. Integrating unstructured data from various sources into a cohesive dataset is complex. This process often involves data transformation, normalization, and enrichment to ensure consistency and usability for AI models.

- **Security and compliance**: With the increasing sensitivity and volume of data used in AI systems, ensuring data security and regulatory compliance is paramount. Protecting data from unauthorized access and breaches involves robust encryption, access control, and authentication mechanisms. Security measures must be integrated throughout the data lifecycle, from ingestion to storage and processing. Compliance with data protection regulations such as the **General Data Protection Regulation (GDPR)**, **California Consumer Privacy Act (CCPA)**, and **Health Insurance Portability and Accountability Act (HIPAA)** adds another layer of complexity to AI data management. Organizations must establish processes for data anonymization, consent management, and auditability to meet regulatory requirements.

- **Data lineage and versioning**: Tracking the lineage and versions of data is essential for reproducibility, accountability, and debugging in AI systems. Data lineage involves tracing the origin and transformations of data throughout its lifecycle. This provides transparency and helps identify the source of errors or biases in AI models. Managing versions of datasets ensures that changes are tracked and can be reverted if necessary. Version control systems for data, like those used for code, are increasingly important for collaborative AI development and maintaining historical records.

- **Bias and fairness**: AI systems are susceptible to biases in the training data, which can lead to unfair or unethical outcomes. Identifying biases in datasets involves analyzing the data for imbalances or anomalies that could influence model predictions. This requires specialized tools and techniques to detect and quantify bias. Ensuring fairness in AI models involves implementing strategies to mitigate identified biases and promote equitable treatment across different demographic groups. This may include resampling, reweighting, or modifying the training process to address disparities.

Managing data for AI systems is fraught with challenges, from scalability and real-time processing to ensuring data quality, security, and compliance. Handling unstructured data, tracking lineage and versions, and addressing bias and fairness further complicate the landscape. Navigating these challenges requires a combination of advanced technologies, robust processes, and a deep understanding of the underlying principles of AI data management. As we move on to the subsequent chapters, we will look into how we can address these challenges effectively.

Data lakes and data warehouses

In the landscape of AI data management, data lakes and data warehouses have emerged as critical components. They serve as the backbone for storing, organizing, and accessing the vast amounts of data essential for AI applications. Understanding these concepts is key to grasping the complexities and capabilities of modern data architectures.

Understanding data lakes

Data lakes are extensive storage repositories capable of holding vast amounts of raw, unstructured, and semi-structured data. Unlike traditional databases that enforce a schema-on-write approach, data lakes adopt a schema-on-read methodology, allowing data to be ingested in its native format. This flexibility is a significant advantage, as it enables the storage of diverse data types, including text, images, videos, and log files. For AI applications, which often require a variety of data sources, this flexibility is crucial.

The scalability of data lakes is another notable feature. Built on distributed storage systems like HDFS or cloud-based object storage services such as Amazon S3 or Azure Blob Storage, data lakes can efficiently handle petabytes of data. This scalability ensures that organizations can store large datasets necessary for training AI models without facing significant storage limitations. Additionally, the cost-effectiveness of storing data in its raw form reduces expenses associated with data transformation and simplifies the data ingestion process.

However, data lakes are not without their challenges. The lack of enforced schema and governance can lead to what is often termed as data swamps, where data becomes disorganized and difficult to manage. Ensuring data quality and implementing robust governance policies are critical to maintaining the usability of data lakes. Furthermore, querying raw data directly from a data lake can be slow and resource-intensive, necessitating additional processing steps to format and optimize the data for analytical queries.

Understanding data warehouses

Data warehouses, on the other hand, are designed specifically for structured data storage and are optimized for analytical queries. They enforce a schema-on-write approach, which means that data must be structured and formatted before ingestion. This approach ensures data consistency and integrity, making data warehouses ideal for **business intelligence** (**BI**) and reporting applications.

The high-performance querying capabilities of data warehouses are one of their most significant advantages. By employing indexing, partitioning, and optimized storage formats, data warehouses ensure fast and efficient data retrieval, which is essential for generating timely insights. Moreover, their seamless integration with BI and analytics tools allows for straightforward data analysis and visualization, facilitating data-driven decision-making within organizations.

However, the benefits of data warehouses come with certain limitations. Storing and processing large volumes of data can be expensive, particularly when dealing with extensive historical datasets. Additionally, the rigid schema structure can make it challenging to handle unstructured or semi-structured data, often requiring additional transformation steps before ingestion.

Modern solutions

Modern data solutions like Delta Lake aim to combine the strengths of both data lakes and data warehouses, providing flexible, scalable, and high-performance data storage and management.

Delta Lake, an open-source storage layer, introduces ACID transactions to data lakes. This addition ensures data consistency through reliable transactions, making Delta Lake suitable for concurrent read and write operations. Furthermore, Delta Lake allows for schema enforcement, which helps maintain data quality and consistency while retaining the flexibility of a data lake. The support for time travel in Delta Lake is another innovative feature, enabling users to query historical versions of data, which is particularly useful for debugging, auditing, and ensuring reproducibility.

Use cases and best practices

Data lakes are suitable for ML and AI training data, log storage, and raw data ingestion from various sources. In contrast, data warehouses excel in BI, reporting, and structured data analysis. Delta Lake is ideal for scenarios requiring reliable data lakes with ACID guarantees, such as real-time analytics and data science. Snowflake is best for organizations needing scalable, high-performance data warehousing with cloud-native features and multi-cloud capabilities.

Implementing robust data governance policies is essential to maintain data quality and prevent data swamps in data lakes. Adopting a hybrid approach, where raw data is stored in data lakes and curated, high-value data is stored in data warehouses, allows organizations to leverage the strengths of both. Additionally, optimizing query performance through caching, indexing, and partitioning strategies is crucial for efficient data management in both data lakes and data warehouses.

The evolution of data architecture has introduced powerful solutions like data lakes and data warehouses, each with distinct strengths and challenges. Modern hybrid solutions like Delta Lake and Snowflake offer the best of both worlds, providing scalable, flexible, and high-performance data management tailored for AI applications. By understanding these foundational concepts, organizations can build robust data architectures that meet the demands of contemporary AI systems, setting the stage for more detailed technical exploration in subsequent chapters.

Distributed computing frameworks

In AI data management, distributed computing frameworks play a critical role in processing and analyzing large-scale datasets. These frameworks enable the parallel processing of data across multiple nodes, ensuring scalability, fault tolerance, and performance. This section introduces two foundational distributed computing frameworks, Apache Hadoop and Apache Spark, which have revolutionized the way organizations handle big data and AI workloads.

Apache Hadoop

Apache Hadoop, introduced in the mid-2000s, marked a significant milestone in the evolution of data processing. It was designed to handle the growing need for processing vast amounts of data, which traditional systems struggled to manage efficiently. Hadoop consists of two main components: the HDFS and the MapReduce programming model.

HDFS is a scalable and fault-tolerant file system that distributes data across multiple nodes in a cluster. It breaks down large data files into smaller blocks and replicates them across different nodes to ensure data availability and reliability. This distributed storage mechanism allows organizations to store petabytes of data inexpensively while maintaining high availability.

MapReduce, Hadoop's processing engine, enables parallel data processing by dividing tasks into smaller sub-tasks that can be executed concurrently across the nodes in the cluster. The MapReduce model consists of two main functions: the **Map** function, which processes input data and produces intermediate key-value pairs, and the **Reduce** function, which aggregates these pairs to produce the final output. This model simplifies the development of distributed applications and provides a robust framework for large-scale data processing.

While Hadoop has been instrumental in advancing big data analytics, it also has certain limitations. MapReduce's batch-processing nature can result in high latency, making it less suitable for real-time analytics. Additionally, the complexity of writing MapReduce programs and managing Hadoop clusters can pose challenges for organizations.

Apache Spark

Apache Spark, introduced in 2014, emerged as a more versatile and efficient alternative to Hadoop. Spark builds on the concepts of distributed data processing but offers significant advancements in performance, ease of use, and versatility. Spark's core innovation lies in its in-memory processing capabilities, which allow data to be processed and stored in memory, reducing I/O operations and significantly speeding up data processing tasks.

One of Spark's key components is the **Resilient Distributed Dataset (RDD)**, an immutable collection of objects that can be processed in parallel. RDDs provide fault tolerance by tracking lineage information, which allows for the reconstruction of lost data partitions. This feature ensures that Spark can handle node failures without losing data or processing progress.

In addition to in-memory processing, Spark supports a variety of workloads, including batch processing, stream processing, ML, and graph processing. Its unified engine allows developers to perform complex data transformations and analyses using a single framework. For instance, Spark Streaming extends the core Spark API to support real-time data streams, enabling low-latency processing of continuous data flows.

Another significant advantage of Spark is its ease of use. It provides high-level APIs in Java, Scala, Python, and R, allowing developers to write concise and expressive code. Spark also integrates seamlessly with other big data tools and frameworks, such as Hadoop, HDFS, and Apache Kafka, making it a versatile addition to existing data ecosystems.

Despite its advantages, Spark also presents certain challenges. In-memory processing requires substantial memory resources, which can be costly for large-scale deployments. Additionally, tuning Spark applications for optimal performance requires a deep understanding of the framework and its configuration parameters.

Advancements in distributed computing

The field of distributed computing continues to evolve, with new frameworks and technologies emerging to address the limitations of existing solutions. For instance, Apache Flink and Apache Beam offer advanced stream processing capabilities and more flexible programming models, respectively. These frameworks aim to provide even lower latency, greater scalability, and improved ease of use.

Integrating distributed computing frameworks with cloud-native platforms also represents a significant trend. Cloud providers like AWS, Azure, and Google Cloud offer managed services for Hadoop, Spark, and other frameworks, simplifying deployment and management while providing scalable infrastructure. These cloud-native solutions enable organizations to leverage the power of distributed computing without the overhead of managing physical hardware and software stacks.

A notable advancement in the field is Databricks, a unified analytics platform founded by the creators of Apache Spark. Databricks extends the capabilities of Spark by providing an integrated environment for data engineering, data science, and ML. It offers features such as collaborative notebooks, automated cluster management, and optimized performance for Spark workloads. Databricks also supports Delta Lake, which brings ACID transactions and schema enforcement to data lakes, ensuring high data reliability and consistency.

We will look further into these concepts and their practical implementation in the subsequent chapters.

Cloud-native data solutions

As organizations increasingly seek to leverage big data and AI, cloud-native data solutions have become indispensable. These solutions offer the scalability, flexibility, and efficiency needed to manage and process vast datasets. Major cloud providers like AWS, Microsoft Azure, and GCP have developed comprehensive suites of data services that cater to the diverse needs of modern enterprises. This section introduces the concept of cloud-native data solutions and explores the offerings from these leading providers.

Rise of cloud-native data solutions

Cloud-native data solutions are designed to exploit the advantages of cloud computing fully. Unlike traditional on-premises systems, cloud-native architectures are built to be scalable, resilient, and agile. They allow organizations to store, process, and analyze data without the constraints of physical hardware, enabling rapid deployment and scaling in response to changing demands.

One of the primary benefits of cloud-native data solutions is their ability to manage and process large volumes of data efficiently. By leveraging the elasticity of cloud resources, organizations can scale their data infrastructure up or down based on workload requirements, optimizing both performance and cost. Additionally, cloud-native solutions offer robust security features, ensuring data privacy and compliance with regulatory standards. In this book, we will explore three public cloud providers: AWS, GCP, and Microsoft Azure.

Amazon Web Services

AWS is a pioneer in cloud computing, offering a comprehensive set of data services designed to meet the needs of enterprises of all sizes. AWS provides scalable storage solutions like Amazon S3 for object storage and Amazon Redshift for data warehousing. These services are designed to handle petabytes of data, providing high availability and durability.

For data processing and analytics, AWS offers services like Amazon **Elastic MapReduce (EMR)**, simplifying the deployment and management of big data frameworks such as Hadoop and Spark. Additionally, AWS Glue provides a fully managed **Extract, Transform, Load (ETL)** service that automates the process of preparing data for analysis. AWS also offers advanced analytics services like Amazon Athena, a serverless query service that allows users to analyze data directly in S3 using standard SQL.

AWS's ML services, such as Amazon SageMaker, enable organizations to build, train, and deploy ML models at scale. SageMaker integrates seamlessly with other AWS data services, facilitating end-to-end ML workflows.

Microsoft Azure

Microsoft Azure offers a rich ecosystem of data services that cater to various data management and analytics needs. Azure Data Lake Storage provides scalable and secure storage for large datasets, while Azure SQL Data Warehouse (now known as **Azure Synapse Analytics**) offers powerful data warehousing capabilities with integrated analytics.

Azure Databricks, a collaborative analytics platform powered by Apache Spark, allows data engineers and data scientists to work together seamlessly. It provides an interactive workspace for data exploration, visualization, and ML, with built-in support for various data sources and formats.

Azure also offers a suite of analytics services, including Azure Stream Analytics for real-time data processing and Azure Machine Learning for building and deploying ML models. These services are designed to integrate with Azure's broader ecosystem, enabling comprehensive data management and analytics workflows.

Google Cloud Platform

Google Cloud Platform (GCP) provides a versatile suite of cloud-native data solutions designed for modern enterprises. Central to GCP's offerings is Google Cloud Storage, which supports scalable object storage for diverse data types. For relational data, Google Cloud SQL and Google Cloud Spanner offer fully managed database services with high availability and global consistency, respectively. Google BigQuery is a powerful, serverless data warehouse, enabling real-time analytics on massive datasets without infrastructure management.

GCP excels in data processing with tools like Google Cloud Dataflow, a fully managed service for stream and batch processing using Apache Beam, and Google Cloud Dataproc, a managed Hadoop and Spark service. Google Cloud Pub/Sub facilitates real-time event ingestion and delivery, supporting scalable event-driven architectures.

GCP's AI and ML capabilities are particularly robust. Google Cloud AI Platform supports the entire AI lifecycle, from data preparation to model deployment, and is compatible with popular frameworks like TensorFlow and PyTorch. For users without extensive ML expertise, Google Cloud AutoML offers simple interfaces to train custom models for image recognition, text analysis, and structured data.

Vertex AI, GCP's unified AI platform, integrates various ML services, streamlining workflows from data preparation to deployment and monitoring. This unified environment fosters collaboration and accelerates AI solution development.

GCP's comprehensive data storage, processing, and AI/ML tools make it a compelling choice for leveraging advanced analytics and ML. Subsequent chapters will explore these tools in greater detail, providing practical insights for building scalable, intelligent data architectures.

Containerization and orchestration

As the complexity and scale of AI applications continue to grow, containerization and orchestration have become essential technologies for managing and deploying these applications efficiently. Containers offer a lightweight, portable, and consistent environment for running applications, while orchestration tools automate the deployment, scaling, and management of these containers. This section introduces the concepts of containerization and orchestration, focusing on key technologies like Docker and Kubernetes.

Understanding containerization

Containerization is a method of packaging applications and their dependencies into isolated units called containers. Unlike traditional **virtual machines** (**VMs**), containers share the host system's kernel but run in their own isolated user spaces. This approach provides several advantages, including lightweight resource utilization, portability, and consistency across different environments.

Docker is the leading platform for containerization and has revolutionized the way applications are developed and deployed. Docker allows developers to create container images that include all the necessary components for an application to run, such as code, runtime, libraries, and configuration files. These images can be built once and run anywhere, ensuring that applications behave consistently across development, testing, and production environments.

One of Docker's key features is its ability to create and manage container images through Dockerfiles. A Dockerfile is a script that contains a series of instructions for building a Docker image. By using Dockerfiles, developers can automate the process of creating container images, making it easier to maintain and update applications.

Containers also efficiently manage dependencies and avoid conflicts between different applications. By encapsulating an application's dependencies within a container, developers can ensure that it runs with the exact versions of libraries and tools it needs, regardless of the host system's configuration.

Role of orchestration

While containers simplify the deployment and management of individual applications, managing many containers in a production environment can be challenging. Orchestration tools automate the deployment, scaling, and management of containerized applications, ensuring that they run smoothly and efficiently.

Kubernetes is the most widely adopted container orchestration platform. Originally developed by *Google*, Kubernetes provides a robust framework for automating the deployment, scaling, and operation of containerized applications. It manages clusters of containers, ensuring that they are deployed reliably and can scale to meet demand.

Kubernetes introduces several key concepts, including pods, services, and deployments. A pod is the smallest deployable unit in Kubernetes, consisting of one or more containers that share the same network namespace and storage. Pods are typically used to host a single instance of an application or a microservice.

Services in Kubernetes provide a stable network endpoint for accessing pods. They enable load balancing and service discovery, ensuring that applications can communicate with each other reliably. Deployments automate the process of updating and scaling applications. They define an application's desired state, and Kubernetes continuously monitors and adjusts the application to match this state.

Kubernetes also provides features for managing applications' lifecycles, such as rolling updates, which ensure that updates are deployed without downtime, and self-healing, which automatically replaces failed containers to maintain application availability.

Advancements and emerging trends

The combination of containerization and orchestration has led to significant advancements in the development and deployment of AI applications. These technologies enable organizations to adopt microservices architectures, where applications comprise small, independent services that can be developed, deployed, and scaled independently. This approach enhances agility and enables **continuous integration and continuous delivery** (**CI/CD**) pipelines, allowing organizations to deliver new features and updates more rapidly.

Emerging trends in containerization and orchestration include the integration of serverless computing and the use of service meshes. Serverless computing allows developers to run functions responding to events without managing the underlying infrastructure. Platforms like Kubernetes increasingly support serverless frameworks, enabling more flexible and scalable application architectures.

Service meshes, such as Istio, provide advanced networking capabilities for microservices, including traffic management, security, and observability. By integrating with Kubernetes, service meshes enhance the reliability and performance of containerized applications.

Containerization and orchestration have transformed the way AI applications are developed, deployed, and managed. Docker provides a lightweight and portable environment for running applications, while Kubernetes automates the deployment, scaling, and management of these containers. Together, these technologies enable organizations to build and deploy complex AI applications with greater efficiency, reliability, and scalability. Subsequent chapters will examine the technical details and best practices for implementing and managing containerized AI applications using Docker, Kubernetes, and related tools.

Data formats and serialization

Efficient data storage and transfer are critical in the era of big data and AI. The choice of data formats and serialization techniques can significantly impact performance, storage efficiency, and the ease of data processing. This section introduces key data formats and serialization methods, focusing on Apache Parquet and Apache Avro, which are widely used in modern data architectures.

Importance of data formats and serialization

Data formats and serialization are essential for organizing, compressing, and transmitting data in a way that optimizes storage and processing. They play a crucial role in ensuring that data can be efficiently read and written, enabling faster analytics and reducing storage costs. Different data formats are optimized for various use cases, such as batch processing, streaming, or real-time analytics, and selecting the right format is vital for achieving optimal performance.

Serialization is the process of converting data structures or objects into a format that can be easily stored or transmitted and later reconstructed. Effective serialization formats ensure that data is compact, consistent, and easily accessible, particularly important for distributed systems and big data platforms.

Apache Parquet

Apache Parquet is a columnar storage format for efficient data processing and analytics. Unlike row-based storage formats, which store data sequentially by rows, Parquet stores data in columns. This design choice offers several advantages, particularly for analytical workloads.

One key benefit of Parquet's columnar format is its ability to significantly reduce the amount of data that needs to be read during query execution. When querying specific columns in a dataset, only the relevant columns are read from disk, reducing I/O operations and improving query performance. This columnar storage also allows for better data compression, as similar data types are stored together, leading to more effective compression algorithms.

Parquet supports advanced encoding schemes and compression techniques, such as run-length encoding and dictionary encoding, which further enhance storage efficiency. These features make Parquet an excellent choice for large-scale data processing tasks, such as those performed in data warehouses, data lakes, and big data analytics platforms.

Additionally, Parquet is optimized for use with distributed computing frameworks like Apache Spark and Apache Hadoop. Its integration with these frameworks enables efficient data ingestion, transformation, and querying, making it a popular choice for ETL processes and analytical workloads.

Apache Avro

Apache Avro is a data serialization system that provides a compact, fast, and binary format for data exchange. Avro is particularly well-suited for data serialization in distributed systems, where data needs to be transmitted across different services or stored in a consistent format.

One of Avro's key features is its support for schema evolution. Avro data is serialized with its schema, allowing the reader to understand the data structure without relying on external schema definitions. This self-describing nature simplifies data interchange between systems and facilitates forward and backward compatibility. Schema evolution allows for changes to the data schema, such as adding or removing fields, without breaking existing applications, which is crucial for maintaining long-term data compatibility in dynamic environments.

Avro's compact binary format ensures efficient data storage and transfer. Its serialization and deserialization processes are highly performant, making Avro an excellent choice for high throughput data pipelines and real-time data processing. Avro is commonly used in conjunction with message brokers like Apache Kafka, where its efficient serialization and schema evolution capabilities are particularly valuable.

Avro also integrates well with big data frameworks like Apache Hadoop and Apache Spark, enabling efficient data processing and analytics. Its support for complex data types, such as nested records and arrays, allows for the serialization of rich and complex data structures, making it a versatile choice for various data processing scenarios.

Other data formats

While Parquet and Avro are widely used, other data formats like Apache **Optimized Row Columnar** (**ORC**) and **JavaScript Object Notation** (**JSON**) also play important roles in specific use cases. ORC, like Parquet, is a columnar storage format optimized for high-performance analytics, particularly in Hadoop ecosystems. JSON, on the other hand, is a widely used text-based format that is easy to read and write, making it suitable for data interchange in web applications and APIs.

Data formats and serialization techniques are fundamental to the efficiency and performance of modern data architectures. Apache Parquet and Apache Avro are two widely adopted formats that offer distinct advantages for different use cases. Parquet's columnar storage format excels in analytical workloads, providing efficient data compression and fast query performance. Avro's compact binary format and schema evolution capabilities make it ideal for data serialization in distributed systems and real-time data pipelines. In subsequent chapters, we will explore the technical details and best practices for implementing and optimizing these data formats, enabling you to leverage their full potential in your AI and big data projects.

Emerging trends

As the field of data management and analytics continues to advance, several emerging trends are poised to significantly influence how organizations handle and analyze their data. Two such transformative trends are federated learning and quantum computing. This section introduces these concepts, highlighting their potential impact on modern data architectures and their relevance to AI-driven initiatives.

Federated learning

Federated learning represents a paradigm shift in how ML models are trained. Traditionally, training an ML model involves aggregating all the data into a central location, which can raise privacy and security concerns, especially with sensitive data. Federated learning addresses these issues by enabling the training of models across decentralized data sources without transferring raw data.

The core idea behind federated learning is to bring the model to the data rather than bringing the data to the model. In this approach, a global model is sent to various data sources (for example, mobile devices and edge servers), where local models are trained using the local data. The local models' updates are then aggregated centrally to update the global model. This process is iterative and continues until the global model converges.

One of the primary benefits of federated learning is enhanced data privacy. Since raw data never leaves the local devices, the risk of data breaches and unauthorized access is significantly reduced. This is particularly important in domains like healthcare, finance, and IoT, where data sensitivity and privacy concerns are paramount.

Federated learning also mitigates the challenges associated with data transfer and storage. By keeping data locally, organizations can save on bandwidth and storage costs and reduce the latency associated with data movement. This approach is well-suited for applications where data is generated at the edge, such as in connected vehicles or smart homes.

Another advantage is the ability to leverage diverse data sources. Federated learning can combine insights from various data sets without centralizing them, resulting in more generalized and robust models. This is particularly useful for applications that require learning from geographically or contextually diverse data, such as personalized recommendations or predictive maintenance across different environments.

Quantum computing

Quantum computing is an emerging field that promises to revolutionize data processing and analytics by harnessing the principles of quantum mechanics. Unlike classical computers, which use bits to represent data as 0s and 1s, quantum computers use quantum bits, or qubits, which can represent multiple states simultaneously due to superposition and entanglement.

One of the most significant potential impacts of quantum computing is its ability to solve complex problems that are infeasible for classical computers. For instance, quantum algorithms can exponentially speed up tasks like factoring large numbers, optimizing complex systems, and simulating quantum processes, which have direct applications in cryptography, logistics, and material science.

In the context of data management and AI, quantum computing can enhance the efficiency and capabilities of various processes. For example, quantum ML algorithms can process and analyze massive data sets much faster than classical algorithms, enabling real-time insights and more accurate predictive models. This can significantly benefit applications in finance, healthcare, and scientific research, where rapid data analysis is crucial.

Quantum computing also promises to improve optimization problems, such as supply chain management, portfolio optimization, and traffic routing. Quantum algorithms can explore a vast number of possible solutions simultaneously, identifying optimal or near-optimal solutions more efficiently than classical methods.

However, integrating quantum computing into existing data architectures poses several challenges. Quantum computers are still nascent, with limited qubit counts and high error rates. Additionally, developing quantum algorithms requires specialized knowledge and expertise. Despite these challenges, ongoing research and development are steadily advancing the field, bringing practical quantum computing applications closer to reality.

Convergence and synergy

While federated learning and quantum computing are distinct trends, they can complement each other and offer synergistic benefits in the future. For example, quantum computing could enhance federated learning by optimizing the aggregation of local model updates or by improving the efficiency of privacy-preserving techniques.

In a modern data architecture, federated learning can provide a scalable and privacy-preserving approach to training ML models. At the same time, quantum computing can offer unparalleled computational power for solving complex data processing tasks. Together, these trends can lead to more efficient, secure, and powerful data systems.

Conclusion

In this introductory chapter, we have explored the foundational concepts of modern data architecture for AI, emphasizing the importance of efficient data management, processing, and storage solutions. We highlighted emerging trends like federated learning and quantum computing and examined cloud-native platforms that offer robust tools for data and AI/ML needs. Understanding these principles sets the stage for deeper technical exploration in subsequent chapters, equipping you with the knowledge to build scalable, intelligent data architectures that drive innovation and competitive advantage.

In the next chapter, we will look at the critical processes of data collection and ingestion, which form the foundation of any data-driven initiative. We will explore strategies and best practices for gathering data from diverse sources, including structured databases, unstructured files, IoT devices, and streaming data. The chapter will provide detailed insights into different data ingestion techniques, such as batch processing, real-time streaming, and micro-batching, along with their respective use cases and advantages. We will also examine the tools and technologies that facilitate efficient data ingestion, including ETL frameworks, data pipelines, and cloud-native services. Additionally, the chapter will cover essential topics such as data validation, transformation, and integration, ensuring that the ingested data is clean, consistent, and ready for analysis.

Join our Discord space

Join our Discord workspace for latest updates, offers, tech happenings around the world, new releases, and sessions with the authors:

https://discord.bpbonline.com

CHAPTER 2
Data Collection and Ingestion Strategies

Introduction

In the realm of data-driven decision-making, the journey begins with effective data collection and ingestion strategies. This chapter explores the foundational aspects of gathering and importing data, which are the bedrock for advanced analytics or AI-driven initiatives. The chapter aims to comprehensively understand the various methodologies, tools, and best practices involved in collecting and ingesting data from diverse sources.

We start by exploring the fundamental concepts of data ingestion, highlighting its importance in ensuring data quality, integrity, and timeliness. This sets the stage for discussing the different types of data ingestion, batch and real-time, and their respective use cases. Understanding when to use each type is crucial for optimizing performance and meeting business requirements.

The chapter then transitions into security and compliance, emphasizing the need to protect sensitive information during the ingestion process. We cover essential techniques such as encryption, access controls, and data masking, along with compliance mandates like GDPR, HIPAA, and CCPA.

Next, we introduce cloud-native ingestion services, such as AWS Glue, Azure Data Factory, and Google Cloud Dataflow. These services offer scalable, flexible, and efficient solutions for handling data ingestion tasks, making them indispensable in modern data architectures. We also discuss real-time streaming solutions like Amazon Kinesis and Azure Stream Analytics, which enable real-time data processing and analytics.

Finally, we present a sample architecture for data collection and ingestion tailored for AI applications. This architecture integrates various components discussed in the chapter, providing a practical blueprint for building robust, secure, and compliant data ingestion pipelines.

Structure

The chapter covers the following topics:

- Data sources and types for AI systems
- Batch vs. stream processing
- Stream processing frameworks
- Data quality and validation techniques
- Data integration validation
- Scalable ingestion architectures
- Security and compliance in data ingestion
- Implementing security and compliance in practice
- Cloud-native ingestion services
- Sample architecture for data collection and ingestion

Objectives

This chapter provides a comprehensive overview of data ingestion, equipping you with the essential knowledge and skills to effectively collect and import data from various sources. You will look into the fundamentals of data ingestion, including batch and real-time methods, and learn how to implement robust security measures to protect sensitive information. Additionally, you will explore popular cloud-native ingestion services like AWS Glue, Azure Data Factory, and Google Cloud Dataflow, understanding their benefits and how to leverage them for efficient and scalable data pipelines. By the end of this chapter, you will be able to design and implement data ingestion architectures that are secure, compliant, and optimized for AI applications, laying a solid foundation for your journey into advanced analytics and data-driven initiatives.

Data sources and types for AI systems

In the intricate landscape of AI, the essence of powerful models lies in the richness and diversity of data. The efficacy of any AI endeavor is deeply rooted in the quality and appropriateness of its data sources. This section embarks on a journey through the various data sources and types that fuel AI systems, elucidating their characteristics and pivotal roles.

Data sources for AI can be broadly categorized into three principal types: structured, semi-structured, and unstructured data. Each type presents distinct challenges and opportunities, shaping how data is ingested and utilized.

Structured data

Structured data epitomizes organization and predictability. It resides in highly organized formats, typically stored in relational databases and data warehouses. This data is neatly arranged in tables, with each entry adhering to a predefined schema.

Structured data is schema-driven, which means it often adheres to a strict schema, making it easily searchable and manageable.

Tables and schemas

Structured data is stored in tables, each consisting of rows and columns. Each row represents a unique record, while columns represent data attributes. For instance, a customer table might include columns such as CustomerID, Name, Email, and PhoneNumber. A schema defines the table's structure, specifying the data types for each column (for example, integer, varchar, date). This schema ensures data integrity and consistency, enabling efficient querying and data manipulation. In relational databases, data is often modeled using **entity-relationship** (**ER**) diagrams. These diagrams visually represent the entities (for example, customers, orders) and the relationships between them. For example, a customer entity might have a one-to-many relationship with an orders entity, indicating that one customer can place multiple orders. ER models help design the database schema, ensuring that relationships between different data entities are accurately captured. This modeling is crucial for maintaining data integrity and supporting complex queries that span multiple tables. *Figure 2.1* represents an ER diagram with tables and relationships between them:

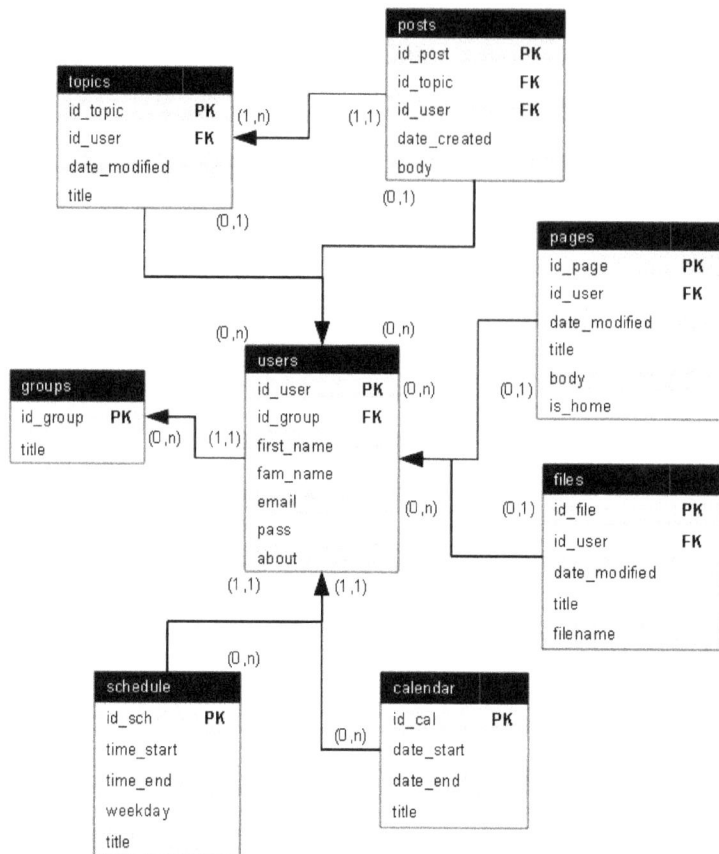

Figure 2.1: *A sample ER diagram*

Importance for AI

Structured data forms the backbone of many AI applications, particularly those requiring precision and clarity. Its well-defined nature simplifies data ingestion and preprocessing, which is crucial for training ML algorithms that depend on clean and consistent data. The use of schemas, tables, and ER models ensures that the data is organized and can be efficiently queried, making it easier to extract valuable insights for AI models.

Semi-structured data

Semi-structured data strikes a balance between structure and flexibility. While it does not conform to a rigid schema, it includes tags and markers delineating data elements. Common formats include JSON, XML, and CSV files. It is characterized by allowing for varying fields and data types within a single dataset. Weblogs, social media posts, and email metadata are some common examples. Semi-structured data is inherently flexible, allowing for the inclusion of diverse data types and structures within a single dataset. For instance, a JSON document might contain nested objects and arrays, enabling complex data representations. This flexibility makes semi-structured data particularly suited for applications where the data schema may evolve.

The following script shows the general structure of a JSON document for an entity called **pantry**:

```
{
"pantry": {
    "snacks": [
        { "name": "Chips",
          "expirationDate": "2024-07-15"
         }
    ],
     "spices": [
        { "name": "Cumin",
          "expirationDate": "2025-08-01"
        }
    ],
     "vegetables": [
     { "name": "Carrots",
       "expirationDate": "2024-12-15"
      }
    ],
     "fruits": [
    { "name": "Apples",
      "expirationDate": "2024-01-25"
     }
     ]
     }
}
```

Importance for AI

Semi-structured data is invaluable for AI applications that require adaptability, such as **natural language processing** (**NLP**) and sentiment analysis. The ability to parse and extract insights from this data type is essential for developing models that understand and interpret human language and context. The flexible nature of semi-structured data allows for dynamic schema evolution, making it easier to integrate diverse data sources and adapt to changing requirements.

By leveraging the inherent flexibility of semi-structured data and imposing some structure on unstructured data, AI systems can achieve a more comprehensive understanding of complex datasets. This approach bridges the gap between raw, unstructured data and actionable insights, enabling more effective and adaptive AI models.

Unstructured data

Unstructured data, as its name suggests, lacks a predefined format or organization. This type of data encompasses a broad array of content, including text, images, audio, and video. It is characterized by diverse forms and can be vast in volume. Social media content, multimedia files, and documents are some examples.

Interestingly, unstructured data can sometimes be semi-structured to a certain extent to enhance usability. For instance, textual data from emails can be parsed to extract key attributes like sender, recipient, timestamp, and subject, which can then be stored in a semi-structured format such as JSON. Similarly, multimedia files can have associated metadata (for example, file type, resolution, and creation date) that provides a semi-structured layer, facilitating easier querying and analysis.

Unstructured data presents unique challenges but also offers immense potential. For instance, computer vision relies on image and video data, while NLP leverages textual data. Effectively processing unstructured data can lead to more sophisticated AI models capable of understanding complex and nuanced information.

Types of data for AI systems

Understanding the specific types of data that can drive AI systems is crucial for devising effective data ingestion and analysis strategies. In the following section, we explore some common types of data utilized in AI applications.

Time-series data

Time-series data comprises sequences of data points collected over intervals of time. This type of data is pivotal in applications such as stock price prediction, weather forecasting, and monitoring sensor data. It is characterized by its temporal aspect, requiring specialized techniques for analysis. AI systems that leverage time-series data can identify patterns, trends, and anomalies, enhancing predictive capabilities across various domains.

The following is an example of time-series data:

https://data.cityofnewyork.us/Health/New-York-City-Leading-Causes-of-Death/jb7j-dtam/about_data

Categorical data

Categorical data represents discrete categories or labels. Examples include attributes like gender, color, or location. Categorical data can be nominal (without a specific order) or ordinal (with a meaningful order). Numerical data is crucial for regression tasks, which aim to predict a continuous outcome based on input features. It also provides valuable insights when used alongside categorical data.

Emerging data sources

The advent of new technologies continually introduces novel data sources, offering fresh opportunities for AI applications. Some emerging sources are as follows:

- **Internet of Things (IoT)**: IoT devices generate vast amounts of data in real-time, ranging from sensor readings to user interactions. This data is invaluable for applications like predictive maintenance and smart city development. The real-time nature of IoT data enables AI systems to make timely decisions based on current conditions, enhancing efficiency and responsiveness.

- **Social media**: Social media platforms are rich reservoirs of unstructured data, capturing user sentiments, trends, and interactions. This data can be harnessed for market analysis, brand sentiment tracking, and customer engagement. AI models can analyze social media data to gain insights into consumer behavior and preferences, enabling businesses to customize their strategies effectively.

- **Open data repositories**: Open data repositories, maintained by governments and organizations, provide access to diverse datasets across various domains, including health, transportation, and education. This data can be utilized for research, policy formulation, and predictive modeling. Open data fosters innovation and collaboration, allowing AI practitioners to develop models that address significant societal challenges.

Understanding the diverse data sources and types available for AI systems is essential for crafting effective data collection and ingestion strategies. From structured databases to the rich, unstructured content from social media, each data type brings a unique set of challenges and opportunities. As AI technology continues to evolve, the ability to harness these varied data sources will be crucial in driving the success of AI applications across industries. The subsequent sections will explore the methodologies and technologies for efficiently ingesting this data into AI systems, ensuring that organizations can fully leverage their data assets.

Batch vs. stream processing

Two primary paradigms exist in data processing for AI systems: batch processing and stream processing. Each approach has its own set of advantages and is suited to different types of applications. Understanding these paradigms is crucial for designing effective data ingestion and processing pipelines.

Batch processing

Batch processing involves collecting data over a period and then processing it in bulk. This approach is characterized by its ability to handle large volumes of data and perform complex computations. It is particularly useful for tasks that do not require immediate results. Examples include data warehousing, ETL operations, and historical data analysis.

Efficiency and complexity

One of the main advantages of batch processing is its efficiency in handling large datasets. By processing data in bulk, systems can optimize resource utilization and perform intricate computations. This makes batch processing ideal for tasks that involve significant data transformations and aggregations. However, this efficiency comes at the cost of higher latency. The time taken to accumulate and process the data means that insights derived from batch processing may lag real-time events.

Stream processing

Stream processing, on the other hand, deals with continuous data flow. Data is processed in real-time as it arrives, enabling immediate insights and actions. This approach is essential for applications that require real-time analytics, such as monitoring live data streams, fraud detection, and IoT applications. The primary advantage of stream processing is its ability to provide immediate insights. By processing data as events occur, stream processing systems offer real-time visibility and quick decision-making, making them ideal for applications where timely responses are critical. Stream processing is achieved through various techniques and technologies designed to handle continuous data streams efficiently. Some of the key techniques are as follows:

- **Event-driven architecture**: Processes data based on events, ensuring immediate action as each event occurs.

- **Windowing**: Divides the data stream into manageable chunks or windows, allowing for periodic analysis and aggregation.

- **Stateful processing**: Maintains state information across events, enabling complex computations and pattern recognition.

- **Backpressure handling**: Manages the flow of data to prevent system overload by adjusting the data intake rate.

Real-time responsiveness

The primary advantage of stream processing is its ability to provide immediate insights. By processing data as events occur, stream processing systems can offer real-time visibility and quick decision-making. This makes them ideal for applications where timely responses are critical. However, stream processing can be resource-intensive, requiring constant processing power and memory. It also demands robust systems to handle continuous data streams and ensure fault tolerance.

Choosing between batch and stream processing

The choice between batch and stream processing depends on the application's specific requirements and the nature of the data being processed. Applications needing real-time insights will benefit from stream processing, while those that can tolerate delays may opt for batch processing. Batch processing is well-suited for large volumes of historical data, whereas stream processing excels with continuous, high-velocity data. *Table 2.1* compares the various aspects of these two data processing paradigms:

Aspect	Batch processing	Stream processing
Data handling	Processes large volumes of data in bulk	Processes data continuously as it arrives
Latency	High latency; results available after the entire batch is processed	Low latency; near real-time results
Execution	Scheduled at intervals (e.g., nightly, weekly)	Continuous, event-driven execution
Complexity of computation	Ideal for complex, resource-intensive computations	Suited for simpler, real-time analytics
Resource management	Easier resource allocation for scheduled jobs	Requires constant resource availability and robust fault tolerance
Use cases	Data warehousing, ETL operations, historical data analysis	Real-time analytics, fraud detection, IoT applications
Advantages	Efficient for bulk data, supports complex transformations and aggregations	Provides immediate insights, ideal for applications requiring quick responses

Table 2.1: Comparison of batch and stream processing

Hybrid approaches

In many cases, a hybrid approach combining batch and stream processing can offer the best of both worlds. This approach leverages the strengths of each paradigm to meet diverse data processing needs. For example, the Lambda architecture combines batch and stream processing to provide both real-time and historical data analysis. The batch layer handles large-scale data processing, while the speed layer processes real-time data streams. Another example is the Kappa architecture, which focuses on stream processing but allows for reprocessing historical data by replaying data streams.

Flexibility and resilience

Hybrid approaches offer flexibility, resilience, and scalability. They can handle various data processing requirements, from real-time analytics to deep historical analysis. By providing redundancy and fault tolerance through multiple processing paths, hybrid approaches ensure that systems remain robust and reliable. Additionally, they offer scalable solutions for both real-time and batch data processing needs, making them an attractive option for complex data environments.

Tools and technologies

Several tools and technologies are available to implement batch and stream processing. Choosing the right tools depends on the specific requirements of the application and the existing technology stack. Popular tools for batch processing include Apache Hadoop, Apache Spark, and AWS Glue. These tools are optimized for processing large datasets and performing complex computations. For stream processing, widely used tools include Apache Kafka, Apache Flink, and Amazon Kinesis. These platforms are designed to handle real-time data feeds and provide low-latency processing.

Selecting the right tools

Selecting the appropriate tools is crucial for the success of data processing pipelines. Organizations must consider scalability, ease of integration, and support for specific data formats and protocols. By leveraging the right tools, they can ensure efficient and effective data processing, enabling their AI systems to deliver valuable insights and drive intelligent decision-making.

In summary, both batch and stream processing play crucial roles in the data processing landscape for AI systems. Batch processing excels at handling large volumes of data and performing complex computations, while stream processing provides real-time insights and immediate responsiveness. Understanding the strengths and limitations of each approach is essential for designing effective data pipelines that meet the specific needs of AI applications. By carefully considering factors such as latency requirements, data volume, and computational complexity and by leveraging the appropriate tools and technologies, organizations can harness the full potential of their data to drive intelligent decision-making and innovation.

Stream processing frameworks

Stream processing frameworks are pivotal in handling continuous data flows, enabling real-time analytics and immediate decision-making. These frameworks provide the tools and infrastructure to process data streams efficiently and effectively. Understanding the key frameworks and their features is essential for selecting the right solution for your needs.

Apache Kafka

Apache Kafka is a distributed streaming platform widely used for building real-time data pipelines and streaming applications. Originally developed by *LinkedIn*, it has become a cornerstone in stream processing. One of Kafka's standout features is its scalability. It can handle high throughput data streams, making it suitable for large-scale applications. Kafka achieves fault tolerance through data replication across multiple nodes, ensuring that data is not lost even if some nodes fail. Kafka is often used for log aggregation, real-time analytics, and event sourcing. Its ability to integrate with various data sources and sinks makes it a versatile choice for building robust data pipelines.

Apache Flink

Apache Flink is another powerful stream processing framework known for its high performance and low latency. Flink provides both stream and batch processing capabilities, making it a flexible choice for various data processing needs. Flink excels in stateful stream processing, maintaining state information across events. This feature is crucial for applications requiring complex event processing and pattern recognition. Flink's state management is both efficient and fault-tolerant, ensuring reliable processing. Flink supports event time processing, allowing it to gracefully handle out-of-order events. This capability is particularly useful when data arrives with varying delays, such as IoT applications and user activity tracking.

Apache Storm

Apache Storm is a real-time computation system designed for processing large streams of data. It provides a simple and flexible API for defining and executing stream processing topologies. One of Storm's key strengths is its low latency. It is designed to process data streams with minimal delay, making it suitable for applications requiring immediate responses, such as fraud detection and real-time monitoring. Storm's API is straightforward, allowing developers to build and deploy stream processing applications quickly. Its modular architecture enables easy integration with other systems and tools.

Apache Samza

Apache Samza is a stream processing framework developed by LinkedIn, designed to work seamlessly with Apache Kafka. Samza provides robust support for stateful stream processing and fault tolerance. Samza's tight integration with Kafka makes it an excellent choice for building end-to-end streaming solutions. It leverages Kafka's scalability and fault tolerance to ensure reliable data processing. Samza offers efficient state management, enabling applications to maintain and query state information across events. This feature is essential for applications requiring complex event processing and real-time analytics.

Spark Streaming

Spark Streaming is an extension of Apache Spark that enables scalable and fault-tolerant stream processing. It integrates seamlessly with the Spark ecosystem, providing a unified platform for batch and stream processing. Spark Streaming processes data streams in small batches, known as **micro-batches**. This approach simplifies stream processing while providing fault tolerance and scalability. Micro-batching is suitable for applications that can tolerate slight processing delays. One of Spark Streaming's key advantages is its integration with the broader Spark ecosystem. This integration allows developers to use the same APIs for both batch and stream processing, simplifying the development and maintenance of data pipelines.

Amazon Kinesis

Amazon Kinesis is a fully managed service for real-time data streaming on AWS. It provides a suite of tools for ingesting, processing, and analyzing data streams. As a fully managed service, Kinesis manages the underlying infrastructure, allowing developers to focus on building applications. This managed approach simplifies deployment, scaling, and maintenance. Kinesis integrates seamlessly with other AWS services, such as AWS Lambda, Amazon S3, and Amazon Redshift. This integration enables the creation of comprehensive data pipelines and analytics solutions within the AWS ecosystem.

Google Cloud Dataflow

Google Cloud Dataflow is a fully managed stream and batch processing service on the Google Cloud Platform. It is based on the Apache Beam programming model and provides a unified approach to data processing. Dataflow's use of the Apache Beam model allows developers to write code once and run it in both batch and stream processing modes. This unified approach simplifies the development and maintenance of data pipelines. Dataflow provides auto-scaling capabilities, dynamically adjusting resources based on the workload. This feature ensures efficient resource utilization and cost management.

Table 2.2 does a comparison between the four most popular stream processing frameworks from an AI architecture perspective:

Aspect	Data lake	Data warehouse
Data type	Stores raw, unprocessed data in its native format (structured, semi-structured, unstructured)	Stores structured data with predefined schema
Schema	Schema-on-read: schema applied when data is read	Schema-on-write: schema applied when data is written
Storage cost	Generally lower due to inexpensive storage solutions	Higher due to optimized storage and performance

Aspect	Data lake	Data warehouse
Data processing	Suitable for big data analytics, ML, and exploratory analysis	Optimized for querying, reporting, and business intelligence
Performance	May require additional processing for querying and analysis	High performance for read-heavy operations and complex queries
Flexibility	Highly flexible, can handle diverse data types and formats	Less flexible, designed for structured data and predefined queries
Scalability	Highly scalable, can store petabytes of data	Scalable but often with higher costs for large volumes
Data governance	Requires robust management to avoid becoming a data swamp	Easier to govern due to structured and organized data
Use cases	Data science, exploratory data analysis, ML, IoT	Business intelligence, operational analytics, financial reporting
Tools and technologies	Apache Hadoop, Amazon S3, Azure Data Lake	Amazon Redshift, Google BigQuery, Snowflake
Data freshness	Can ingest data in real-time but may need processing before use	Data is transformed and loaded (ETL) before use, ensuring consistency
Integration	Often integrated with data processing frameworks like Apache Spark	Integrated with ETL tools for data transformation and loading
Security and compliance	Requires comprehensive strategies for data security and compliance	Easier to implement security and compliance measures due to structure
Advantages	Cost-effective, flexible, supports a wide range of data types	High performance, reliable, optimized for structured data
Challenges	Risk of becoming a disorganized data swamp, requires robust governance	Higher storage costs, less flexibility with data types

Table 2.2: Comparison of data lake and data warehouse

By understanding the strengths and use cases of these top frameworks, organizations can make informed decisions and build effective real-time data processing solutions. Each of these frameworks has proven its mettle in the industry, powering some of the world's most demanding real-time applications and demonstrating their robustness, scalability, and versatility.

Data quality and validation techniques

Ensuring data quality is critical for any organization that relies on data-driven decision-making. Poor data quality can lead to incorrect insights, flawed strategies, and, ultimately, business failures. Data validation techniques are essential for maintaining high data quality by ensuring that data is accurate, complete, and consistent. This section explores the key concepts, techniques, and best practices for achieving and maintaining data quality.

Importance of data quality

Data quality refers to data conditions based on factors such as accuracy, completeness, consistency, reliability, and timeliness. High-quality data is crucial for effective decision-making, operational efficiency, and regulatory compliance. The explanation of the factors is as follows:

- **Accuracy**: Ensures that data correctly represents the real-world entities it is meant to model. Inaccurate data can lead to incorrect conclusions and misguided actions. For example, inaccurate sales data can result in poor inventory management and lost revenue.

- **Completeness**: This means that all required data is present. Missing data can lead to incomplete analyses and decisions based on partial information. For instance, missing customer information can hinder personalized marketing efforts.

- **Consistency**: Ensures that data is uniform across different datasets and systems. Inconsistent data can cause confusion and errors in data integration and analysis. For example, inconsistent product names across sales and inventory systems can lead to discrepancies in reporting.

- **Reliability**: Refers to the dependability of data over time. Reliable data is stable and trustworthy, ensuring that analyses and decisions based on it remain valid. Unreliable data can erode trust in data-driven processes.

- **Timeliness**: Ensures that data is up-to-date and available when needed. Outdated data can lead to decisions based on obsolete information, negatively impacting business outcomes.

Data validation techniques

Data validation techniques ensure that data meets the required quality standards. These techniques can be applied at various stages of the data lifecycle, from data entry to data integration and analysis.

Input validation

Input validation involves checking data at the entry point to ensure it meets predefined criteria. This technique helps prevent errors from entering the system in the first place. Common input validation methods are as follows:

- **Format checks**: Ensuring that data follows a specific format, such as email addresses or phone numbers.

- **Range checks**: Verifying that numerical data falls within a specified range, such as ages between 0 and 120.

- **Mandatory field checks**: Ensuring that required fields are not left empty.

Data profiling

Data profiling involves analyzing existing data to understand its structure, content, and quality. This technique helps identify data quality issues and informs the development of data validation rules. Key data profiling activities are as follows:

- **Frequency analysis**: Determining the frequency of different values in a dataset to identify anomalies.

- **Pattern analysis**: Identifying patterns and inconsistencies in data, such as unexpected null values or duplicate records.

- **Statistical analysis**: Using statistical methods to detect outliers and determine data distributions. Some data distributions include uniform, normal (Gaussian), binomial, poisson, exponential, log-normal, and chi-square. From an AI/ML perspective, data distribution helps determine the model selection, feature engineering, performance metrics, anomaly detection, and parameter tuning.

Data cleansing

Data cleansing, or data scrubbing, involves correcting or removing inaccurate, incomplete, or inconsistent data. This technique is essential for improving data quality before analysis or integration. Common data cleansing methods include the following:

- **Standardization**: Converting data to a common format or standard, such as date formats or units of measurement.

- **Deduplication**: Identifying and removing duplicate records to ensure data uniqueness.

- **Error correction**: Fixing data errors, such as typos or incorrect values, based on predefined rules or reference data.

Data enrichment

Data enrichment involves enhancing existing data by adding additional information from external sources. This technique improves data quality by filling in missing details and providing a more comprehensive view of the data. Examples of data enrichment are as follows:

- **Appending missing information**: Adding missing customer details from third-party databases.

- **Geocoding**: Adding geographic coordinates to address data for location-based analysis.

- **Categorization**: Classifying data into predefined categories, such as industry sectors or product types.

Enforcing constraints and handling violations

Enforcing constraints is a crucial aspect of data validation. Constraints ensure data adheres to specific rules and standards, maintaining integrity and quality.

The types of constraints are as follows:

- **Uniqueness constraints**: Ensure that each record is unique, preventing duplicate entries.

- **Referential integrity constraints**: Ensure relationships between tables, such as foreign key constraints, are maintained.

- **Domain constraints**: Ensure data values, such as valid ranges or permissible values, fall within a specific domain.

- **Business rules constraints**: Ensure data adheres to specific business rules, such as age restrictions or credit limits.

Handling constraint violations

When data fails to meet constraints, handling violations effectively is essential to maintain data quality. Common approaches include rejecting invalid data, using quarantine tables for review and correction, logging errors for auditing, and automated correction with predefined rules. Quarantine tables are a practical solution for handling constraint violations without losing valuable data. When data fails validation checks, it is moved to a quarantine table where it can be reviewed, corrected, and reprocessed. This approach ensures that data quality issues are addressed while preserving the original data for analysis and correction.

Handling missing data

Missing data is a common issue that can compromise data quality and analysis, especially when the data is used to train a ML model. Effectively addressing missing data is crucial for maintaining the integrity of datasets and the effectiveness of an ML model.

Types of missing data can be broadly categorized as follows:

- **Missing completely at random (MCAR)**: Data missing with no apparent pattern.

- **Missing at random (MAR)**: Data missing with a pattern related to other observed data.

- **Missing not at random (MNAR)**: Data missing with a pattern related to the missing data itself.

Data imputation techniques help deal with missing values in data. They involve filling in missing values using various techniques. Modern AI and ML methods offer advanced imputation capabilities. Techniques include mean/median/mode imputation, **k-nearest neighbors** (**KNN**) imputation, multiple imputation, and using ML models to predict and impute missing values.

Data integration validation

Data integration validation ensures that data remains accurate and consistent as it is combined from multiple sources. This technique is crucial for maintaining data quality in warehouses and lakes. Data integration validation methods include schema matching, data lineage tracking, and reconciliation. Automated data validation uses software tools and algorithms to monitor and validate data quality continuously. This technique helps maintain high data quality with minimal manual intervention. Common automated data validation methods include rule-based validation, ML for anomaly detection, and real-time monitoring.

Ensuring data quality is essential for accurate and reliable data-driven decision-making. By understanding the importance of data quality and implementing effective data validation techniques, organizations can maintain high data quality and derive meaningful insights from their data. Key techniques such as input validation, data profiling, data cleansing, data enrichment, enforcing constraints, handling constraint violations, and automated data validation play crucial roles in achieving and maintaining data quality. Additionally, addressing missing data through data imputation techniques, including AI/ML methods, further enhances data integrity. Adhering to best practices, such as establishing data governance, defining data quality metrics, implementing data quality tools, fostering a data quality culture, and continuous improvement, further enhances data quality management efforts. Organizations can build a solid foundation for successful data-driven initiatives by prioritizing data quality.

Scalable ingestion architectures

In the era of big data, scalable ingestion architectures are fundamental to efficiently and reliably move vast amounts of data from various sources into data lakes, warehouses, and real-time analytics platforms. This section examines the concepts and techniques for building scalable ingestion architectures, focusing on **Change Data Capture** (**CDC**) as a pivotal method.

The need for scalable ingestion

As organizations generate and consume data at unprecedented rates, traditional data ingestion methods often fall short in scalability and performance. Scalable ingestion architectures are designed to handle high throughput data streams, ensure low latency, and maintain data integrity across distributed systems. The following features are desirable in data ingestion from a scalability perspective:

- **High throughput**: Modern applications generate large volumes of data in real time. Scalable ingestion architectures must support high throughput data ingestion to keep up with the pace of data generation. This includes handling data from IoT devices, social media, transactional systems, and more.

- **Low latency**: In real-time analytics and decision-making scenarios, low latency is crucial. Scalable ingestion architectures minimize the delay between data generation and data availability for analysis. This is essential for fraud detection, real-time monitoring, and personalized recommendations.

- **Data integrity**: Maintaining data integrity during ingestion is critical. Scalable architectures ensure data is accurately captured, transformed, and loaded without loss or corruption. This involves handling various data formats, ensuring schema compatibility, and managing data quality.

Change Data Capture

CDC is a technique for identifying and capturing changes made to data in a source system and applying those changes to a target system. CDC plays a vital role in scalable ingestion architectures by enabling real-time data replication and synchronization.

CDC captures data changes by monitoring transaction logs, database triggers, or timestamp columns. When a change occurs in the source system, CDC captures the change event and propagates it to the target system. This approach ensures that the target system remains in sync with the source system in near real-time.

There are several benefits of implementing the CDC in the scalable implementation architecture. They are as follows:

- **Real-time data replication**: CDC enables real-time data replication, ensuring that changes in the source system are immediately reflected in the target system.

- **Reduced load on source systems**: CDC reduces the load on source systems compared to full data extraction methods by capturing only the changes.

- **Efficient data movement**: CDC efficiently moves data by transmitting only incremental changes, reducing network bandwidth and storage requirements.

Implementing CDC

Implementing CDC involves selecting the right tools and techniques based on the specific requirements of the data sources and target systems. The following are some common approaches:

- **Log-based CDC**: It captures changes directly from the database transaction logs. This method is highly efficient and minimally invasive, as it leverages the existing logging mechanisms of the database. Tools like Debezium and Oracle GoldenGate are popular for log-based CDC.

- **Trigger-based CDC**: It uses database triggers to capture changes. When a data modification occurs, the trigger records the change in a separate table or log. This method is relatively easy to implement but can introduce additional overhead on the database.

- **Timestamp-based CDC**: This method relies on timestamp columns to identify changes. By comparing the timestamps of the last extraction with the current data, this method captures only the new or modified records. While simple to implement, it may not capture all changes, such as deletions.

Best practices for scalable ingestion

Building scalable ingestion architectures requires careful planning and adherence to best practices. The following are some key considerations:

- **Scalability and flexibility**: Design your ingestion architecture to scale horizontally. Use distributed systems and cloud-based services to handle increasing data volumes and workloads. Ensure the architecture is flexible enough to accommodate new data sources and changing requirements.

- **Data partitioning**: Partitioning data helps distribute the load across multiple nodes, improving performance and scalability. Use partitioning strategies that align with your data access patterns, such as time-based or key-based partitioning.

- **Fault tolerance and reliability**: Implement fault-tolerant mechanisms to ensure data availability and reliability. Use replication, data backups, and failover strategies to handle hardware failures, network issues, and other disruptions.

- **Monitoring and alerting**: Continuously monitor your ingestion pipelines to detect and resolve issues promptly. Use monitoring tools to track performance metrics, data quality, and system health. Set up alerts to notify you of anomalies or failures.

- **Data security and compliance**: Ensure that your ingestion architecture complies with data security and privacy regulations. Implement encryption, access controls, and audit logging to protect sensitive data. Regularly review and update your security policies to address emerging threats.

Scalable ingestion architectures are essential for handling the growing volume, velocity, and variety of data in modern enterprises. Techniques like CDC are pivotal in enabling real-time data replication and synchronization. By implementing scalable ingestion patterns such as batch processing, stream processing, and Lambda architecture, organizations can efficiently ingest and process data to derive valuable insights. Adhering to best practices for scalability, fault tolerance, monitoring, and security ensures that the ingestion architecture remains robust and reliable. As data grows, scalable ingestion architectures will be the backbone of successful data-driven initiatives.

Security and compliance in data ingestion

In the age of data-driven decision-making, the security and compliance of data ingestion processes are paramount. Ensuring that data is ingested securely and in compliance with regulatory requirements protects sensitive information, builds trust, and mitigates risks. This section explores the key concepts, techniques, and best practices for achieving security and compliance in data ingestion.

Importance of security in data ingestion

Data ingestion involves transferring data from various sources into centralized storage systems. This process often handles sensitive and confidential information, making it a prime target for cyberattacks. Data ingestion is necessary to protect against the following:

- **Data breaches**: Data breaches can have severe consequences, including financial losses, reputational damage, and legal penalties. Securing data ingestion pipelines helps prevent unauthorized access and data leaks, safeguarding the organization's assets.

- **Unauthorized access**: Unauthorized access to data can lead to data manipulation, theft, and misuse. Implementing robust access controls and authentication mechanisms ensures that only authorized personnel can access and modify data.

- **Data integrity**: Maintaining data integrity during ingestion is crucial. Ensuring that data is not altered or corrupted during transfer protects its accuracy and reliability, which are essential for decision-making and analysis.

- **Compliance in data ingestion**: Compliance with regulatory requirements is a critical aspect of data ingestion. Various laws and regulations govern how data should be handled, stored, and protected. Adhering to these regulations ensures legal compliance and helps avoid penalties and sanctions.

- **GDPR**: The **General Data Protection Regulation** (**GDPR**) governs the processing of EU citizens' personal data. Organizations must ensure that data ingestion processes comply with GDPR requirements, including data minimization, consent, and the right to be forgotten.

- **HIPAA**: The **Health Insurance Portability and Accountability Act** (**HIPAA**) sets standards for protecting sensitive health information. Ensuring compliance with HIPAA involves implementing safeguards to protect patient data during ingestion and storage.

- **CCPA**: The **California Consumer Privacy Act** (**CCPA**) provides California residents with data privacy rights. Organizations must ensure that data ingestion processes comply with CCPA requirements, including access, deletion, and opt-out provisions.

Techniques for securing data ingestion

Implementing security measures during data ingestion protects against threats and vulnerabilities. The following are some key techniques for securing data ingestion:

- **Encryption**: Encryption is a fundamental technique for protecting data during ingestion. Encrypting data in transit and at rest ensures that even if data is intercepted, it remains unreadable without the decryption key.

- **TLS/SSL**: **Transport Layer Security** (**TLS**) and **Secure Sockets Layer** (**SSL**) protocols encrypt data during transmission, protecting it from eavesdropping and tampering.

- **AES**: **Advanced Encryption Standard** (**AES**) is commonly used to encrypt data at rest, ensuring that stored data remains secure.

Access controls

Implementing access controls ensures that only authorized personnel can access and modify data. **Role-based access control** (**RBAC**) and **attribute-based access control** (**ABAC**) are common methods for managing access permissions. The description is as follows:

- **RBAC**: Assigns access permissions based on user roles, ensuring that users have only the necessary access to perform their duties.

- **ABAC**: This method uses attributes such as user, resource, and environment characteristics to determine access permissions, providing fine-grained access control.

Authentication and authorization

Strong authentication and authorization mechanisms prevent unauthorized access to data ingestion pipelines. **Multi-factor authentication** (**MFA**) and **single sign-on** (**SSO**) are effective methods for enhancing security:

- **MFA**: Requires users to provide multiple forms of identification, such as passwords and biometric data, to access the system.

- **SSO**: Allows users to authenticate once and gain access to multiple systems, simplifying the authentication process while maintaining security.

Data masking

Data masking involves obfuscating sensitive data to protect it from unauthorized access. Masked data retains its usability for testing and analysis while protecting sensitive information. The types are as follows:

- **Static data masking**: Masks data in storage, ensuring that sensitive information is hidden in non-production environments.

- **Dynamic data masking**: Masks data in real-time, protecting sensitive information during access and processing.

Network security best practices

Opening ports only to the required traffic minimizes the attack surface and reduces the risk of unauthorized access. Configuring firewalls and network security groups to allow only necessary traffic ensures that data ingestion pipelines remain secure. Managing access permissions using IAM roles provides a secure and scalable way to control access to data ingestion resources. IAM roles allow you to define and enforce access policies without hardcoding user IDs and passwords, enhancing security and compliance. Hardcoding user IDs and passwords in code or configuration files is a security risk. Using secure methods such as environment variables, secret management tools, or IAM roles ensures that credentials are protected and not exposed in source code.

Compliance best practices

Adhering to best practices ensures that data ingestion processes comply with regulatory requirements and industry standards. The following are some key best practices for achieving compliance:

- **Data minimization**: Data minimization involves collecting only the necessary data for specific purposes. Reducing the amount of collected data minimizes the risk of exposure and ensures compliance with privacy regulations.

- **Consent management**: Obtaining and managing user consent is crucial for compliance with data privacy regulations. Implementing consent management mechanisms ensures that data is collected and processed with user consent.

  o **Explicit consent**: Users must provide clear and affirmative consent before data collection.

  o **Granular consent**: Allows users to consent to specific data processing activities, providing greater control over their data.

- **Data auditing and monitoring**: Regularly auditing and monitoring data ingestion processes ensures compliance and identifies potential security issues. Implementing auditing and monitoring tools helps track data access, modifications, and transfers.

o **Audit logs**: Maintain detailed data access and modification records, providing a trail for compliance and forensic investigations.

o **Real-time monitoring**: Continuously monitors data ingestion pipelines for anomalies and unauthorized activities, enabling prompt detection and response.

- **Data retention and deletion**: Implementing data retention and deletion policies ensures compliance with regulations that govern data storage duration. Regularly reviewing and deleting unnecessary data reduces the risk of exposure and ensures compliance with data retention requirements.

Implementing security and compliance in practice

Implementing security and compliance measures requires technology, policies, and procedures. The following are practical points for achieving security and compliance in data ingestion:

- **Security policies and procedures**: Establishing security policies and procedures provides a framework for protecting data during ingestion. Policies should address encryption, access controls, authentication, data masking, network security, and incident response.

- **Training and awareness**: Training employees on best security and compliance practices ensures they understand their roles and responsibilities. Regular training and awareness programs help maintain a security-conscious culture within the organization.

- **Technology solutions**: Leveraging technology solutions enhances security and compliance efforts. Implementing encryption tools, access control systems, authentication mechanisms, network security configurations, and monitoring tools provides robust protection for data ingestion processes.

- **Regular assessments**: Conducting regular security and compliance assessments identifies potential vulnerabilities and ensures that measures are effective. Assessments should include penetration testing, vulnerability scanning, and compliance audits.

Security and compliance are critical components of data ingestion processes. Ensuring that data is ingested securely and in compliance with regulatory requirements protects sensitive information, builds trust, and mitigates risks. Techniques such as encryption, access controls, authentication, data masking, IAM roles, and network security enhance security, while best practices like data minimization, consent management, auditing, and data retention ensure compliance. By implementing a combination of technology, policies, and procedures, organizations can achieve robust security and compliance in their data ingestion processes. As data grows in volume and complexity, prioritizing security and compliance will be essential for successful data-driven initiatives.

Cloud-native ingestion services

Cloud-native ingestion services have revolutionized the way organizations handle data ingestion, offering unparalleled scalability, flexibility, and ease of use. These services, provided by major cloud platforms like AWS, Azure, and Google Cloud, simplify ingesting data from various sources into data lakes, warehouses, and real-time analytics platforms. This section explores some of the most popular cloud-native ingestion services, their features, and their applications.

AWS Glue

AWS Glue is a fully managed ETL service that streamlines data preparation and loading for analytics. With AWS Glue, you can effortlessly discover, catalog, clean, enrich, and move data between various data stores.

The key features are as follows:

- **Data catalog**: AWS Glue automatically discovers and catalogs metadata about your data stores, facilitating easy search and query of data.

- **ETL jobs**: Create and run ETL jobs to transform and move data between sources and destinations. AWS Glue supports both code-based and visual ETL development.

- **Serverless**: AWS Glue is serverless, eliminating the need to manage infrastructure. It scales automatically to handle varying data volumes.

AWS Glue is ideal for building data lakes, preparing data for ML, and integrating data from multiple sources for analytics. It supports various data sources, including S3, RDS, and Redshift.

Azure Data Factory

Azure Data Factory (**ADF**) is a cloud-based data integration service that allows you to create, schedule, and orchestrate data workflows. ADF supports seamless data movement and transformation across various data stores and services.

The key features are as follows:

- **Data pipelines**: ADF enables the creation of data pipelines that define the workflow for data movement and transformation. You can design these pipelines using a visual interface or code.

- **Integration runtime**: ADF provides a scalable and secure integration runtime that enables data movement and transformation across cloud and on-premises environments.

- **Activity library**: ADF offers a rich library of data transformation activities, including data flow, copy, and lookup.

Azure Data Factory is suitable for hybrid data integration, ETL processes, and data orchestration across diverse data sources and destinations. It supports various data stores, including Azure Blob Storage, SQL Database, and Cosmos DB.

Google Cloud Dataflow

Google Cloud Dataflow is a fully managed service for stream and batch data processing. It allows you to build data pipelines capable of processing data in real-time or in batches.

The key features are as follows:

- **Unified programming model**: Dataflow uses Apache Beam, which allows you to write both batch and stream processing pipelines.

- **Auto-scaling**: Dataflow automatically scales your data pipelines based on data volume, ensuring optimal performance and cost-efficiency.

- **Integration**: Dataflow integrates seamlessly with other Google Cloud services, such as BigQuery, Cloud Storage, and Pub/Sub.

Google Cloud Dataflow is ideal for real-time analytics, ETL processes, and data preparation for ML. It supports batch and stream processing, making it versatile for various data processing needs.

Amazon Kinesis

Amazon Kinesis is a platform for real-time data streaming and analytics. It enables you to ingest, process, and analyze real-time data streams at scale.

The key features are as follows:

- **Kinesis data streams**: Capture and store real-time data streams from various sources, such as IoT devices, application logs, and social media.

- **Kinesis data firehose**: Fully managed service for loading real-time data streams into data lakes, warehouses, and analytics services.

- **Kinesis data analytics**: Analyze real-time data streams using SQL queries and build real-time dashboards and alerts.

Amazon Kinesis is suitable for real-time monitoring, log and event data processing, and real-time analytics. It integrates with other AWS services, such as S3, Redshift, and Lambda.

Azure Stream Analytics

Azure Stream Analytics is a real-time service that processes and analyzes streaming data from various sources.

The key features are as follows:

- **Stream processing**: Write SQL-like queries to process and analyze streaming data in real-time.

- **Integration**: Integrates with Azure services like Event Hubs, IoT Hub, and Blob Storage for seamless data ingestion and processing.

- **Scalability**: Automatically scales to handle varying data volumes, ensuring high availability and performance.

Azure Stream Analytics is ideal for real-time analytics, IoT data processing, and alerting. It supports various data sources, including Azure Event Hubs, IoT Hubs, and Blob Storage.

Google Cloud Pub/Sub

Google Cloud Pub/Sub is a messaging service that ingests and delivers real-time messages between independent applications.

The key features are as follows:

- **Publish-subscribe model**: Decouples data producers and consumers, enabling scalable and reliable data ingestion.

- **Real-time messaging**: Supports real-time message delivery with low latency, ensuring timely data processing and analytics.

- **Integration**: Integrates with other Google Cloud services, such as Dataflow, BigQuery, and Cloud Functions, for seamless data processing.

Google Cloud Pub/Sub suits real-time messaging, event-driven architectures, and data integration. It supports various data sources and destinations, making it versatile for use cases.

Cloud-native ingestion services offer robust capabilities for efficiently ingesting and processing data at scale. Services like AWS Glue, Azure Data Factory, Google Cloud Dataflow, Amazon Kinesis, Azure Stream Analytics, and Google Cloud Pub/Sub provide comprehensive solutions for various data ingestion needs. Organizations can build reliable and efficient data ingestion pipelines by leveraging these services, enabling data-driven insights and decision-making. As data grows in volume and complexity, cloud-native ingestion services will be pivotal in driving successful data initiatives.

Sample architecture for data collection and ingestion

Designing an architecture for data collection and ingestion for AI involves integrating various components to ensure efficient, secure, and compliant data processing. This architecture leverages scalable ingestion methods, cloud-native services, and robust security measures. The following is a detailed description of a sample architecture encompassing all the aspects covered in this chapter.

In our sample architecture, which is based on the AWS ecosystem, we can have the following components:

- **Data sources**: Transactional databases including line item and master data (structured data containing categorical values), IoT data (in this case, time series data), social media data (images and videos which are largely unstructured), log files in XML format, which is semi-structured.

- **Data ingestion**: We use AWS Glue for data ingestion, batch processing for transactional data sources, and trigger-based CDC to ingest IoT data.

   o **Real-time processing**: We use Amazon Kinesis to process real-time data from IoT, social media, and application logs.

   o **Data processing:** We use AWS Glue ETL jobs for transformation and Kinesis data analytics for real-time streams using SQL queries.

   o **Data storage:** Amazon S3 is used for a data lake, and Amazon Redshift is used for a data warehouse to run managed queries.

- **Data security and compliance**: Use TLS/SSL protocols to encrypt data during transmission at various stages, along with at-rest encryption when storing in a data lake or warehouse. Use MFA in conjunction with SSO to maintain security across all systems. Configure firewalls and security groups to allow only necessary traffic and assign proper IAM roles to various entities in the architecture. Lastly, firewalls and security groups should be configured to allow only necessary traffic, minimizing the attack surface.

In subsequent chapters, we will explore additional components like data storage, management, and processing. By the end of *Chapter 4, Data Processing and Transformation for AI*, we will have a schematic diagram connecting the components discussed in this chapter to create an end-to-end data ingestion framework.

Conclusion

This chapter has provided a comprehensive exploration of the foundational processes essential for any data-driven enterprise. We began by delving into the core principles of data ingestion, understanding its critical role in ensuring that data is both high-quality and timely. Recognizing the nuances between batch and real-time ingestion methods has equipped you with the knowledge to choose the right approach for various business scenarios.

We then navigated the complex landscape of data security and compliance, emphasizing the importance of safeguarding sensitive information throughout the ingestion process. By implementing robust security measures such as encryption, access controls, and data masking and adhering to regulatory requirements like GDPR, HIPAA, and CCPA, you can ensure that your data practices are both secure and compliant.

The chapter also introduced you to the powerful capabilities of cloud-native ingestion services. Tools like AWS Glue, Azure Data Factory, and Google Cloud Dataflow offer scalable and flexible solutions for managing data ingestion tasks, while real-time streaming services such as Amazon Kinesis and Azure Stream Analytics enable instantaneous data processing and analytics. These services are indispensable in modern data architectures, providing the scalability and efficiency required to handle large volumes of data.

Finally, we synthesized the chapter's concepts into a sample architecture for data collection and ingestion tailored for AI applications. This architecture integrates the discussed methodologies, tools, and best practices, offering a practical blueprint for building robust, secure, and compliant data ingestion pipelines.

By mastering the strategies and tools covered in this chapter, you are now well-prepared to lay a strong foundation for advanced analytics and AI-driven insights. As you move forward, the knowledge and skills gained here will be instrumental in navigating the increasingly complex data landscape, enabling you to harness the full potential of your data assets.

In the next chapter, we will transition from data ingestion to data storage and management. We will explore the intricacies of data lakes, data warehouses, and hybrid storage solutions, examining their respective architectures, benefits, and use cases. You will learn about the best practices for organizing, partitioning, and optimizing your data storage to ensure seamless access and efficient querying. Additionally, we will look into data governance and metadata management, which are crucial for maintaining data integrity and enabling effective data discovery.

Join our Discord space

Join our Discord workspace for latest updates, offers, tech happenings around the world, new releases, and sessions with the authors:

https://discord.bpbonline.com

CHAPTER 3
Data Storage and Management for AI Workloads

Introduction

In the era of big data and AI, robust data storage and management are the backbone of successful AI initiatives. This chapter examines these crucial components, emphasizing their role in the overall AI architecture.

We explore data storage architectures, on-premises, cloud-based, and hybrid models. Each offers unique benefits and challenges, impacting storage capacity, accessibility, scalability, and cost-efficiency. Understanding these architectures is vital for aligning your storage strategy with AI objectives.

Next, we tackle data integration and interoperability. Seamless data flow across diverse sources enhances AI model accuracy and efficiency, making it a cornerstone of AI projects. We also discuss maintaining data consistency and synchronization in real-time applications, highlighting techniques to ensure data integrity and minimize latency.

Security and compliance are paramount. This chapter covers encryption techniques, access controls, and regulatory compliance to protect sensitive data, crucial in today's landscape of data breaches and stringent regulations.

Cost management is another key focus. We offer insights into cost optimization strategies that balance expenses with performance, ensuring sustainable AI initiatives. Performance optimization techniques like load balancing, strategic data placement, and caching are also discussed to enhance system efficiency.

Structure

The chapter covers the following topics:

- Database types for AI
- Distributed storage systems
- Data lakes and data warehouses for AI
- Delta Lake, the backbone of lakehouse
- Data versioning and lineage tracking
- Metadata management and cataloging
- Partitioning and indexing strategies
- Hybrid and multi-cloud storage solutions

Objectives

By the end of this chapter, you will have a solid grasp of the essential data storage architectures for AI workloads, including on-premises, cloud-based, and hybrid models. You will learn to evaluate and select the best storage strategy that aligns with your AI goals and organizational needs.

We will study data integration and interoperability complexities, offering best practices to ensure seamless data flow across diverse systems. A key focus will be understanding how to maintain data consistency and synchronization in real-time AI applications, equipping you with techniques to ensure data integrity and minimize latency.

Security and compliance are critical in the AI landscape. You will explore advanced encryption methods and stringent access controls to protect sensitive data and strategies for navigating regulatory frameworks to ensure compliance.

Cost management will be another important topic where you will discover strategies to balance expenses without sacrificing performance. We will also cover performance optimization techniques, including load balancing, strategic data placement, and caching, to ensure your AI systems run efficiently.

Finally, we will address the risks of vendor lock-in and provide strategies to maintain flexibility and portability, such as using open standards, APIs, containerization, and orchestration tools. By mastering these objectives, you will be well-equipped to manage data storage for scalable, secure, and efficient AI workloads.

Database types for AI

In AI, data is the lifeblood that fuels algorithms and models. The choice of database systems can significantly impact AI workloads' efficiency, scalability, and performance.

This section explores the primary database types, relational, NoSQL, and NewSQL, and examines their characteristics, strengths, and suitability for various AI applications.

Relational databases

Relational databases have been the cornerstone of data management for decades. They organize data into tables with rows and columns, utilizing **structured query language (SQL)** for data manipulation. These databases are known for their ACID properties, ensuring reliable transactions and data integrity.

Characteristics and strengths

The characteristics and strengths are as follows:

- **Structured data**: Relational databases excel at handling structured data with predefined schemas. This makes them ideal for applications where data relationships are well-defined and consistent.
- **ACID compliance**: Ensures data integrity and reliability, which is crucial for transactional systems.
- **Mature ecosystem**: Extensive tooling, robust performance tuning options, and widespread support in the developer community.

Suitability for AI workloads

While relational databases are excellent for structured data, they face challenges with the scalability and flexibility required for AI workloads:

- **Scalability**: Traditional relational databases can struggle with horizontal scaling, which is critical for large-scale AI applications.
- **Flexibility**: AI often involves unstructured or semi-structured data (for example, text and images), which relational databases are not optimized for.

Some popular relational databases include the following

- **MySQL**: Open-source and highly popular, known for its ease of use and reliability.
- **PostgreSQL**: Offers advanced features like support for JSON and XML, making it more flexible for semi-structured data.
- **Oracle database**: Known for its robustness and extensive feature set, often used in enterprise environments.

NoSQL databases

NoSQL databases emerged to address the limitations of relational databases, particularly in terms of scalability and flexibility. They are designed to handle various data types and are optimized for distributed architectures.

Characteristics and strengths

The characteristics and strengths are as follows:

- **Schema-less design**: Allows for flexible data models, accommodating unstructured and semi-structured data.

- **Horizontal scalability**: Designed to scale out by distributing data across multiple nodes, making them ideal for large-scale AI applications.

- **Diverse data models**: Includes document stores, key-value stores, column-family stores, and graph databases, each optimized for different data types and queries.

Types of NoSQL databases

The types of NoSQL databases are as follows:

- **Document stores**: MongoDB and Couchbase store data in JSON-like documents, making them flexible and easy to use for hierarchical data.

- **Key-value stores**: Redis and DynamoDB are optimized for simple key-value pair storage, providing high performance for specific use cases.

- **Column-family stores**: Apache Cassandra and HBase are designed for high write throughput and are often used in big data applications.

- **Graph databases**: Neo4j and Amazon Neptune are optimized for storing and querying graph structures, making them ideal for applications involving complex relationships.

Suitability for AI workloads

NoSQL databases are well-suited for AI workloads due to their scalability and flexibility:

- **Handling diverse data types**: Can easily store and manage unstructured data like text, images, and sensor data.

- **Scalability**: Their distributed nature allows them to handle large volumes of data, which is common in AI applications.

- **Performance**: Optimized for specific use cases, providing high performance for read and write operations.

Popular NoSQL databases include the following:

- **MongoDB**: Known for its flexibility and ease of use, it is widely adopted in AI and big data applications.

- **Apache Cassandra**: Offers high availability and scalability, making it suitable for large-scale AI applications.

- **Neo4j**: Optimized for graph data, used in applications involving social networks, recommendation systems, and fraud detection.

NewSQL databases

NewSQL databases aim to combine the best of both relational and NoSQL worlds, offering the scalability of NoSQL systems while maintaining the ACID properties of traditional relational databases.

Characteristics and strengths

The characteristics and strengths are as follows:

- **Scalability**: Designed to scale out horizontally, similar to NoSQL databases, but with the reliability and consistency of relational databases.

- **ACID compliance**: Ensures data integrity and reliability, which is crucial for applications requiring transactional support.

- **SQL interface**: Provides a familiar SQL interface, making it easier for developers to adopt and integrate with existing systems.

Suitability for AI workloads

NewSQL databases are particularly suited for AI workloads that require both scalability and strong consistency:

- **Transactional AI applications**: Ideal for applications that need to handle large volumes of data while ensuring data integrity, such as financial services and healthcare.

- **Mixed workloads**: Can efficiently handle both transactional and analytical workloads, making them versatile for various AI use cases.

Popular NewSQL databases include the following:

- **Google Spanner**: A globally distributed NewSQL database known for its strong consistency and scalability.

- **CockroachDB**: Offers horizontal scalability and strong consistency, designed to survive data center failures.

- **VoltDB**: Optimized for high throughput transactional workloads, often used in real-time analytics and ML applications.

Comparative analysis

To understand how these three types of databases fit into the overall AI landscape, it is essential to compare them based on key criteria relevant to AI workloads: scalability, flexibility, data integrity, and performance. The following table summarizes how each database type is from an AI workload perspective.

Table 3.1 is a comparison of relational, NoSQL, and NewSQL databases on multiple aspects:

Criteria	Relation databases	NoSQL databases	NewSQL databases
Scalability	Limited horizontal scalability	Designed for horizontal scalability	Horizontal scalability with ACID
Flexibility	Best for structured data	Highly flexible for diverse data types	Balance of flexibility and structure
Data integrity	Strong ACID compliance	Often eventual consistency	Strong ACID compliance
Performance	High for structured data, transactions	Optimized for specific use cases	High for both transactional and analytical workloads
Overall fit in AI	Best for smaller-scale, structured data	Ideal for large-scale, diverse data	Suitable for large-scale, mixed workloads requiring consistency

Table 3.1: Comparison of relational, NoSQL and NewSQL databases

Distributed storage systems

The need for robust and scalable storage solutions becomes paramount as AI workloads grow in complexity and scale. Distributed storage systems have emerged as a cornerstone in the modern data architecture for AI, offering the ability to store and manage massive volumes of data across multiple nodes. This section explores the key distributed storage systems, including **Hadoop Distributed File System (HDFS)** and object storage solutions, examining their characteristics, strengths, and suitability for AI applications.

Introduction to distributed storage systems

Distributed storage systems are designed to spread data across multiple physical or virtual nodes, providing high availability, fault tolerance, and scalability. These systems are essential for AI workloads, which often involve processing large datasets that exceed the capacity of a single machine. By distributing data, these systems ensure that data remains accessible and resilient, even in the face of hardware failures or network issues. This architecture is crucial for AI applications that demand uninterrupted access to vast amounts of data for training, inference, and real-time analytics.

Hadoop Distributed File System

The HDFS is a pivotal component of the Apache Hadoop ecosystem, engineered specifically for storing and managing large datasets in a distributed environment. HDFS divides large files into smaller blocks and distributes them across multiple nodes, enabling parallel processing and efficient storage management. This block storage mechanism is complemented by data replication, where each data block is typically replicated across three different nodes. This replication ensures fault tolerance and high availability, as the system can continue to function even if some nodes fail.

Figure 3.1 shows the basic architecture of a HDFS:

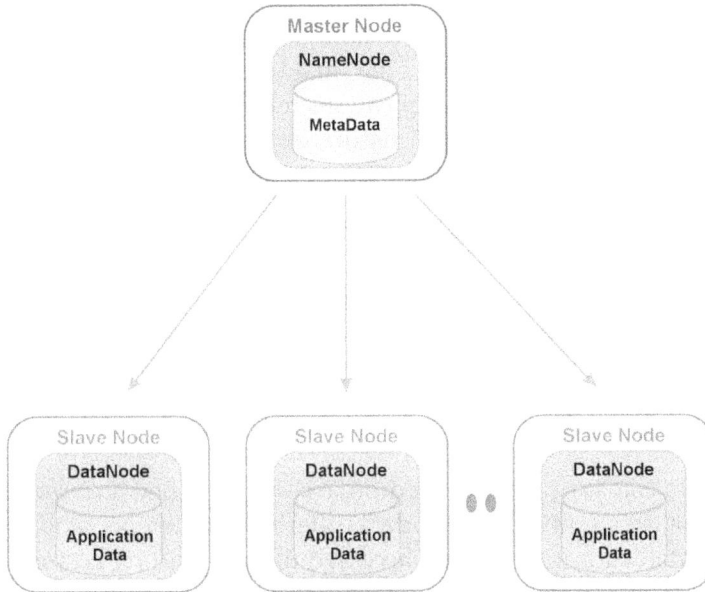

Figure 3.1: *Basic architecture of a HDFS*

HDFS's scalability is one of its most significant advantages. It can easily scale out by adding more nodes to the cluster, making it capable of handling petabytes of data. This scalability is particularly beneficial for AI applications that require processing and analyzing massive datasets. For instance, in an ML pipeline, HDFS can store vast amounts of training data, facilitating efficient data retrieval and processing. Integrating HDFS with other Hadoop components, such as MapReduce, Apache Hive, and Apache Spark, further enhances its utility in big data and AI applications. These integrations enable seamless data processing workflows, from data ingestion to model training and evaluation.

HDFS is often used as the underlying storage layer for data lakes, where raw data from various sources is stored and processed. In this context, HDFS provides a cost-effective storage solution, often deployed on commodity hardware. This cost efficiency, its robustness, and scalability make HDFS an ideal choice for AI applications requiring large-scale data processing.

Object storage

Object storage represents a modern storage architecture that manages data as objects rather than files or blocks. Each object in an object storage system contains the data itself, metadata, and a unique identifier, making it highly scalable and flexible. This architecture is particularly well-suited for storing unstructured data types, such as images, videos, and text, which are common in AI applications.

One of the defining characteristics of object storage is its scalability. Object storage systems can scale horizontally by adding more nodes, making them capable of handling exabytes of data. Scalability is essential for AI applications requiring vast data for training complex models. Additionally, the metadata-rich nature of object storage enables advanced data management and retrieval capabilities, allowing AI systems to access and process the data they need efficiently.

Public cloud services like Amazon S3, Google Cloud Storage, and Azure Blob Storage offer highly scalable and durable object storage solutions with global availability. These services provide a robust infrastructure for AI applications, enabling seamless data storage and retrieval across different regions. For example, an AI application that involves image recognition can store millions of images in a cloud-based object storage system, allowing for efficient data access and processing.

Object storage tiers categorize data based on access frequency and retention needs. Hot storage is ideal for frequently accessed data, offering low latency and high throughput. Cold storage is suitable for infrequently accessed data, providing cost-effective long-term storage. Glacier storage is designed for very low-frequency access and long-term retention, offering the lowest cost per terabyte.

On-premises object storage solutions, such as MinIO, Ceph, and OpenStack Swift, offer similar capabilities for organizations that prefer maintaining control over their data and compliance. These solutions provide the flexibility to deploy object storage within a private data center, ensuring data security and compliance with regulatory requirements.

Object storage is often used as the storage layer for data lakes, providing a scalable and cost-effective solution for storing raw data. In ML and deep learning applications, object storage facilitates the storage of large datasets used for training models. For instance, a deep learning application that requires vast amounts of video data for training can leverage object storage to store and manage these large files efficiently.

Comparison of HDFS and object storage

To understand the fit of HDFS and object storage in the AI landscape, it is essential to compare them based on key criteria relevant to AI workloads. *Table 3.2* does the comparison between HDFS and object storage based on multiple criteria:

Criteria	HDFS	Object storage
Scalability	High, scales out by adding nodes	Very high, scales out horizontally
Flexibility	Optimized for large-scale batch processing	Highly flexible, supports diverse data types
Performance	High for batch processing workloads	High for unstructured data access
Cost efficiency	Cost-effective on commodity hardware	Generally cost-effective, especially in the cloud
Use cases	Data lakes, ML pipelines	Unstructured data storage, cloud-native AI applications, **content delivery networks (CDNs)**

Table 3.2: Comparison of HDFS and object storage

Distributed storage systems like HDFS and object storage are critical components in modern data architecture for AI. HDFS excels in handling large-scale batch processing workloads, making it suitable for data lakes and ML pipelines. On the other hand, object storage offers unparalleled scalability and flexibility, which makes it ideal for storing unstructured data and supporting a wide range of AI applications. Understanding the strengths and limitations of each system enables architects to design robust and scalable storage solutions tailored to the specific needs of their AI workloads. As AI evolves, distributed storage systems will play an increasingly vital role in managing the vast amounts of data required to drive innovation and insights in this dynamic field.

Data lakes and data warehouses for AI

Two essential components in modern data architecture are data lakes and data warehouses, each designed for specific functions and optimized for distinct types of workloads. Recently, the **data lakehouse** concept has emerged, offering a hybrid approach that seeks to blend the strengths of both data lakes and data warehouses.

Data lakes

A data lake is a centralized repository that can store vast quantities of structured, semi-structured, and unstructured data. Unlike traditional databases, data lakes store data in raw format, enabling flexibility and scalability. This structure is ideal for AI workloads, which often need massive, diverse datasets for tasks like training, testing, and validation of ML models.

Characteristics and advantages

Data lakes can handle various data types, such as structured data from databases, semi-structured data (for example, JSON and XML), and unstructured data like images, videos, and text. This versatility allows organizations to centralize data from multiple sources, making it easier to manage and analyze.

A key benefit of data lakes is their scalability. Built on distributed storage systems, data lakes can expand horizontally by adding more storage nodes, supporting petabytes or even exabytes of data. This feature is crucial for AI, where large datasets are required for training complex models. Additionally, data lakes are cost-effective because they store data in its raw form without the upfront cost of data transformation. The **schema-on-read** approach enables data scientists to define data structures when needed for analysis, allowing for more exploratory data investigation.

Figure 3.2 shows the architectural overview of a typical data lake:

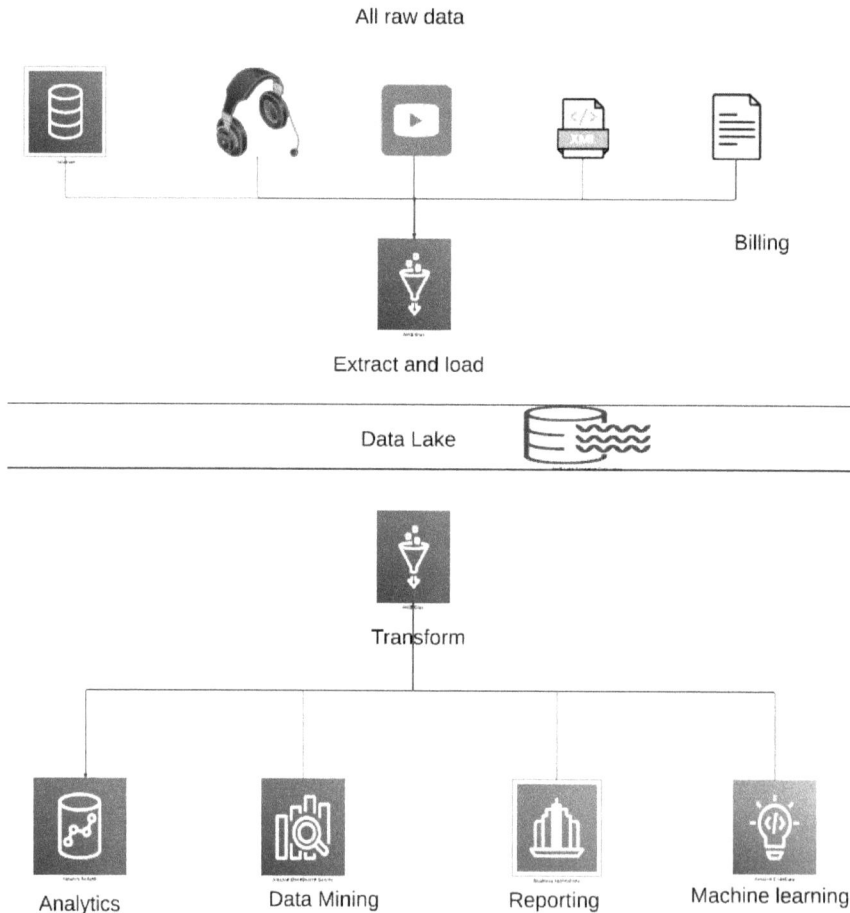

Figure 3.2: Data lake overview

Object storage options in public clouds like Amazon S3 and Google Cloud Storage are often used as data lakes to store large amounts of unstructured and semi-structured data, including logs, media files, and user interaction data.

Use cases in AI

Data lakes serve as the foundational layer for many AI applications. In ML pipelines, raw data can be ingested into the data lake, where it is stored for later processing. Data scientists access this raw data for feature engineering, model training, and evaluation.

Data lakes are also critical for IoT applications. IoT devices generate vast amounts of real-time data, and data lakes offer a scalable and affordable storage solution. AI models can analyze this data to provide insights, such as predictive maintenance for industrial machinery or real-time traffic management.

Data warehouses

In contrast to data lakes, data warehouses are designed specifically for structured data. They use a **schema-on-write** approach, meaning data is organized and transformed before loading it into the warehouse. This design results in optimized performance for complex queries and analytical tasks, making data warehouses particularly useful for business intelligence.

Characteristics and advantages

Data warehouses excel at handling read-heavy workloads and complex queries, offering fast response times thanks to indexing, partitioning, and parallel processing techniques. This makes them ideal for tasks that involve aggregating, filtering, and joining large datasets.

One of the main advantages of data warehouses is their ability to ensure data consistency and reliability. The schema-on-write model enforces strict data quality standards, which are crucial for business intelligence and reporting, where accurate insights are needed for decision-making.

Data warehouses also provide strong security and compliance features, such as access controls and encryption, making them suitable for industries with stringent data protection requirements, like healthcare and finance.

Snowflake is an example of a cloud-based data warehouse solution for storing and analyzing structured data, mainly for BI and data analytics. AWS Redshift and Google BigQuery are examples of other public cloud-based data warehousing solutions.

Figure 3.3 shows the architectural overview of a typical data warehouse:

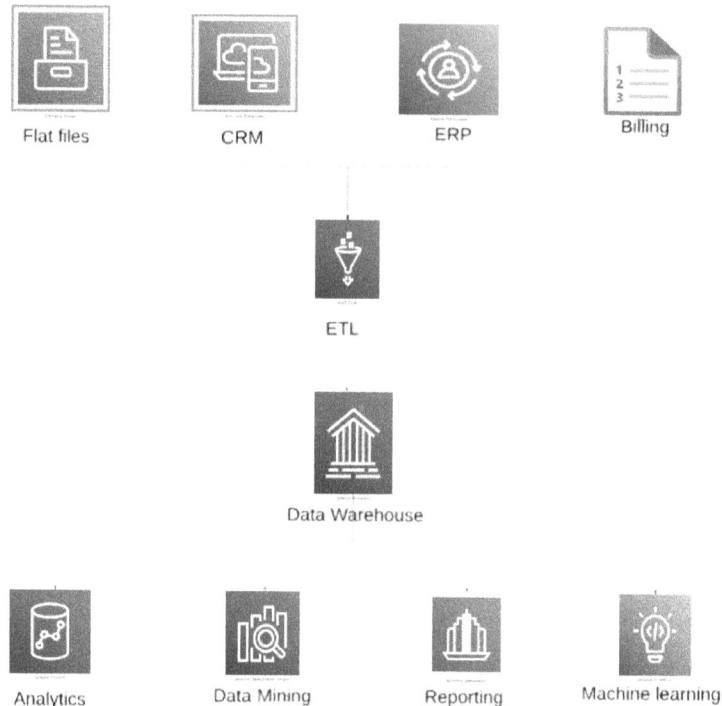

Figure 3.3: A basic data warehouse architecture

Use cases in AI

Although data warehouses are traditionally associated with business intelligence, they also have significant applications in AI. For instance, data warehouses can store and analyze historical data, which provides valuable context for AI models. Predictive analytics, a common AI application, often combines historical data from data warehouses with real-time data from other sources to generate accurate insights.

Data warehouses are also essential for customer analytics in AI. Organizations can create detailed customer profiles by integrating customer data from CRM systems, transactional databases, and social media. AI models can then use these profiles to identify trends, segment customers, and tailor marketing campaigns.

Data lakehouse

Data lakehouse is a relatively new architectural approach designed to combine a data lake's flexibility and scalability with a data warehouse's performance and reliability. It is a unified architecture capable of supporting both structured and unstructured data, making it highly suitable for AI workloads.

Characteristics and advantages

Data lakehouses offer the versatility of data lakes, allowing organizations to store diverse data types in one repository. This integration reduces data silos and simplifies data management. The architecture supports open data formats and ACID transactions, ensuring data quality and consistency across workloads.

Lakehouses also deliver high performance for complex queries by incorporating advanced indexing, caching, and query optimization, like traditional data warehouses. This high performance is particularly important for AI applications that require real-time data processing.

Data governance and security are other areas where lakehouses excel. They offer built-in access control, encryption, and auditing capabilities. These features protect sensitive data, which is crucial for AI applications dealing with personal or confidential information.

Databricks is an example of a solution that stores data in its lakehouse platform to process both BI and AI/ML workloads on a single silo. Another example is the AWS Lake Formation.

Use cases in AI

Data lakehouses are ideal for various AI applications, including ML pipelines. Raw data can be ingested into the lakehouse and stored in native format. Data scientists can then access this data for feature engineering, model training, and evaluation while benefiting from the system's scalability and performance.

Lakehouses are also valuable for real-time analytics and decision-making. By combining historical data with real-time data streams, organizations can generate insights and make decisions on the fly, which is essential for applications such as fraud detection and personalized recommendations.

Comparative analysis

Table 3.3 briefly summarizes the comparison of three data management paradigms from the data type, scalability, performance, cost efficiency, and use cases:

Criteria	Data lakes	Data warehouses	Data lakehouse
Data types	Structured, semi-structured, unstructured	Structured only	Structured, semi-structured, unstructured
Scalability	Very high, scales horizontally	High, but more rigid	Very high, scales horizontally
Performance	Moderate for complex queries	High for complex queries	High for complex queries

Criteria	Data lakes	Data warehouses	Data lakehouse
Cost efficiency	Cost-effective for diverse data types	Can be costly due to transformation	Cost-effective for diverse data types
Use cases	AI-driven analytics, IoT	Business intelligence, predictive analytics	Real-time analytics, AI-driven decision-making

Table 3.3: Comparison of data management paradigms

Data lakes, data warehouses, and data lakehouse are crucial elements in the modern data architecture that supports AI. Data lakes provide scalability and flexibility, data warehouses offer reliability and performance, and data lakehouse combine the strengths of both.

Delta Lake, the backbone of lakehouse

Delta Lake is an open-source storage layer that enhances data lakes with the reliability and performance necessary to support the lakehouse paradigm. Built on top of Apache Spark, Delta Lake provides a unified data management platform that addresses the limitations of traditional data lakes, making them more suitable for AI and analytics workloads.

Characteristics and advantages

Delta Lake introduces several key features that are essential for the lakehouse paradigm. One of the most important features is support for ACID transactions. By providing transactional guarantees, Delta Lake ensures data reliability and consistency, enabling organizations to perform complex data transformations and analytics with confidence.

Another significant feature of Delta Lake is its ability to handle both batch and streaming data. This capability allows organizations to process data in real-time and perform continuous data integration and analytics. By supporting both batch and streaming workloads, Delta Lake enables organizations to build more flexible and responsive AI applications.

Delta Lake also offers advanced data management capabilities, such as schema enforcement and evolution. Schema enforcement ensures that data adheres to a predefined schema, preventing data quality issues and ensuring consistency. Schema evolution allows organizations to modify the schema as their data requirements change, providing greater flexibility and adaptability.

Use cases in AI

Delta Lake is well-suited for a wide range of AI applications and is the backbone of the lakehouse paradigm. For example, raw data from various sources can be ingested in a ML pipeline into Delta Lake, where it is stored in its native format. Data scientists can then access this data for feature engineering, model training, and evaluation, leveraging Delta Lake's high performance and scalability.

Another common use case is real-time analytics and decision-making. By combining historical data with real-time data streams, Delta Lake enables organizations to generate insights and make decisions in real-time. This capability is particularly valuable for AI applications such as fraud detection, predictive maintenance, and personalized recommendations.

Delta Lake enables the lakehouse paradigm by providing a unified data platform that supports both structured and unstructured data. This unified approach simplifies data management and reduces the need for multiple systems. By consolidating data from various sources into a single repository, Delta Lake makes managing and analyzing data easier, providing greater flexibility and versatility for AI and analytics.

Data versioning and lineage tracking

Data versioning and lineage tracking are critical practices ensuring data reliability, reproducibility, and accountability. These practices enable data scientists and engineers to manage data changes effectively, track data origins and transformations, and maintain a clear history of data usage. This section explores the concepts of data versioning and lineage tracking, their significance in the AI landscape, and the methods used to achieve them.

Data versioning

Data versioning involves creating and managing multiple versions of datasets over time. Like version control in software development, data versioning allows data scientists to track changes, revert to previous versions, and collaborate more effectively. In the context of AI, data versioning is essential for maintaining the integrity of datasets used for training, testing, and validating models.

Importance of data versioning

Data versioning is crucial for several reasons. First, it ensures reproducibility. In AI research and development, reproducing results is essential for validating findings and building trust in models. By maintaining a history of dataset versions, data scientists can recreate the exact conditions under which a model was trained, tested, and evaluated.

Second, data versioning facilitates collaboration. In collaborative AI projects, multiple team members may work on the same dataset simultaneously. Versioning allows team members to track changes, avoid conflicts, and merge updates seamlessly. This collaborative approach enhances productivity and reduces the risk of errors.

Third, data versioning supports data governance and compliance. Organizations must often adhere to regulatory requirements that mandate the tracking and auditing of data usage. Versioning provides a clear record of dataset changes, helping organizations demonstrate compliance with data governance standards.

Data versioning provides several benefits in AI workflows, as follows:

- **Reproducibility**: Data scientists can recreate experiments using specific versions of datasets, ensuring consistent results.

- **Collaboration**: Team members can work on different versions of datasets without conflicts, merging changes when necessary.

- **Audit trails**: Versioning creates a historical record of data changes, which is valuable for compliance and debugging.

- **Rollback capability**: If issues are discovered in a dataset, teams can easily revert to a previous, stable version.

Implementation in AI landscape

In a typical AI environment, data versioning is implemented through specialized tools and practices, as follows:

- **Version control systems**: While traditionally used for code, version control systems like Git have been adapted for data versioning. Git-based solutions such as **Data Version Control** (**DVC**) allow teams to version large datasets alongside their code.

- **Data lake versioning**: Modern data lakes often come with built-in versioning capabilities. For instance, Delta Lake, an open-source storage layer that brings ACID transactions to Apache Spark and big data workloads, provides time travel (data versioning) for reproducible ML experiments.

- **Metadata management**: Versioning often involves storing metadata about each version, including timestamps, changes made, and the responsible party. This metadata is crucial for understanding the evolution of datasets over time.

Lineage tracking

Data lineage tracking involves capturing the complete lifecycle of data, from its origin to its final form. Lineage tracking provides a comprehensive view of how data is generated, transformed, and consumed, enabling data scientists to trace the path of data through various processing and analysis stages. In the AI landscape, lineage tracking is essential for ensuring data quality, understanding data dependencies, and maintaining transparency.

Importance of lineage tracking

Lineage tracking is vital for several reasons. First, it ensures data quality. By tracking the data lineage, data scientists can identify and address data quality issues at their source. Understanding the transformations and processes that data undergoes helps diagnose problems and implement corrective measures.

Second, lineage tracking enhances transparency and accountability. It is important to understand how data influences model outcomes in AI projects. Lineage tracking provides a clear record of data transformations, enabling data scientists to explain and justify model decisions. This transparency is crucial for building trust in AI systems and addressing ethical concerns.

Third, lineage tracking supports data governance and compliance. Organizations must often demonstrate how data is used and processed to comply with regulatory requirements. Lineage tracking provides a detailed audit trail of data usage, helping organizations meet compliance standards and avoid legal and reputational risks.

Implementation in AI landscapes

In AI environments, data lineage tracking is often implemented using specialized tools and practices listed as follows:

- **Workflow management systems**: Tools like Apache Airflow or Kubeflow include features for tracking data lineage as part of their workflow orchestration capabilities. These systems record each step in the data processing pipeline, creating a visual representation of data flow.

- **Data catalogs**: Modern data catalogs not only inventory datasets but also track their lineage. For example, tools like Collibra or Alation provide detailed lineage information, showing how datasets are created, transformed, and used across the organization.

- **Automated lineage capture**: Advanced data processing frameworks, such as Apache Spark and Apache Flink, provide built-in support for lineage tracking. These frameworks capture metadata about data transformations and processing steps, enabling data scientists to trace the data lineage through various stages of analysis.

Key components of lineage tracking

Effective lineage tracking in AI projects typically involves capturing the following key pieces of information:

- **Data sources**: The origin of the data, including external sources or internal systems.

- **Transformations**: Any changes applied to the data, such as cleaning, aggregation, or feature engineering.

- **Dependencies**: Relationships between different datasets or between datasets and AI models.

- **Usage information**: How and where the data is used, including in which ML models or analytical processes.

- **Output destinations**: Where the processed data or AI model results are stored or used.

Integration in AI workflows

In practice, data versioning and lineage tracking are often integrated into broader data management and **ML operations** (**MLOps**) processes:

- **Feature stores**: Modern feature stores, which are centralized repositories for storing and serving ML features, often incorporate both versioning and lineage tracking. This integration ensures that AI teams can track the evolution of features and understand their provenance.

- **Model registry integration**: Data versioning and lineage information are frequently linked to model registries. This linkage allows teams to understand which versions of datasets were used to train specific model versions, enhancing reproducibility and auditability.

- **Automated pipelines**: In mature AI workflows, data versioning and lineage tracking are automated as part of **continuous integration/continuous deployment** (**CI/CD**) pipelines. This automation ensures that every data transformation and model training run is automatically versioned and recorded.

Metadata management and cataloging

Metadata, often described as **data about data**, provides essential context that enables data scientists, engineers, and analysts to understand, find, and utilize data efficiently. Metadata management and cataloging ensure that data assets are well-documented, discoverable, and governed, forming the backbone of a robust data infrastructure. This section explores the importance of metadata management and cataloging, their roles in the AI landscape, and the methods used to achieve them.

Understanding metadata in AI context

Metadata encompasses a wide range of information that describes dataset's characteristics, structure, and context. In AI landscapes, metadata takes on additional dimensions, including information about data quality, lineage, and usage in ML models. Effective metadata management is essential for several reasons. First, it enhances data discoverability. Finding relevant data can be challenging in large organizations with vast data repositories. Metadata provides the necessary context to locate and understand data assets quickly, enabling data scientists and analysts to spend less time searching and more time analyzing.

Metadata management supports data governance and compliance. Organizations must often adhere to regulatory requirements that mandate the tracking and auditing of data usage. Metadata provides a clear record of data lineage, transformations, and access, helping organizations demonstrate compliance with data governance standards.

Metadata management improves data quality and consistency. By documenting data sources, transformations, and usage, metadata helps identify and resolve data quality issues. It ensures that data is accurate, consistent, and fit for its intended purpose, which is crucial for AI and analytics applications.

Types of metadata

The types of metadata are as follows:

- **Technical metadata**: This includes information about the overall structure, data formats, schema definitions, and storage locations. In AI contexts, it also covers details about data distributions, feature encodings, and preprocessing steps applied to datasets.

- **Business metadata**: This type of metadata provides context about the business relevance of datasets, including data owners, stewards, and the business processes that generate or consume the data. Provides information about the content and context of data, such as titles, authors, and creation dates. For AI projects, this might include information about the intended use cases for specific datasets.

- **Operational metadata**: This covers information about data pipelines, including execution times, data freshness, and quality metrics. In AI workflows, this might extend to include details about model training runs and feature extraction processes. It also includes information related to data management, such as access controls, ownership, and versioning.

- **AI-specific metadata**: Unique to AI and ML workflows, this includes information about model versions, hyperparameters, training datasets, and model performance metrics.

Metadata management in AI landscapes

Effective metadata management in AI environments involves systematically capturing, organizing, and maintaining metadata throughout the data lifecycle. This process is crucial for ensuring data discoverability, understanding data lineage, and compliance with data governance policies. The following are the crucial aspects of metadata and the role they play in the overall AI landscape:

- **Automated metadata extraction**: In AI workflows, many metadata management systems integrate with data processing and model training pipelines to extract metadata automatically. This might include capturing information about data transformations, feature engineering steps, and model training parameters.

- **Metadata standards and schemas**: Adopting standardized metadata schemas helps ensure consistency and interoperability. For AI projects, this might involve extending existing standards like Dublin Core or **Data Catalog Vocabulary (DCAT)** to include AI-specific metadata elements.

- **Metadata repositories**: Centralized metadata repositories serve as the single source of truth for metadata across the organization. These repositories often integrate with various data sources, data lakes, and AI platforms to aggregate and manage metadata holistically.

- **Metadata governance**: Establishing clear policies and procedures for metadata creation, update, and deletion is essential. This includes defining roles and responsibilities for metadata management within AI teams.

Several tools and platforms have emerged to address the unique metadata management needs in AI environments, as follows:

- **Apache Atlas**: An open-source metadata management and governance platform that provides a scalable and extensible foundation for enterprise-wide data governance. It is particularly useful in AI landscapes for its ability to capture complex data lineage and integrate with big data ecosystems.

- **Collibra**: A commercial data intelligence platform that offers robust metadata management capabilities. It is well-suited for AI environments due to its strong focus on data lineage, impact analysis, and integration with ML workflows.

- **Alation**: This data catalog platform includes powerful metadata management features. It is notable for its ML-driven approach to metadata discovery and its ability to capture tribal knowledge through collaborative features, making it valuable in AI-driven organizations.

Metadata cataloging in AI

Data catalogs are comprehensive inventories of an organization's data assets, providing a searchable interface for discovery and exploration. In AI landscapes, data catalogs are crucial in helping data scientists and ML engineers find relevant datasets for their projects. Metadata cataloging involves creating and maintaining a centralized metadata repository, known as a **data catalog**. A data catalog provides a searchable interface that enables users to discover, understand, and access data assets. It serves as a single source of truth for metadata, facilitating data management and governance.

Key features of AI-oriented data catalogs

The key features of AI-oriented data catalogs are as follows:

- **Semantic search and discovery**: Advanced data catalogs leverage natural language processing and ML techniques to enable intuitive, semantic-based search capabilities. This allows AI practitioners to find relevant datasets based on context and meaning, not just exact keyword matches.

- **Dataset profiling**: AI-oriented data catalogs often include automated profiling capabilities that analyze datasets to extract statistical information, data quality metrics, and potential issues. This information helps data scientists quickly assess the suitability of datasets for specific AI tasks.

- **Collaboration and annotation**: Modern data catalogs often include features for collaborative tagging, rating, and commenting on datasets. This social aspect can be particularly valuable in AI environments, where insights about dataset quality and usefulness can significantly impact model development.

- **Integration with AI/ML platforms**: Data catalogs in AI landscapes often integrate with popular ML platforms and notebooks, allowing data scientists to discover and access datasets directly from their development environments.

Implementing data catalogs in AI workflows

The implementation of data catalogs in AI environments typically involves several key phases. They are as follows:

- **Data discovery and indexing**: Automated processes scan various data sources, including data lakes, databases, and file systems, to discover and index datasets. This process often involves extracting schema information and generating data profiles.

- **Metadata enrichment**: The initial metadata extracted during indexing is often enriched with additional information, either through automated processes or manual curation. In AI contexts, this might include tagging datasets with relevant ML task categories or noting their use in successful models.

- **Access control integration**: Data catalogs need to integrate with existing access control systems to ensure that users can only discover and access datasets for which they have appropriate permissions. This is particularly important in AI projects that may involve sensitive or regulated data.

- **Usage tracking**: Advanced data catalogs in AI environments often include features for tracking how datasets are used in various projects and models. This information can be valuable for understanding the impact and importance of different datasets across the organization.

The following can be considered as examples of how data catalogs integrate into AI workflows:

- **Jupyter Notebook integration**: Many metadata management tools, such as Alation and Collibra, offer plugins or extensions for Jupyter Notebooks. This allows data scientists to search for datasets, view metadata, and even load data directly within their notebook environment.

- **MLflow integration**: Some catalog solutions integrate with MLflow, an open-source platform for managing the ML lifecycle. For instance, Databricks Unity Catalog can be used to manage and version ML models tracked in MLflow, providing a comprehensive view of both data and model lineage.

- **Automated data profiling**: Tools like Informatica Enterprise Data Catalog and AWS Glue Data Catalog offer automated data profiling capabilities. These can automatically generate statistics and quality metrics for datasets, which is particularly useful for AI practitioners in assessing dataset suitability for specific ML tasks.

Partitioning and indexing strategies

As AI workloads often involve massive datasets, optimizing data storage and retrieval becomes crucial. Two key techniques that significantly enhance data processing performance are partitioning and indexing. These strategies ensure that data is organized and accessible in a manner that minimizes latency and maximizes throughput. This section looks at the concepts of data partitioning and indexing, their importance in AI workloads, and the methods used to implement them effectively.

Data partitioning

Data partitioning involves dividing a large dataset into smaller, more manageable pieces or partitions. Each partition is stored separately, allowing for parallel processing and more efficient data retrieval. In the context of AI, data partitioning is essential for handling large-scale datasets used in training, testing, and deploying ML models.

Data partitioning offers several benefits that are particularly valuable for AI workloads. First, it improves query performance. By dividing data into partitions based on certain criteria, such as time, geography, or categorical values, queries can be directed to specific partitions rather than scanning the entire dataset. This targeted approach reduces query latency and enhances performance.

Second, partitioning enhances parallel processing capabilities. In distributed computing environments like Hadoop or Apache Spark, data partitioning allows multiple nodes to process different partitions simultaneously. This parallelism accelerates data processing tasks, making it feasible to handle large-scale AI workloads efficiently.

Third, partitioning facilitates data management and maintenance. Organizing data into partitions makes it easier to manage data lifecycle operations, such as archiving, purging, and updating. For example, old data partitions can be archived or deleted without affecting the rest of the dataset, ensuring efficient storage management.

Data partitioning in AI environments

Data partitioning involves dividing large datasets into smaller, more manageable pieces. In AI workloads, effective partitioning can significantly improve data processing speed, enable parallel processing, and facilitate efficient data distribution across cluster resources.

Horizontal partitioning

Horizontal partitioning, often referred to as sharding in distributed systems, is a common strategy in AI data architectures. It involves dividing data based on rows or documents, typically using a partitioning key.

In AI workflows, horizontal partitioning can be particularly beneficial for the following:

- **Parallel model training**: By distributing partitions across multiple nodes, data scientists can train models in parallel, significantly reducing training time for large datasets.

- **Efficient cross-validation**: Partitions can be used as natural folds for cross-validation, enabling more efficient model evaluation processes.

- **Scalable inference**: For AI systems serving real-time predictions, horizontal partitioning allows for distributing the inference workload across multiple nodes, improving response times and system scalability.

Vertical partitioning

While less common in AI workloads, vertical partitioning, dividing data based on columns or features, can be useful in certain scenarios:

- **Feature-based processing**: Some AI workflows may benefit from grouping related features together, allowing for more efficient feature engineering or selection processes.

- **Privacy-preserving AI**: In scenarios where certain features are sensitive, vertical partitioning can help implement privacy-preserving ML techniques by isolating sensitive data.

Time-based partitioning

For AI systems dealing with time-series data or requiring historical analysis:

- **Efficient time-window processing**: Partitioning data by time intervals (for example, daily, monthly) can significantly speed up time-based queries and analyses, which are common in many AI applications like forecasting or anomaly detection.

- **Model versioning**: Time-based partitions can naturally align with model versions, facilitating easier management of model lifecycles and dataset versions used for training.

Indexing strategies

Indexing involves creating data structures that enable fast data retrieval. An index acts like a roadmap, allowing the system to locate and access data quickly without scanning the entire dataset. In AI workloads, indexing is crucial for optimizing query performance and ensuring efficient data access.

Indexing offers several benefits that are essential for AI workloads. First, it significantly improves query performance. Indexes reduce the time and resources required to execute queries by providing a shortcut to the desired data. This performance boost is significant for AI applications that require real-time data access and analysis.

Second, indexing enhances data retrieval efficiency. In large datasets, finding specific records can be time-consuming. Indexes provide a structured way to locate data quickly, ensuring that AI models can access the necessary data without delays.

Third, indexing supports complex queries. In AI workloads, queries often involve filtering, sorting, and aggregating data. Indexes enable these complex operations to be performed efficiently, ensuring that AI models receive accurate and timely results.

Indexing strategies for AI workloads

Indexing is crucial for speeding up data retrieval operations, particularly in AI workflows where rapid data access can significantly impact overall system performance.

The following are some of the most commonly used indexing strategies in AI workloads:

- **B-tree and B+ tree indexes**: These traditional indexing structures remain relevant in AI data storage systems, particularly for exact Match Queries. This is useful for quickly retrieving specific training examples or feature values and range queries which is beneficial for filtering datasets based on feature value ranges, a common operation in data preprocessing and analysis for AI.

- **Bitmap indexes**: Bitmap indexes can be highly efficient for AI workloads involving feature selection, which helps quickly identify relevant features based on certain criteria. Multidimensional filtering, which helps efficiently filter datasets based on multiple categorical features, is common in many machine-learning preprocessing steps.

- **Inverted indexes**: Particularly useful in AI systems dealing with text data in cases like **natural language processing** (**NLP**) for enabling quick lookup of documents containing specific words or phrases. It is also crucial for many NLP tasks as well as information retrieval for supporting efficient retrieval of relevant documents or data points based on textual queries.

- **Spatial indexes**: For AI applications dealing with geographical or multidimensional data, like Geospatial AI, for efficiently querying and processing location-based data for applications like recommendation systems or autonomous vehicles, and similarity search for supporting nearest neighbor searches in high-dimensional spaces, which is fundamental to many ML algorithms.

Implementing partitioning and indexing

Integrating data partitioning and indexing involves combining the benefits of both techniques to achieve optimal performance. For example, a dataset can be partitioned by date to facilitate time-based queries, and each partition can be indexed to enable fast data retrieval. This integrated approach ensures that queries are directed to specific partitions and executed efficiently using indexes. Implementing these strategies in AI landscapes often leverages specialized tools and frameworks, provided as follows:

- **Distributed storage systems**: Systems like HDFS, which is often used as the underlying storage layer in big data AI workflows, implement partitioning through its block storage mechanism, and Apache Cassandra, which provides flexible partitioning strategies and supports various index types, making it suitable for AI workloads requiring high write throughput.

- **AI-optimized data formats**:

  o **Apache Parquet**: This columnar storage format includes built-in support for partitioning and is widely used in AI data pipelines for its compression and query performance.

  o **Delta Lake**: Built on top of Parquet, Delta Lake adds ACID transactions and time travel capabilities, along with optimized layout and indexing for AI workloads.

- **Specialized AI data storage solutions**:

  o **NVIDIA RAPIDS cuDF**: For GPU-accelerated AI workflows, **CUDA DataFrame (cuDF)** provides GPU-based partitioning and indexing capabilities, significantly speeding up data manipulation tasks.

  o **Feast (Feature Store)**: Implements efficient indexing and retrieval mechanisms specifically designed for ML features, supporting both online and offline AI use cases.

Considerations and best practices

When implementing partitioning and indexing strategies for AI workloads, several factors should be considered, such as the following:

- **Workload characteristics**: The choice of partitioning and indexing strategies should align with the specific access patterns of AI workflows, such as batch processing for model training versus real-time access for online inference.

- **Data skew**: Careful selection of partition keys is crucial to avoid data skew, which can lead to hotspots and reduced performance in distributed AI systems.

- **Index maintenance overhead**: While indexes can significantly speed up queries, they also introduce maintenance overhead. This trade-off should be carefully evaluated, especially in write-heavy AI data pipelines.

- **Adaptive strategies**: As AI workloads evolve over time, consider implementing adaptive partitioning and indexing strategies that automatically adjust based on changing query patterns and data distributions.

Note: **The details of the aforementioned principles are out of the book's scope and are essentially very important data engineering principles. It is highly recommended that you have a good grasp of these best practices.**

Hybrid and multi-cloud storage solutions

The landscape of AI is characterized by the need for massive computational power and vast amounts of data storage. As AI workloads continue to grow in complexity and scale, organizations are increasingly turning to hybrid and multi-cloud storage solutions. These approaches offer the flexibility, scalability, and resilience needed to support advanced AI applications. This section explores how hybrid and multi-cloud storage solutions are implemented and utilized in AI landscapes.

Hybrid cloud storage

Hybrid cloud storage combines on-premises storage infrastructure with public cloud services, creating a unified storage environment. This approach leverages the strengths of both private and public clouds, offering a balance between control, security, and scalability.

Hybrid cloud storage is essential for several reasons. First, it provides flexibility. Organizations can choose to store sensitive or critical data on-premises, where they have greater control and security, while leveraging the scalability and cost-effectiveness of public cloud storage for less sensitive data. This flexibility allows organizations to optimize their storage strategy based on specific needs and constraints.

Second, hybrid cloud storage enhances data availability and resilience. By distributing data across on-premises and cloud environments, organizations can ensure that their data is always accessible, even in the event of a failure in one environment. This redundancy is crucial for maintaining the continuity of AI workloads.

Third, hybrid cloud storage supports data locality and compliance. Some organizations are subject to regulatory requirements that mandate storing certain data within specific geographic regions. Hybrid cloud storage allows organizations to comply with these requirements by storing data locally while still benefiting from the cloud's scalability.

Methods for achieving hybrid cloud storage

A hybrid cloud approach combines on-premises infrastructure with public cloud services. In AI workflows, this might involve the following:

- **Data lake on premises, compute in cloud**: Maintaining sensitive training data on-premises while leveraging cloud resources for computationally intensive model training.

- **Edge AI with cloud backup**: Deploying AI models at the edge (on-premises) for low-latency inference, with cloud storage for data aggregation and model updates.

- **Common approach 1**: To achieve such arrangements, one common approach is to use cloud storage gateways, which act as a bridge between on-premises storage and cloud storage. These gateways provide seamless access to cloud storage, allowing organizations to move data between environments without disrupting their workflows.

- **Common approach 2**: Another approach is to use hybrid cloud storage platforms, such as Microsoft Azure Stack or Google Anthos. These platforms provide a consistent storage environment across on-premises and cloud environments, enabling organizations to manage their data seamlessly.

Multi-cloud storage

Multi-cloud storage involves using services from multiple cloud providers, creating a diversified storage environment. This approach leverages different cloud providers' unique strengths and capabilities, offering enhanced flexibility, resilience, and performance.

Multi-cloud storage is crucial for several reasons. First, it prevents vendor lock-in. Organizations can avoid being dependent on a single provider by using storage services from multiple cloud providers. This diversification reduces the risk of service disruptions and provides greater bargaining power when negotiating contracts.

Second, multi-cloud storage enhances resilience and availability. By distributing data across multiple cloud providers, organizations can ensure their data is always accessible, even if one provider experiences an outage. This redundancy is vital for maintaining the continuity of AI workloads.

Third, multi-cloud storage optimizes performance and cost. Different cloud providers offer varying performance characteristics and pricing models. By leveraging the strengths of multiple providers, organizations can optimize their storage strategy to achieve the best performance and cost-efficiency for their specific workloads.

Additionally, it ensures data sovereignty compliance by storing and processing data in specific geographic regions to comply with data regulations, which may require using multiple cloud providers.

Methods for achieving multi-cloud storage

Achieving multi-cloud storage involves integrating storage services from multiple cloud providers into a cohesive storage environment. One common approach is to use multi-cloud management platforms, such as Terraform by HashiCorp Terraform or CloudBolt. These platforms provide a unified interface for managing storage resources across multiple cloud providers, enabling organizations to orchestrate and automate their storage workflows.

Another approach is to use storage abstraction layers, such as NetApp Cloud Volumes or IBM Cloud Satellite. These solutions provide a consistent storage interface across different cloud providers, allowing organizations to manage their data seamlessly. They offer features such as data replication, migration, and synchronization, ensuring that data is always available and consistent across environments.

Implementing hybrid and multi-cloud storage

The implementation of hybrid and multi-cloud storage solutions in AI landscapes often involves several key strategies.

Data tiering and lifecycle management

Implementing intelligent data tiering across hybrid and multi-cloud environments is crucial for optimizing both cost and performance in AI workloads:

- **Hot data on high-performance storage**: Keeping frequently accessed training data or features on high-performance, low-latency storage, either on-premises or in the cloud.

- **Cold data on cost-effective cloud storage**: Moving historical or infrequently accessed data to cost-effective cloud storage tiers, such as Amazon S3 Glacier or Azure Archive Storage.

Figure 3.4 illustrates this strategy of placing data in various tiers based on its usage and accessibility:

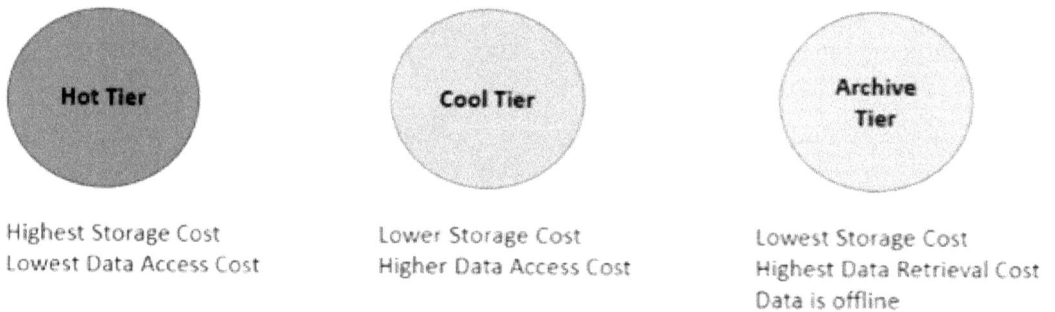

Hot Tier

Cool Tier

Archive Tier

Highest Storage Cost
Lowest Data Access Cost

Lower Storage Cost
Higher Data Access Cost

Lowest Storage Cost
Highest Data Retrieval Cost
Data is offline

Figure 3.4: *Three tiers of storage*

Data replication and synchronization

Ensuring data consistency across hybrid and multi-cloud environments is critical for AI workflows:

- **Asynchronous replication**: Implementing asynchronous data replication between on-premises and cloud storage to maintain up-to-date copies of critical AI datasets. Data is written to the primary storage system (for example, on-premises), then the primary system acknowledges the write operation as complete, and then data is then copied to the secondary system (for example, cloud storage) in the background. Cloud offerings like AWS DataSync or Azure File Sync and database-specific tools like PostgreSQL's logical replication are some tools for asynchronous replication.

- **Multi-region synchronization**: For global AI operations, synchronizing data across multiple cloud regions to ensure low-latency access and compliance with data sovereignty requirements.

- **Active-active replication**: Data can be read and written in all regions, with changes synchronized across regions.

- **Active-passive replication**: One region serves as the primary for writes, with others acting as read-only replicas.

- **Eventual consistency**: Changes are propagated asynchronously, allowing for temporary inconsistencies between regions.

- **Strong consistency**: Ensures that all regions always have the same data, often at the cost of higher latency.

Cloud providers like Amazon Aurora global database or Azure Cosmos DB provide built-in multi-region synchronization. Many databases used in AI, like PostgreSQL or MongoDB, offer multi-region replication features.

Cloud-agnostic AI platforms

A cloud-agnostic AI platform is designed to operate across multiple cloud environments without dependency on any single cloud provider. These platforms offer a consistent development and deployment experience, enabling organizations to run their AI workloads on any cloud infrastructure or on-premises environment. By abstracting the underlying cloud infrastructure, cloud-agnostic AI platforms provide the flexibility to choose the best storage and compute resources for specific AI workloads. Some cloud-agnostic AI platforms include:

- **Kubflow/Kubernetes for AI orchestration**: Kubeflow is an open-source platform designed to make deploying, scaling, and managing ML workflows on Kubernetes simple, portable, and scalable. As a cloud-agnostic platform, Kubeflow allows organizations to run their AI workloads on any Kubernetes cluster, regardless of the underlying cloud provider.

- **Databricks unified analytics platform**: It is a cloud-agnostic AI platform that provides a collaborative environment for data engineering, data science, and ML. Built on Apache Spark, Databricks supports multiple cloud providers, enabling organizations to run their AI workloads seamlessly across different environments.

- **H2O.ai**: It is an open-source AI platform that provides a suite of ML and AI tools for building, deploying, and managing AI applications. As a cloud-agnostic platform, H2O.ai allows organizations to run their AI workloads on any cloud infrastructure or on-premises environment.

- **Apache Airflow**: Apache Airflow is an open-source platform for orchestrating complex workflows and data pipelines. It is cloud-agnostic, allowing organizations to run their AI workflows on any cloud infrastructure or on-premises environment, providing flexibility and scalability.

Subsequent chapters will provide further details on the use and implementation of these tools from an AI architecture perspective.

Challenges and considerations

Implementing hybrid and multi-cloud storage solutions entails navigating complex challenges and considerations. The following are some key points to consider:

- **Data integration**: Achieving seamless interoperability between varied storage systems and cloud providers is crucial. Integrating disparate data sources can lead to data silos and complicate data management. It is recommended to utilize data integration platforms and middleware that support multiple cloud providers and on-premises systems. Standardize data formats and protocols to facilitate smooth data exchange.

- **Data consistency and synchronization**: Ensuring data consistency across multiple environments is complex and prone to latency issues. Synchronizing data in real-time can be resource-intensive and technically challenging.

  One should implement distributed databases and data replication strategies that ensure data consistency. Use eventual consistency models where appropriate and employ conflict resolution mechanisms to handle discrepancies.

- **Security and compliance**: Robust encryption and stringent access controls are essential to protect sensitive data. Adhering to diverse regulatory frameworks across different jurisdictions is a significant challenge. Adopt a Zero Trust security model, enforce strong encryption for data at rest and in transit, and implement **multi-factor authentication** (**MFA**). Regularly audit compliance with regulations such as GDPR, HIPAA, and others relevant to your industry.

- **Cost management**: Balancing the costs of on-premises infrastructure with variable cloud pricing models requires careful planning. Hidden costs, such as data transfer fees and storage overheads, can complicate budget management.

  Use cost management tools and cloud cost calculators to forecast expenses accurately. Implement policies for automated scaling and resource optimization to avoid over-provisioning and reduce unnecessary costs.

- **Performance optimization**: Sophisticated load balancing and strategic data placement are necessary to minimize latency and maximize throughput. Performance tuning across hybrid and multi-cloud environments can be complex and time-consuming. Employ **content delivery networks** (**CDNs**) and edge computing to reduce latency. Use performance monitoring tools to track and optimize workload distribution continuously. Implement caching strategies to improve access speeds.

- **Vendor lock-in**: The risk of becoming dependent on a single provider can hinder flexibility and complicate future migrations. A strategic approach is needed to ensure interoperability and avoid long-term vendor lock-in. Design your architecture using open standards and APIs to ensure portability. Use containerization and orchestration tools like Kubernetes to abstract workloads from the underlying infrastructure. Regularly review and test migration plans to ensure readiness.

Conclusion

In this chapter, we explored the intricate world of data storage and management tailored for AI workloads. We began by exploring the various data storage architectures, on-premises, cloud-based, and hybrid models, providing you with the knowledge to choose the most suitable strategy for your AI initiatives. We then tackled the challenges of data integration and interoperability, offering best practices to ensure seamless data flow across diverse systems.

Another critical focus was maintaining data consistency and synchronization in real-time AI applications. We equipped you with techniques to ensure data integrity and minimize latency. We emphasized the importance of robust security measures, including advanced encryption and stringent access controls, to protect sensitive data. Additionally, we navigated the complexities of regulatory compliance to ensure your data management practices meet industry standards.

Cost management strategies were discussed to help you balance expenses without compromising performance. We also covered performance optimization techniques such as load balancing, strategic data placement, and caching, ensuring your AI systems run efficiently. Finally, we addressed the risks of vendor lock-in, providing strategies to maintain flexibility and portability using open standards, APIs, containerization, and orchestration tools.

In the next chapter, we will focus on the critical aspects of data preprocessing and feature engineering for AI models. We will begin by discussing the importance of data quality and the techniques to clean and preprocess raw data effectively. You will learn about various feature extraction methods and how to select the most relevant features to improve model performance. We will also cover advanced topics such as dimensionality reduction, handling imbalanced datasets, and using automated feature engineering tools. By the end of the next chapter, you will be equipped with the skills to transform raw data into a refined dataset that enhances the accuracy and efficiency of your AI models.

Join our Discord space

Join our Discord workspace for latest updates, offers, tech happenings around the world, new releases, and sessions with the authors:

https://discord.bpbonline.com

CHAPTER 4
Data Processing and Transformation for AI

Introduction

In the ever-evolving landscape of AI, the transformation of raw data into actionable insights is a critical and nuanced process. The success of AI systems hinges on the quality of data they consume, making data processing and transformation foundational to any AI endeavor. This chapter explores these essential processes, highlighting how raw, unstructured data is meticulously prepared to fuel intelligent models.

We will explore traditional and contemporary methodologies, starting with the **Extract, Transform, Load (ETL)** and **Extract, Load, Transform (ELT)** approaches. Understanding these paradigms is crucial, as they dictate how data is handled, processed, and optimized for AI consumption.

Beyond these foundational methods, the chapter will cover advanced data transformation techniques such as feature engineering, data normalization, and strategies for handling imbalanced datasets. These techniques are vital for refining data quality and enhancing AI model performance.

Additionally, we will examine the role of distributed processing frameworks like Apache Spark and GPU-accelerated data processing in managing large-scale AI data. We will also discuss the integration of automated data preprocessing pipelines with ML workflows, illustrating how these pipelines streamline data preparation and boost efficiency.

Structure

The chapter covers the following topics:

- ETL vs. ELT approaches for AI data
- Distributed processing frameworks
- Feature engineering, selection, and data normalization
- Handling imbalanced datasets and data augmentation
- GPU-accelerated data processing
- Automated data preprocessing pipelines
- Integration of data processing with ML workflows

Objectives

By the end of this chapter, you will be able to distinguish between ETL and ELT approaches, understanding their unique roles and suitability in AI data processing workflows. You will also explore essential data transformation techniques, such as feature engineering and data normalization, which are crucial for preparing high-quality datasets that enhance AI model performance. Additionally, you will examine the utility of distributed processing frameworks like Apache Spark and the advantages of GPU-accelerated data processing in handling large-scale AI datasets efficiently.

Furthermore, you will understand the importance of automated data preprocessing pipelines and their seamless integration with ML workflows to streamline the data preparation process. You will also be able to identify strategies for managing imbalanced datasets and implementing data augmentation techniques to ensure robust and accurate AI models.

Finally, you will learn best practices for designing scalable and efficient data processing pipelines tailored to the specific needs of AI applications. You will gain practical insights into the tools and platforms that facilitate efficient data processing and transformation, enabling the creation of robust AI solutions. By achieving these objectives, you will be equipped with the knowledge and skills to design and implement effective data processing and transformation pipelines, ensuring that your AI systems are built on a solid foundation of high-quality, well-prepared data, ultimately leading to more accurate and reliable AI insights and applications.

ETL vs. ELT approaches for AI data

In AI data processing, the methodologies employed to transform raw data into actionable insights are paramount. Two primary approaches dominate this landscape, which are, ETL and ELT. While they may seem similar at first glance, their underlying mechanics, use cases, and implications for AI systems differ significantly. This section unravels these methodologies, highlighting their relevance, advantages, and challenges in the context of AI data processing.

Understanding ETL and ELT

The basic understanding of ETL and ELT is as follows:

- **ETL**: ETL is a traditional data processing approach that has been the backbone of data warehousing for decades. The process involves three sequential steps:
  1. **Extract**: Data is extracted from various source systems, which can include databases, APIs, flat files, and more. This step focuses on gathering raw data from disparate sources.
  2. **Transform**: Once extracted, the data undergoes transformation. This involves cleaning, filtering, aggregating, and converting the data into a suitable format. Transformations can include operations such as joining tables, applying business rules, and calculating derived metrics.
  3. **Load**: The transformed data is then loaded into a target system, typically a data warehouse or a data mart, where it becomes available for analysis and reporting.
- **ELT**: ELT, on the other hand, is a more modern approach that leverages the power of scalable data storage and processing platforms. The steps are as follows:
  1. **Extract**: Like ETL, data is extracted from various source systems.
  2. **Load**: The raw data is immediately loaded into the target system, often a data lake or a cloud-based storage solution.
  3. **Transform**: Transformation occurs within the target system. This approach capitalizes on the processing power of modern data platforms, allowing for more flexible and scalable transformations.

Differences between ETL and ELT

The key differences between ETL and ELT are as follows:

- **Processing location**: The primary difference between ETL and ELT lies in the location where the transformation occurs. In ETL, data is transformed before it is loaded into the target system. Conversely, in ELT, raw data is loaded first, and transformations are performed within the target system. This distinction has significant implications for performance, scalability, and flexibility.
- **Scalability and performance**: ELT benefits from the scalability of modern data platforms. By leveraging the computational power of data lakes and cloud-based solutions, ELT can handle large volumes of data and complex transformations

more efficiently. ETL, while still effective, may struggle with scalability, particularly when dealing with massive datasets or intricate transformations.

- **Flexibility**: ELT offers greater flexibility in data processing. Since raw data is loaded first, it allows for more dynamic and iterative transformations. Analysts and data scientists can experiment with different transformation logic without the need to re-extract and re-load data. ETL, being more rigid, requires predefined transformation logic, making it less adaptable to changing requirements.

The following figure elucidates the overall architecture of ETL and ELT:

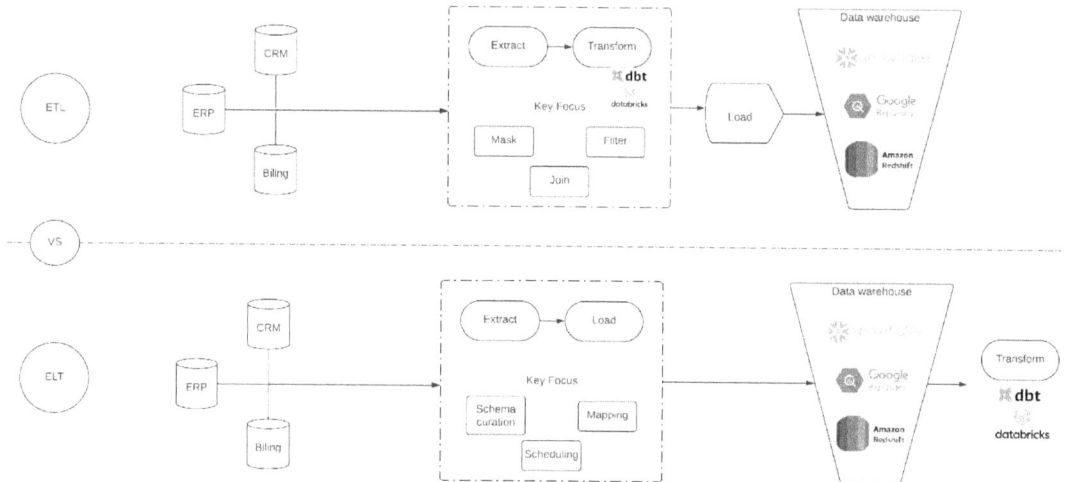

Figure 4.1: ETL vs. ELT

Suitability for AI data processing

AI-specific data processing is often required when compared to traditional data processing methods due to the unique demands of AI algorithms and the massive scale of data they often work with. Here are a few key reasons why AI-specific data processing is required:

- **Data variety and volume**: AI systems often deal with diverse and voluminous datasets, including structured, semi-structured, and unstructured data. ELT's ability to handle raw data of varying formats and sizes makes it particularly suitable for AI applications. Data lakes, commonly used in ELT, can store vast amounts of raw data, enabling AI models to access and process diverse datasets seamlessly.

- **Real-time processing**: In AI applications requiring real-time or near-real-time data processing, ELT can be advantageous. By loading raw data immediately, ELT supports real-time transformations and analytics. ETL, with its sequential processing steps, may introduce delays, making it less ideal for time-sensitive AI use cases.

- **Data exploration and experimentation**: AI development often involves iterative experimentation with different features and models. ELT's flexibility allows data scientists to explore and experiment with raw data without the need for extensive reprocessing. This accelerates the AI development lifecycle, enabling faster iterations and more efficient model training.

Choosing between ETL and ELT

The choice between ETL and ELT for AI data processing depends on several factors:

- **Data characteristics**: For large volumes of diverse data typical in AI projects, ELT often provides better scalability and flexibility.

- **Project requirements**: If the AI project requires extensive data cleansing and complex transformations before analysis, ETL might be more suitable. For exploratory projects with evolving requirements, ELT offers more agility.

- **Infrastructure**: Organizations with investments in traditional data warehouses may find ETL more aligned with their existing processes. Cloud-native organizations or those using data lakes may find ELT more natural.

- **Real-time needs**: For AI applications requiring real-time or near-real-time data processing, ELT's ability to make raw data immediately available can be advantageous.

- **Compliance and governance**: If strict data governance is required before data can be used, ETL's upfront transformation step may be preferable. However, ELT can also support robust governance when properly implemented.

The following table briefly summarizes the various aspects to consider in choosing between ETL and ELT in a typical AI data architecture:

Aspect	ETL	ELT
Process order	Data is transformed before being loaded into the target system.	Data is loaded into the target system first and transformed in place.
Performance	Can be slower for large datasets due to transformations happening outside the data warehouse.	Faster with modern cloud-native architectures since transformations leverage the target system's computational power.
Scalability	Less scalable for large-scale AI workloads due to potential bottlenecks in external transformation layers.	Highly scalable with modern data platforms (e.g., Snowflake, BigQuery) optimized for in-database transformations.

Aspect	ETL	ELT
Complexity	Typically more complex due to the need to predefine and maintain transformation rules outside the storage layer.	Simpler for handling evolving AI/ML data needs, as transformations can be dynamically applied within the data storage environment.
Latency	Higher latency, not suitable for real-time AI/ML workflows.	Lower latency, enabling near real-time analytics and AI/ML model development.
Infrastructure dependency	Relies on external ETL tools for transformations, requiring dedicated compute resources.	Leverages the computational power of the target system, reducing dependency on external transformation tools.
Cost	Higher cost due to separate infrastructure for transformation and potential delays in processing.	Cost-efficient with pay-as-you-go cloud solutions for transformation in the target system.
Use case fit	Suitable for structured, legacy systems where transformations need to be controlled and predefined.	Ideal for modern, cloud-based, AI-driven systems requiring flexibility, scalability, and rapid prototyping.
AI/ML workflow alignment	Limited integration with iterative AI/ML workflows, as transformations are static and harder to modify.	Better aligned with AI/ML workflows due to dynamic transformation capabilities and seamless integration with model pipelines.
Data quality	Ensures data quality before loading but may delay data availability.	Requires robust data governance in the target system, as raw data is loaded first.
Compliance and governance	Easier to enforce data compliance as transformations happen upfront.	Requires stricter monitoring and governance tools since raw data is accessible in the target system.
Tool ecosystem	Common tools: Informatica, Talend, IBM DataStage.	Common tools: Snowflake, BigQuery, Databricks.

Table 4.1: Choosing between ETL and ELT

Challenges and considerations

Implementing ETL or ELT processes for AI workloads involves several critical challenges and considerations that must be carefully addressed to ensure data quality, resource efficiency, and security:

- **Data quality and governance**: Both ETL and ELT must address data quality and governance. In ETL, data quality checks are typically integrated into the transformation step, ensuring that only clean and validated data is loaded into the target system. In ELT, raw data is loaded first, necessitating robust data quality and governance mechanisms within the target platform to maintain data integrity.

- **Resource management**: ELT's reliance on the target platform for transformations can lead to increased resource consumption, particularly in cloud environments. Organizations must carefully manage and optimize resource usage to avoid excessive costs. ETL, while less resource-intensive in the target system, may require substantial processing power during the transformation step.

- **Security and compliance**: Security and compliance are critical considerations in both ETL and ELT. Data must be protected throughout the extraction, transformation, and loading processes. ELT, with its immediate loading of raw data, may introduce additional security challenges, particularly when dealing with sensitive or regulated data. Robust encryption, access controls, and compliance measures are essential to safeguard data.

Real-world use cases

The following are some real-world use cases of ETL and ELT:

- **ETL in traditional data warehousing**: ETL remains a staple in traditional data warehousing environments. Organizations with established data warehouses and predefined reporting requirements often rely on ETL to ensure data consistency and accuracy. ETL's structured approach aligns well with scenarios where data transformation logic is well-defined and stable. Numerous ETL tools are available, ranging from traditional solutions like Informatica and Talend to modern cloud-based services such as AWS Glue and Azure Data Factory. These tools offer robust capabilities for data extraction, transformation, and loading, catering to various data integration needs.

- **ELT in modern AI and big data applications**: ELT has gained prominence in modern AI and big data applications. Organizations leveraging cloud-based data lakes and distributed processing frameworks, such as Apache Spark, often adopt ELT to harness the scalability and flexibility of these platforms. ELT is particularly suited for AI use cases involving large-scale data processing, real-time analytics, and iterative experimentation. ELT tools leverage the power of cloud platforms and distributed processing frameworks. Technologies such as Apache Spark, Databricks, and Snowflake are commonly used for ELT workflows. These tools provide scalable and flexible environments for loading and transforming raw data, enabling efficient AI data processing.

In the context of AI data processing, both ETL and ELT have their merits and challenges. ETL's structured approach ensures data consistency and accuracy, making it suitable for traditional data warehousing. With its scalability and flexibility, ELT is well-suited for modern AI and big data applications. Understanding the nuances of each approach allows organizations to choose the methodology that best aligns with their AI data processing requirements. Later in the book, we will examine how ELT/ETL approaches work with data warehouses and data lakes to create a holistic and scalable data pipeline for AI workloads.

Distributed processing frameworks

In the age of big data and AI, data's sheer volume, velocity, and variety necessitate robust and scalable processing solutions. Distributed processing frameworks have emerged as indispensable tools for handling large-scale data transformations efficiently. These frameworks enable the parallel processing of data across multiple nodes, significantly speeding up data preparation tasks and making them more manageable. Let us look at the key distributed processing frameworks pivotal for AI data processing, focusing on their features, advantages, and use cases.

Introduction to distributed processing

Distributed processing involves dividing a large dataset into smaller chunks and processing these chunks concurrently across multiple computing nodes. This approach leverages the combined computational power of multiple machines, enabling the efficient handling of vast amounts of data. Distributed processing frameworks provide the infrastructure to orchestrate and manage these parallel computations seamlessly.

Before diving into specific frameworks, it is essential to understand some fundamental concepts:

- **Data partitioning**: Splitting large datasets into smaller chunks that can be processed independently.

- **Task scheduling**: Assigning computational tasks to available nodes in the cluster.

- **Data locality**: Optimizing task assignment to minimize data movement across the network.

- **Fault recovery**: Mechanisms to handle node failures and ensure job completion.

- **Resource management**: Efficient allocation and utilization of cluster resources.

Popular distributed computing frameworks

Distributed computing frameworks are essential for AI architecture due to their ability to handle massive datasets, accelerate model training, optimize resource utilization, enable real-time processing, and provide cost-effective solutions. By distributing workloads across multiple machines and parallelizing tasks, these frameworks empower organizations to build and deploy complex AI models efficiently.

Apache Hadoop

Apache Hadoop is a pioneering distributed processing framework designed to store and process massive datasets across clusters of commodity hardware. Its architecture is based on the **Hadoop Distributed File System** (**HDFS**) and the MapReduce programming model.

The key features are as follows:

- **HDFS**: A distributed file system that provides high throughput access to data, ensuring fault tolerance and scalability.

- **MapReduce**: A programming model that simplifies the processing of large datasets by breaking down tasks into map and reduce operations.

- **Scalability**: Hadoop can scale horizontally by adding more nodes to the cluster, allowing it to handle growing data volumes.

- **Fault tolerance**: HDFS replicates data across multiple nodes, ensuring data availability even in the event of hardware failures.

- **Cost-effective**: Can run on commodity hardware, making it accessible for organizations with limited resources.

Use cases: Hadoop is well-suited for batch processing tasks, such as data aggregation, ETL workflows, and large-scale data analysis. It is commonly used in scenarios where data processing can be performed in a batch mode without the need for real-time results.

Apache Spark

Apache Spark is a powerful and versatile distributed processing framework known for its speed and ease of use. Unlike Hadoop's MapReduce, Spark provides in-memory processing capabilities, which significantly enhance performance for iterative algorithms and interactive data analysis.

The key features are as follows:

- **In-memory processing**: Spark stores intermediate data in memory, reducing the need for disk I/O and speeding up data processing tasks.

- **Unified analytics engine**: Spark supports various data processing tasks, including batch processing, stream processing, ML, and graph processing.

- **Ease of use**: Spark provides high-level APIs in Java, Scala, Python, and R, making it accessible to a wide range of developers and data scientists. Includes libraries like MLlib for ML and GraphX for graph computation.

- **Resilient Distributed Datasets** (**RDDs**): RDDs are fault-tolerant collections of objects that can be operated on in parallel, providing a robust abstraction for distributed data processing.

Use cases: Spark is ideal for both batch and real-time data processing. Its in-memory processing capabilities make it particularly well-suited for iterative ML algorithms, real-time analytics, and interactive data exploration. Spark's versatility and performance have made it a popular choice for AI data processing tasks.

Apache Flink

Apache Flink is a distributed stream processing framework designed for high throughput, low-latency data processing. Flink's architecture is optimized for both batch and stream processing, allowing it to handle real-time data streams efficiently.

The key features are as follows:

- **Stream processing**: Flink treats batch processing as a special case of stream processing, providing a unified model for handling both types of data.

- **Event time processing**: Flink supports event time semantics, enabling accurate processing of out-of-order events and late arrivals.

- **Stateful computations**: Flink's state management capabilities allow for complex event processing and windowing operations.

- **Fault tolerance**: Flink provides exactly-once processing guarantees, ensuring data consistency and reliability.

Use cases: Flink is particularly well-suited for real-time data processing tasks, such as event-driven applications, real-time analytics, and complex event processing. Its ability to handle high throughput data streams with low latency makes it a valuable tool for AI applications requiring real-time insights.

Dask

Dask is a flexible parallel computing library for Python that scales from single machines to large clusters. It is designed to parallelize existing Python code and integrate seamlessly with popular data science libraries like NumPy, Pandas, and scikit-learn.

The key features are as follows:

- **Dynamic task scheduling**: Dask's task scheduler dynamically schedules and executes tasks, optimizing resource utilization and performance.

- **DataFrame and array abstractions**: Dask extends pandas DataFrames and NumPy arrays to larger-than-memory datasets, enabling scalable data manipulation.

- **Ease of integration**: Dask integrates well with existing Python codebases, making it easy to parallelize workflows without significant code changes.

- **Scalability**: Dask can scale from a single machine to a distributed cluster, providing flexible deployment options.

Use cases: Dask is ideal for data science and ML workflows in Python. It is particularly useful for scaling pandas-based data manipulation tasks, parallelizing ML model training, and handling larger-than-memory datasets. Dask's flexibility and ease of use make it a valuable tool for AI practitioners working in the Python ecosystem.

Choosing the right framework

The choice of a distributed processing framework depends on various factors, including the nature of the data, the specific processing requirements, and the existing technology stack. Here are some considerations to guide the decision:

- **Data volume and velocity**: For high throughput, low-latency stream processing, frameworks like Apache Flink are ideal. For batch processing of large datasets, Apache Hadoop and Apache Spark are strong contenders.

- **Processing requirements**: If in-memory processing and iterative computations are critical, Apache Spark's capabilities make it a suitable choice. For event-driven and real-time applications, Apache Flink's stream processing architecture is advantageous.

- **Integration with existing tools**: Consider the compatibility of the framework with existing tools and libraries. For Python-centric workflows, Dask offers seamless integration with popular data science libraries.

- **Scalability and fault tolerance**: Evaluate the framework's ability to scale horizontally and handle hardware failures. Hadoop's HDFS and Spark's RDDs provide robust fault tolerance mechanisms.

Distributed processing frameworks are essential for managing the complexities of AI data processing. They provide the scalability, performance, and flexibility needed to handle large-scale data transformations efficiently. By leveraging frameworks like Apache Hadoop, Apache Spark, Apache Flink, and Dask, organizations can build robust data pipelines that meet the rigorous demands of modern AI systems. Understanding the strengths and use cases of each framework enables informed decisions, ensuring that AI models are built on a solid foundation of well-processed and high-quality data.

Feature engineering, selection, and data normalization

The journey from raw data to actionable insights is paved with meticulous preprocessing steps. Among these, feature engineering, feature selection, and data normalization/standardization stand out as critical processes that shape the effectiveness of AI models. When dealing with large-scale datasets, these processes must be scalable and efficient to ensure timely and accurate results. This section looks into the intricacies of feature engineering and selection, as well as data normalization and standardization techniques, highlighting the tools and processes that facilitate these tasks in the AI landscape. We will not deep dive into these methodologies as they are part of core ML. However, the details will be sufficient on how to use them in a scalable AI architecture.

Feature engineering

Feature engineering is the art and science of transforming raw data into meaningful features that enhance the predictive power of ML models. This process involves creating new features, modifying existing ones, and ensuring that the data fed into the model is as informative as possible. The following list briefs us on the three common types of feature engineering:

- **Creating new features**: Creating new features can uncover hidden patterns in the data. Common techniques include the following:

  o **Mathematical transformations**: Applying operations like logarithms or square roots to capture non-linear relationships.

  o **Aggregations**: Summarizing data over specific dimensions (for example, mean, sum, count) to create features that capture aggregate information.

  o **Date and time features**: Extracting components like day of the week, month, or hour to capture temporal patterns.

  o **Domain-specific features**: Leveraging domain expertise to create features that provide valuable insights.

- **Handling categorical data**: Categorical data often requires special treatment to be useful in ML models. Techniques include:

  o **One-hot encoding**: Converting categorical variables into binary vectors.

  o **Label encoding**: Assigning unique integers to categories, useful for ordinal variables.

  o **Frequency encoding**: Replacing categories with their frequency counts to capture prevalence.

- **Interaction features**: Interaction features capture relationships between different features. Techniques include:

  o **Polynomial features**: Creating interaction terms by multiplying features together (for example, (x_1 multiply by x_2)).

  o **Crossed features**: Combining categorical features to create new categories that capture interactions.

Feature selection

Feature selection involves identifying and retaining the most relevant features for model training, reducing dimensionality, improving performance, and preventing overfitting. Some common methods to achieve feature selection include:

- **Filter methods**: It evaluates feature relevance based on statistical measures, independent of the learning algorithm. The correlation coefficient measures linear relationships between features and the target variable. The chi-square test assesses the independence of categorical features and the target variable. Mutual information quantifies the amount of information shared between features and the target variable.

- **Wrapper methods**: It evaluates feature subsets based on the performance of a specific learning algorithm. Recursive feature elimination iteratively removes the least important features based on model performance. Forward selection adds features one by one, evaluating model performance at each step. Backward elimination removes features one by one, evaluating model performance at each step.

- **Embedded methods**: It performs feature selection during model training. Lasso Regression applies L1 regularization to shrink less important feature coefficients to zero. Tree-based methods use feature importance scores derived from tree-based algorithms (for example, decision trees and random forests).

Data normalization and standardization

Data normalization and standardization are essential preprocessing steps that ensure features contribute equally to the model. These techniques transform data into a consistent scale, improving model performance and convergence.

Normalization scales features to a specific range, typically [0, 1] or [-1, 1]. Common methods are min-max scaling, which transforms features by scaling each feature to a given range, and max abs scaling, which scales each feature by its maximum absolute value, preserving the sign of the data.

Standardization transforms features to have a mean of zero and a standard deviation of one. This technique is particularly useful for algorithms that assume normally distributed data. One popular method, Z-score standardization, subtracts the mean and divides by the standard deviation for each feature.

Scaling feature engineering, selection, and normalization

When dealing with large-scale datasets, these preprocessing steps must be scalable. Here are some strategies and tools to achieve this:

- As discussed in the previous section, **distributed computing** frameworks (for example, Apache Spark, Dask) enable parallel processing of data across multiple nodes, significantly speeding up feature engineering, selection, and normalization tasks.

- **Incremental processing** involves breaking down the dataset into smaller chunks and processing them sequentially. This approach reduces memory requirements and allows for real-time feature engineering and normalization, which can be achieved in a distributed computing framework.

- **Automated feature engineering tools** can generate and select features automatically, reducing manual effort and time. These tools leverage advanced algorithms to identify the most relevant features of the model. Some examples include tools like:

  o **Feature tools:** An open-source library for automated feature engineering, enabling the creation of new features from relational data.

  o **H2O.ai:** Provides automated ML capabilities, including feature engineering and selection.

- **Dimensionality reduction** techniques reduce the number of features while preserving the most important information, managing the complexity and computational requirements of large-scale datasets. **Principal component analysis** (**PCA**) is one of the most used dimensionality reduction techniques that reduce dimensionality by transforming features into a set of linearly uncorrelated components. Another example is **t-Distributed Stochastic Neighbor Embedding** (**t-SNE**), which is a non-linear dimensionality reduction technique used for visualizing high-dimensional data.

Conducting feature engineering, selection, and normalization

Several tools and processes facilitate feature engineering, selection, and normalization in the typical AI landscape:

- **Scikit-learn**: A popular ML library in Python that provides various tools and libraries for feature engineering, selection, and normalization. While primarily designed for single-machine use, it can be combined with distributed computing frameworks for certain operations.

- **Pandas**: A powerful data manipulation library in Python that supports data cleaning, transformation, and analysis. While not inherently distributed, it is often used in conjunction with Dask or Spark for initial data exploration and feature engineering.

- **TensorFlow and PyTorch**: Deep learning frameworks using autoencoders that offer preprocessing utilities for feature engineering and normalization. Also, transfer learning is used to leverage pre-trained models for feature extraction in new domains.

- **Data preprocessing pipelines**: Automated pipelines (for example, Apache Airflow, Kubeflow) streamline the preprocessing workflow, ensuring consistency and efficiency. In the Apache Spark ecosystem, MLlib offers distributed implementations of feature engineering, selection, and normalization algorithms, while Spark SQL enables complex feature engineering using SQL queries on structured data. Databricks also provides a unified analytics platform that combines the power of Spark with collaborative notebooks, which offers managed solutions for feature stores and MLflow for experiment tracking. We will detail this aspect later in this chapter.

Best practices for feature engineering, selection, and normalization

To ensure effective preprocessing, consider the following best practices:

- **Understand the data**: Gain a deep understanding of the dataset and the problem domain to identify meaningful features. Test ideas on a subset of data before scaling. Combine automated techniques with domain expertise.

- **Iterate and experiment**: Feature engineering and selection are iterative processes. Experiment with different techniques and evaluate their impact on model performance.

- **Avoid data leakage**: Ensure that features are created and selected using only the training data to prevent data leakage and overfitting. Track changes in features and preprocessing steps to ensure reproducibility.

- **Use cross-validation**: Regularly assess the impact of engineered features and normalization on model performance. Evaluate feature selection techniques using cross-validation to ensure their robustness and generalizability.

Feature engineering, selection, and data normalization/standardization are pivotal steps in the AI data preprocessing pipeline. These processes transform raw data into meaningful features, identify the most relevant ones, and ensure that features contribute equally to the model. Scaling these processes to handle large-scale datasets requires leveraging distributed computing, incremental processing, and automated tools. By following best practices and employing effective techniques, you can build robust AI models that deliver accurate and reliable insights.

Handling imbalanced datasets and data augmentation

AI and ML, as well as the quality and distribution of your data, can significantly impact model performance. One common challenge is dealing with imbalanced datasets, where certain classes are underrepresented compared to others. Imbalanced data can lead to biased models that perform poorly on minority classes. Another critical aspect is data augmentation, a technique primarily used to increase the size and diversity of the training dataset artificially. These techniques are essential for improving model accuracy and generalization, especially when dealing with real-world datasets that often have inherent imbalances or limited samples. This section will explore strategies for handling imbalanced datasets and discuss various data augmentation techniques, providing a comprehensive guide to improving model robustness and accuracy.

Understanding imbalanced datasets

Imbalanced datasets occur when the distribution of classes is not uniform, meaning one class significantly outnumbers the others. This imbalance can lead to models that are biased towards the majority class, resulting in poor performance on the minority class. For instance, in a medical diagnosis dataset, if the number of healthy patients far exceeds the number of patients with a rare disease, the model might become biased toward predicting the healthy class.

Imbalanced datasets can lead to significant challenges in overall model performance, notably in the following ways:

- **Bias towards majority class**: Models tend to predict the majority class more frequently, ignoring the minority class. This translates to high overall accuracy but poor prediction of the minority classes.

- **Poor model performance**: Metrics like accuracy can be misleading, as a model might achieve high accuracy by simply predicting the majority class, which results in skewed performance metrics.

- **Overfitting**: The model may be overfit to the majority class, failing to generalize well to new, unseen data.

- **Overlooking important patterns**: Rare but crucial events may be treated as noise and ignored.

Techniques for handling imbalanced datasets

Several techniques can be employed to address the challenges posed by imbalanced datasets. These techniques can be broadly categorized into data-level methods and algorithm-level methods.

- **Data-level methods**: Data-level methods involve modifying the training data to balance the class distribution. Common techniques include:

  o **Resampling**: Adjusting the class distribution by either oversampling the minority class or undersampling the majority class. **Oversampling** techniques like **Synthetic Minority Over-sampling Technique** (**SMOTE**) generate synthetic samples for the minority class while **undersampling** randomly removes samples from the majority class to balance the dataset. Then there are methods that are a combination of using both undersampling and oversampling techniques, like SMOTETomek, which works by combining SMOTE and Tomek link removal.

o **Class weights**: Adjusting the importance of classes during model training.

o **Focal loss**: Modifying the loss function to focus on hard, misclassified examples.

- **Algorithm-level methods**: Algorithm-level methods involve modifying the learning algorithm to account for class imbalance. Common techniques include:

o **Cost-sensitive learning**: Assigning different misclassification costs to different classes, penalizing the model more for misclassifying the minority class.

o **Ensemble methods**: Combining multiple models to improve the performance of the minority class. Techniques like balanced random forests and EasyEnsemble are designed to handle imbalanced data.

o **Anomaly detection**: Treating the minority class as anomalies in extreme imbalance cases.

Data augmentation

Data augmentation is a powerful technique used to increase the size and diversity of the training dataset artificially. It involves creating new, synthetic data points to expand the training dataset. This technique is beneficial when dealing with limited data or to improve model generalization. We can create new data points that help the model generalize better by applying various transformations to the existing data. While data augmentation is commonly used in image processing, it can also be applied to other data types. The following are some of the use cases of data augmentation in a typical AI landscape:

- **Image processing**: Data augmentation in image processing can be done in the following ways.

o **Rotation**: Rotating images by a certain angle to create new perspectives.

o **Flipping**: Flipping images horizontally or vertically.

o **Scaling**: Zooming in or out to create variations in image size.

o **Translation**: Shifting images horizontally or vertically.

o **Noise addition**: Adding random noise to images to make the model more robust to variations.

- **Text processing**: Data augmentation for text data includes:

o **Synonym replacement**: Replacing words with their synonyms to create new sentences.

o **Random insertion**: Inserting random words into sentences.

o **Random deletion**: Removing random words from sentences.

o **Back translation**: Translating a sentence to another language and then back to the original language to create variation

- **Time-series data**: For time-series data, augmentation techniques include:

    o **Time warping**: Stretching or compressing the time series data.

    o **Jittering**: Adding random noise to the data points.

    o **Window slicing**: Creating new samples by slicing the time series data into overlapping windows.

    o **Resampling**: Changing the sampling rate to create variations in the data.

Implementing handling imbalance datasets

When working with large-scale AI systems, implementing these handling imbalance dataset techniques requires careful consideration of computational resources and data pipeline design. Some scalable approaches include the following:

- **Distributed resampling**: Implement resampling techniques in a distributed manner using frameworks like Apache Spark or Dask.

- **Online learning with adaptive sampling**: For streaming data, use adaptive sampling techniques that adjust class ratios on the fly.

- **GPU-accelerated augmentation**: Leverage GPU capabilities for faster data augmentation, especially for image and video data.

- **Parallel augmentation pipelines**: Design data augmentation pipelines that can run in parallel across multiple nodes.

- **Evaluate multiple techniques**: Experiment with different techniques for handling imbalanced data and data augmentation to find the best combination for your specific problem. Accuracy is not always a reliable metric for imbalanced datasets. Use metrics like precision, recall, F1-score, and AUC-ROC to evaluate model performance.

- **Monitor overfitting**: Be cautious of overfitting, especially when applying data augmentation. Ensure that the augmented data is realistic and representative of the real-world data. Use cross-validation to ensure that the techniques you apply generalize well to unseen data.

Several tools and libraries facilitate handling imbalanced datasets and data augmentation in the AI landscape. **Imbalanced-learn** is a Python library that provides various techniques for handling imbalanced datasets, including oversampling, undersampling, and ensemble methods. **Augmentor** is designed to augment image data with various transformations. **NLPAug** is a textual data augmentation library in Python that offers techniques like synonym replacement, random insertion, and back translation. **TSAUG** is a Python library for augmenting time series data, providing techniques like time warping and jittering.

GPU-accelerated data processing

In a typical AI and big data landscape, computational demands have surged, necessitating more powerful and efficient processing solutions. Traditional CPUs, while versatile, often need help to meet the requirements of large-scale data processing and complex AI models. This is where **graphics processing units** (**GPUs**) come into play. Initially designed for rendering graphics, GPUs excel at parallel processing, making them highly effective for a variety of data-intensive tasks. In this section, we will explore the types of workloads and tasks within AI architecture that particularly benefit from GPU-accelerated data processing, highlighting the transformative impact of this technology. GPUs are specialized hardware designed to perform multiple computations simultaneously. Unlike CPUs, which are optimized for sequential processing, GPUs excel at parallel processing, making them ideal for tasks that can be broken down into smaller, independent operations. This capability is particularly beneficial for data processing and ML, where operations on large datasets can be parallelized to achieve significant speedups.

GPU-optimized ML and deep learning

GPU-accelerated data processing is particularly advantageous in ML and deep learning. Training deep neural networks, a cornerstone of modern AI, involves extensive matrix multiplications and other operations that can be parallelized. With their thousands of cores, GPUs are adept at handling these computations simultaneously, drastically reducing training times. For instance, tasks such as image classification, natural language processing, and recommendation systems, which require processing vast amounts of data and performing numerous calculations, see substantial performance improvements when GPUs accelerate. This acceleration speeds up the training process and allows for more complex models, enabling deeper insights and more accurate predictions. Some key advantages of GPU acceleration include the following:

- **Massive parallelism**: GPUs can perform thousands of operations simultaneously.

- **High memory bandwidth**: Faster data transfer between memory and processing units.

- **Specialized hardware**: Built-in tensor cores for optimized matrix operations.

- **Energy efficiency**: Better performance per watt compared to CPUs for certain tasks.

This enables GPUs to significantly speed up various data processing tasks common in AI workflow, like data transformation, feature engineering, and data augmentation (synthetic data generation. Filtering and aggregation, time series processing, graph processing, and text processing.

Implementing GPU-accelerated data processing

A robust ecosystem of tools and frameworks designed to leverage GPUs' capabilities further supports the integration of GPUs into AI architectures. The following are examples of how GPUs are used in AI data processing:

- **GPU-enabled libraries and frameworks**: Several libraries and frameworks support GPU-accelerated data processing:

  o **RAPIDS**: A suite of open-source libraries for end-to-end GPU data processing and ML.

    ▪ **cuDF**: GPU-accelerated pandas-like DataFrame operations.

    ▪ **cuML**: ML algorithms optimized for GPU.

    ▪ **cuGraph**: Graph analytics on GPU.

  o **TensorFlow**: Supports GPU acceleration for data preprocessing operations.

  o **PyTorch**: Offers GPU support for tensor operations and data loading.

  o **Numba**: JIT compiler that can target NVIDIA GPUs for accelerated Python functions.

  o **JAX**: AutoGrad and XLA for high-performance ML research on GPUs.

- **GPU-optimized algorithms**: Many data processing algorithms have been redesigned to take advantage of GPU architecture:

  o **Sorting**: GPU-based algorithms like Thrust for faster sorting of large datasets.

  o **Join operations**: GPU-accelerated database joins for faster data merging.

  o **Matrix operations**: Optimized linear algebra operations using libraries like cuBLAS.

  o **Signal processing**: FFT and other signal processing operations using cuFFT.

- **Distributed GPU processing**: For handling extremely large datasets:

  o **Multi-GPU systems**: Utilizing multiple GPUs in a single machine for increased parallelism.

  o **GPU clusters**: Distributing processing across multiple GPU-enabled nodes.

  o **Cloud GPU services**: Leveraging cloud platforms for scalable GPU resources.

Challenges and best practices of GPU acceleration

While GPU acceleration offers significant benefits, it also comes with several challenges. For one, there is data transfer overhead, which means that the movement of data between the CPU and the GPU is a bottleneck, and this movement of data back and forth is an additional step. As such, keep data on the GPU as much as possible to avoid transfer overhead. GPUs usually have less memory than CPUs; as such, they need more careful memory considerations. Group operations into batches to maximize GPU utilization, and techniques like streaming and out-of-core processing for large datasets. Writing efficient programs for GPUs can be more complex than the corresponding CPU code. As such, it is advisable to leverage optimized libraries like cuDF and cuML for common operations. Lastly, GPUs are expensive when compared to CPUs, and hence there should be utmost attention to using GPUs at the right place in the architecture to avoid cost overruns. GPU profiling tools can be used to identify and address performance bottlenecks.

Comparison of some common GPU processing frameworks

When it comes to GPU-accelerated data processing, choosing the right framework can significantly impact the efficiency and effectiveness of your AI workflows. The following is a comparison table highlighting several popular GPU acceleration frameworks, detailing their key features, typical use cases, and unique advantages:

Framework	Key features	Typical use cases	Unique advantages
CUDA	Low-level GPU programming	Custom GPU applications	Direct access to GPU hardware for fine-grained control
	Extensive library support (for example, cuBLAS, cuDNN)	High-performance computing	Optimized libraries for various computational tasks
RAPIDS	High-level GPU-accelerated data science libraries	ETL	Familiar API similar to pandas and scikit-learn
	cuDF for DataFrames, cuML for ML algorithms, cuGraph for graph analytics	ML model training	End-to-end GPU acceleration from data manipulation to model training
TensorFlow	Deep learning framework with extensive GPU support	Deep neural network training	Robust ecosystem with tools for model building, training, and deployment
	TensorFlow GPU for accelerated computations	NLP	TensorBoard for visualization and monitoring

Framework	Key features	Typical use cases	Unique advantages
PyTorch	Dynamic computation graph for flexible model building	Research and development in Deep learning	Intuitive and easy-to-use interface
	Strong GPU acceleration capabilities	Computer vision	Seamless integration with Python, making it a favorite among researchers
Apache Spark	Distributed data processing framework with GPU support via RAPIDS accelerator	Big data analytics	Scalability across distributed systems
	Integration with existing Spark APIs	Real-time data processing	Compatible with existing Spark workflows, enabling easy adoption of GPU acceleration
Dask	Parallel computing library for Python	Parallel data processing	Scales from single machines to large clusters
	Integrates with RAPIDS for GPU acceleration	Real-time analytics	Flexible and easy integration with existing Python data science stack
cuML	GPU-accelerated ML library	Clustering, regression, classification	Provides GPU-accelerated implementations of popular ML algorithms
	Part of the RAPIDS suite	Data preprocessing	Seamless integration with cuDF for end-to-end GPU-accelerated data science workflows

Table 4.2: Comparison of common GPU processing frameworks

GPU-accelerated data processing is revolutionizing the field of AI and big data analytics. The ability to handle parallel computations efficiently makes GPUs indispensable for a wide range of tasks, from training complex ML models to performing real-time data analytics and scientific simulations. By leveraging the power of GPUs, organizations can achieve significant speedups in their data processing workflows, enabling faster insights and more accurate models. As the AI landscape continues to evolve, the role of GPUs in accelerating data processing will only become more critical, driving innovation and efficiency across various domains.

Automated data preprocessing pipelines

Preprocessing large volumes of data is crucial in a typical AI landscape involving large volumes of data. Automated data preprocessing pipelines have emerged as a key solution, enabling organizations to streamline their data preparation workflows, ensure consistency, and accelerate the path from raw data to actionable insights. Raw data is often messy, incomplete, and inconsistent, necessitating a series of transformations to convert it into a usable format. However, manual data preprocessing can be labor-intensive, time-consuming, and prone to errors. This is where automated data preprocessing pipelines come into play. These pipelines streamline the preprocessing workflow, ensuring consistency, efficiency, and scalability. This section will explore the concept of automated data preprocessing pipelines, their components, benefits, and the tools available to implement them.

Automated data preprocessing pipelines are designed to handle the various data transformation stages with minimal human intervention. These pipelines automate repetitive tasks such as data cleaning, normalization, feature extraction, and integration, allowing data scientists to focus on more strategic aspects of model development. By automating these processes, organizations can ensure that their data is consistently prepared to the highest standards, reducing the risk of errors and improving the overall quality of their AI models.

Components of an automated data preprocessing pipeline

An automated data preprocessing pipeline typically consists of several key components, each responsible for a specific aspect of data transformation. These components work together to convert raw data into a format suitable for ML:

- **Data ingestion**: The first phase in any data preprocessing pipeline is data ingestion, where raw data is collected from various sources. These sources can include databases, APIs, flat files, and streaming data. Automated data ingestion tools can handle diverse data formats and sources, ensuring that data is consistently and efficiently collected. In many cases, data from multiple sources needs to be integrated into a single cohesive dataset. Automated data integration tools can merge datasets based on common keys, ensuring that the integrated data is consistent and accurate. This step is crucial for creating a comprehensive dataset that includes all relevant information.

- **Data cleaning**: This involves identifying and rectifying errors, inconsistencies, and missing values in the dataset. Automated data cleaning tools can detect and correct common issues such as duplicate records, outliers, and incorrect data types. Techniques like imputation, interpolation, and outlier detection are often employed to ensure the data is clean and reliable.

- **Data transformation**: This can include normalization, scaling, encoding categorical variables, and creating new features. Automated data transformation tools can apply these transformations consistently across the dataset, ensuring that the data is prepared according to the requirements of the ML model.

- **Feature engineering**: Automated feature engineering tools can identify and generate relevant features, reducing the need for manual intervention. Techniques such as polynomial features, interaction terms, and domain-specific transformations can be applied to enhance the dataset.

Benefits of automated data preprocessing pipelines

Automated data preprocessing pipelines offer several benefits that can enhance the efficiency and effectiveness of AI workflows. The benefits are as follows:

- **Consistency**: Automating data preprocessing ensures that the same transformations are applied consistently across the dataset. This reduces the risk of errors and inconsistencies, leading to more reliable and accurate models.

- **Efficiency**: Automated pipelines can process large volumes of data quickly and efficiently, reducing the time required for data preparation. This allows data scientists to focus on more strategic tasks such as model development and optimization.

- **Scalability**: Automated data preprocessing pipelines can easily scale to handle growing data volumes and complexity. This makes them ideal for large-scale AI projects where manual data preprocessing would be impractical.

- **Reproducibility**: Automating data preprocessing ensures that the steps taken to prepare the data are documented and reproducible. This is crucial for ensuring the transparency and reliability of AI models, particularly in regulated industries.

Implementing automated preprocessing pipelines

Several tools and frameworks are available to implement automated data preprocessing pipelines. These tools offer a range of features and capabilities to streamline the data preparation process:

- **Workflow orchestration**: Tools like Apache Airflow, Luigi, or Prefect can be used to design and manage automated preprocessing workflows. Workflow orchestration tools can define preprocessing tasks as **directed acyclic graphs (DAGs)**, schedule and monitor pipeline execution, handle dependencies between tasks, and manage retries. A common workflow orchestration tool is Apache Airflow. Apache Airflow is an open-source platform that allows users to define, schedule, and monitor data preprocessing pipelines using a Python-based syntax. Airflow's extensibility and integration capabilities make it a popular choice for building automated data pipelines.

- **Containerization and microservices**: Container orchestration platforms like Kubernetes enable easy scaling of AI workloads based on demand, ensuring optimal resource allocation and performance. Containers package applications and their dependencies into self-contained units, ensuring they run consistently across different environments. This makes deploying and managing AI models easier and more portable. They also help maintain consistent environments for training and deploying AI models, improving reproducibility and reducing the risk of errors. Containerization aligns well with microservices architectures, where applications are broken down into smaller, independent services. This promotes modularity, scalability, and easier maintenance.

- **Serverless architecture**: Serverless platforms automatically scale resources based on demand, ensuring optimal performance for varying workloads. This is especially beneficial for AI pipelines that often deal with fluctuating data volumes. Serverless allows developers to focus on building AI models and data processing logic without worrying about infrastructure management. This accelerates development and reduces time-to-market. It eliminates the need for upfront infrastructure costs and only charges for the resources consumed. This can significantly reduce costs, especially for AI pipelines that might experience intermittent usage. AWS Lambda, Azure Functions, and GCP Cloud Functions are examples of serverless compute platforms that let you execute code without managing the servers.

- **MLOps**: MLOps is crucial for AI architectures, especially when dealing with automated data processing pipelines, because it provides a structured approach to managing the entire ML lifecycle. MLOps automates many of the tasks involved in building, deploying, and maintaining AI models, reducing manual effort and increasing efficiency. fosters collaboration between data scientists, engineers, and other stakeholders, ensuring that AI models are developed and deployed in a consistent and reproducible manner. It enables AI pipelines to scale efficiently as data volumes and complexity increase. In essence, MLOps provides the framework and tools needed to build, deploy, and manage AI pipelines effectively. We will explore MLOps as a concept in more detail in subsequent chapters.

Databricks as a unified ingestion platform

Databricks is a unified analytics platform that revolutionizes the automation of data preprocessing pipelines. By integrating seamlessly with Apache Spark, Databricks offers a comprehensive, scalable, and collaborative environment for automating tasks from data ingestion to feature engineering. A key feature of this platform is **Delta Live Tables** (**DLT**), which enhances automation capabilities and ensures that data pipelines are continuously updated.

From a **data ingestion** perspective, Databricks excels by providing robust tools to efficiently ingest data from various sources such as databases, cloud storage, APIs, and streaming platforms. Using Spark's DataFrame API and built-in connectors, it handles multiple data formats like CSV, JSON, Parquet, and Avro, ensuring consistent and efficient ingestion across various data sources.

Following ingestion, Databricks automates the **data cleaning** process using Apache Spark's distributed computing. Integrated tools like Delta Lake ensure ACID transactions and scalable metadata management for large datasets. Data cleaning workflows, such as removing duplicates, handling missing values, and correcting data types, can be scheduled to run at regular intervals using Databricks Notebooks, which support languages such as Python, SQL, Scala, and R.

Data transformation is another critical part of automated preprocessing. With Spark's built-in functions and the ability to create custom transformations, Databricks automates tasks like normalization, scaling, and encoding categorical variables. A significant enhancement comes from DLT, which automatically applies transformations as new data arrives, keeping the data up to date. DLT also includes built-in quality checks and monitoring, simplifying the creation and maintenance of reliable, high-quality data pipelines.

Databricks automates **feature engineering** using tools like Spark MLlib, a scalable ML library. Users can generate new features through techniques like polynomial expansion and interaction terms, and can experiment interactively with feature engineering in Databricks notebooks. Automated feature selection algorithms help identify the most relevant features, further streamlining the process.

Databricks also shines in **workflow orchestration**. Through Databricks Jobs, users can schedule and automate preprocessing tasks, making the pipeline responsive to events such as new data arrivals. Additionally, Databricks Workflows offers a visual interface for designing and managing complex data workflows, simplifying monitoring and optimization.

The following figure depicts the automated data processing architecture using Databricks and AWS:

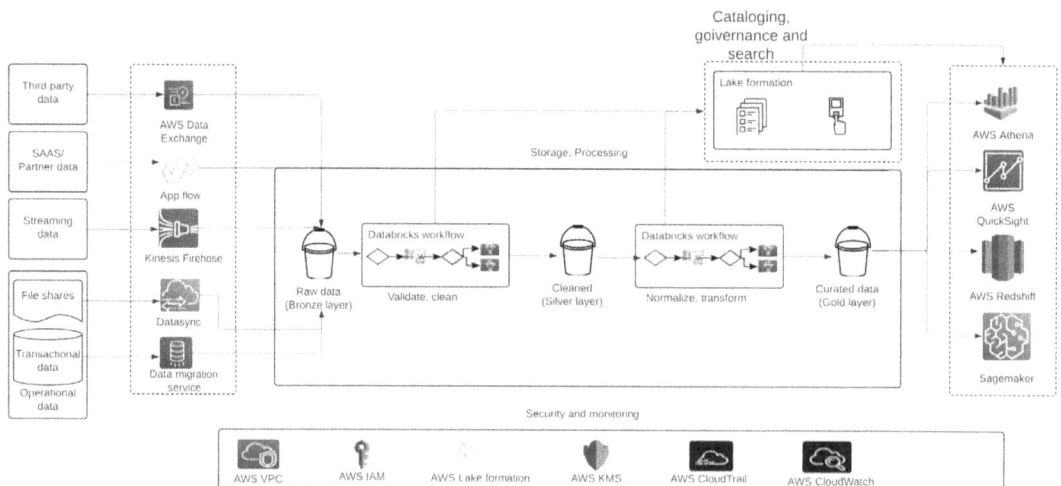

Figure 4.2: Automated data processing architecture

Another key strength is Databricks' collaborative environment. Databricks notebooks support real-time collaboration, allowing data engineers and scientists to work together seamlessly. Integration with GitHub enables version control, ensuring that changes are tracked and best practices are followed consistently. Scalability is a core feature of Databricks, which dynamically adjusts cluster size based on the workload, optimizing resource utilization. This auto-scaling capability is vital for large-scale AI projects, where efficient data preprocessing is crucial to preventing bottlenecks.

Databricks provides a comprehensive suite of tools to automate the data preprocessing pipeline, from ingestion and cleaning to transformation and feature engineering. The addition of DLT further enhances automation, ensuring that data pipelines are continuously maintained with minimal manual intervention. This platform enables organizations to prepare data efficiently and consistently, driving better outcomes in AI projects.

Integration of data processing with ML workflows

The seamless integration of data processing with ML workflows is crucial for building efficient, scalable, and reproducible AI systems. This integration streamlines the entire AI development lifecycle, from data preparation to model deployment, enabling organizations to derive value from their data more quickly and effectively.

The integration of data processing, whose detailed phases we have gone through in this chapter and previous chapters with ML workflow, is extremely important for the efficiency of the overall AI architecture, primarily because of the following reasons:

- **Efficiency and automation**: Integrating data processing with ML workflows eliminates manual handoffs between data engineers and data scientists. This automation reduces the time-to-insight and minimizes human errors, allowing teams to focus on high-value tasks rather than repetitive data manipulations.

- **Consistency and reproducibility**: When data processing is tightly coupled with ML workflows, it ensures that the same transformations are applied consistently across training, validation, and production environments. This consistency is vital for reproducing results and maintaining model performance over time.

- **Scalability**: Integrated workflows can leverage distributed computing resources more effectively, enabling organizations to process larger datasets and train more complex models. This scalability is essential for handling the ever-growing volumes of data in AI applications.

- **Versioning and traceability**: Combining data processing and ML workflows allows for better versioning of both data and models. This integration provides a clear lineage of how data was processed for each model version, which is crucial for debugging, auditing, and complying with regulatory requirements.

- **Agility and experimentation**: Tightly integrated workflows enable data scientists to iterate quickly on feature engineering and model development. They can easily modify data processing steps and immediately see the impact on model performance, fostering a culture of experimentation and continuous improvement.

Architectural considerations

The integration of data processing with ML workflow needs the following careful architectural considerations:

- **Unified platforms**: Modern AI architectures often leverage unified analytics platforms that combine data processing, ML training, and model serving capabilities. These platforms, such as Databricks, provide a seamless environment for end-to-end AI development.

- **Data pipelines as code**: Treating data processing pipelines as code allows for version control, testing, and collaboration. This approach aligns well with MLOps practices and enables the application of software engineering best practices to data workflows.

- **Feature stores**: Integrating feature stores into the AI architecture provides a centralized repository for preprocessed features. This integration ensures consistency between training and inference and allows for efficient reuse of features across multiple models.

- **Metadata management**: Robust metadata management is crucial for tracking the relationships between datasets, processing steps, and ML models. This metadata facilitates reproducibility and helps in understanding the impact of data changes on model performance.

- **Containerization**: Using containerization technologies like Docker ensures that data processing and ML environments are consistent across development, testing, and production. This consistency is vital for reproducible workflows and easy deployment.

We will further explore the amalgamation of the data processing and ML workflows when we discuss MLOps in *Chapter 8, Scalable Machine Learning Infrastructure*.

Challenges and considerations

While integrating data processing with ML workflows offers numerous benefits, it also presents some challenges that can be mitigated with specific best practices as follows:

- **Complexity**: Integrated workflows can become complex, potentially making them harder to maintain and debug. Careful design and modular architecture are essential to manage this complexity.

- **Skill set requirements**: Integrated workflows often require team members to have a broader skill set, spanning data engineering and ML. This may necessitate additional training or collaboration between specialized roles.

- **Performance optimization**: Balancing the needs of data processing and ML training can be challenging. Architects must carefully consider resource allocation and optimization strategies to ensure efficient execution of integrated workflows.

- **Governance and access control**: Integrated workflows may require more sophisticated governance mechanisms to ensure appropriate access controls and data privacy, especially when spanning multiple teams or departments.

The integration of data processing with ML workflows is a cornerstone of modern AI architectures. It enables organizations to build more efficient, scalable, and reproducible AI systems. By carefully considering the architectural implications and addressing potential challenges, organizations can create robust AI pipelines that drive innovation and deliver value from their data assets. As AI evolves, this integration will become increasingly important, forming the foundation for advanced techniques like automated ML and continuous learning systems.

Conclusion

The chapter explored the critical aspects of data processing and transformation for AI, emphasizing the importance of automated data preprocessing pipelines and their seamless integration with ML workflows. We began by understanding the necessity of automated data preprocessing pipelines, which streamline the transformation of raw data into a format suitable for analysis, ensuring consistency, efficiency, and scalability. The role of powerful platforms like Databricks was highlighted, showcasing how tools such as DLT enhance automation capabilities, making data pipelines more robust and adaptive.

We then covered the integration of data processing with ML workflows, underscoring the importance of consistency, efficiency, scalability, and reproducibility. Key components such as data ingestion, cleaning, transformation, and feature engineering were discussed, along with best practices like automation, modular design, monitoring, and collaboration. Tools like Databricks, MLflow, Apache Airflow, and Kubeflow were identified as instrumental in facilitating this integration, offering comprehensive solutions to manage and streamline the entire ML lifecycle.

In essence, the synergy between automated data preprocessing and integrated ML workflows forms the backbone of successful AI projects. By leveraging modern tools and adhering to best practices, organizations can ensure their data is consistently prepared to the highest standards, driving better outcomes in their AI initiatives.

As we progress to the next chapter, we will focus on the orchestration and management of these data processing pipelines. We will discuss workflow management tools, monitoring strategies, and performance optimization techniques. Additionally, we will explore the integration of CI/CD practices and serverless architectures for data pipelines, ensuring scalability and efficiency. As we move forward, we will further investigate specific techniques and advanced tools, providing a more granular understanding of the processes that underpin effective AI development.

Join our Discord space

Join our Discord workspace for latest updates, offers, tech happenings around the world, new releases, and sessions with the authors:

https://discord.bpbonline.com

CHAPTER 5
Modern Data Pipeline Management

Introduction

In modern AI systems, data pipelines serve as the critical infrastructure enabling seamless flow, transformation, and preparation of data for AI workloads. This chapter looks into the intricate data pipeline design and orchestration world, exploring how organizations can build robust, scalable, and efficient data processing systems. The need for sophisticated pipeline architecture becomes paramount as AI applications grow in complexity and scale. From designing flexible workflows to implementing comprehensive testing strategies, we will examine the key components and best practices that form the foundation of successful AI data pipelines. Through a combination of architectural patterns, tool evaluations, and practical implementation guidance, this chapter provides a roadmap for building data pipelines that can handle the demands of modern AI systems.

Structure

The chapter covers the following topics:

- Designing data pipelines for AI workflows
- Workflow management and orchestration tool
- Monitoring and error handling in data pipelines
- Scalability and performance optimization

- CI/CD for data pipelines

- Serverless architectures for data processing

- Testing and validation of data pipelines

- Cloud-native pipeline management

Objectives

By the end of this chapter, readers will gain a comprehensive understanding of modern data pipeline management. They will learn how to automate data pipeline processes through CI/CD, leverage serverless architectures for efficient and scalable data processing, and utilize cloud-native tools like AWS, Azure, and Google Cloud to build robust pipelines. Additionally, they will explore the importance of rigorous testing and validation to ensure data integrity and pipeline reliability. Finally, they will look into best practices for designing, monitoring, and securing data pipelines, ensuring they are resilient, maintainable, and compliant with regulatory standards. This knowledge will empower readers to modernize their data pipelines, harness the full potential of their data, and drive insightful analytics and informed decision-making.

Designing data pipelines for AI workflows

Data pipelines are the backbone of AI workflows, facilitating the seamless flow of data from its source to its destination, where it can be analyzed and used to train models. A well-designed data pipeline ensures data integrity, efficiency, and scalability, which are critical for the success of AI systems. In AI workflows, these pipelines must be designed with specific considerations in mind, ensuring they can handle the unique challenges posed by AI applications while maintaining scalability, reliability, and efficiency. This section will explore the foundational principles of designing data pipelines for AI workflows, emphasizing the importance of scalability, reliability, and flexibility.

Understanding data pipelines

A data pipeline is a series of data processing steps that move data from one system to another and integrate data from various sources to a single location. Data pipelines are mainly used to improve data quality, incorporate data, handle big data, and break down information silos as per business requirements. The pipeline encompasses various stages: data collection, transformation, storage, and analysis. In the context of AI, data pipelines are designed to handle large volumes of data, often in real-time, to support ML and deep learning models. Key components of data pipelines are:

- **Data source**: The origin of the data, which can be databases, APIs, log files, IoT devices, or streaming data. It can also be in a myriad of formats, such as Excel, JSON, image, etc.

- **Ingestion**: The process of collecting and importing data from various sources into the pipeline. It handles data intake from various sources, implements appropriate ingestion patterns (batch, micro-batch, or streaming), ensures data compatibility, and enforces constraints and validation checks.

- **Processing and transformation**: Transforming and cleaning data to make it suitable for analysis. This may involve filtering, aggregating, and enriching the data, making it ideal for consumption by business intelligence applications and ML models. It handles feature engineering and extraction and manages data normalization and standardization. It handles distributed computing when needed and manages resource allocation for computational tasks.

- **Storage**: Storing the processed data in a database, data lake, or data warehouse for further downstream consumption. Implementing appropriate storage solutions for different data types and managing data versioning and lineage. Ensuring efficient data retrieval for BI and ML operations.

- **Delivery**: Using the data in the storage layer to deliver business intelligence applications like interactive reports and dashboards, as well as the development and deployment of ML models using the CI/CD paradigm, which we will explore later in this chapter.

Designing a data pipeline involves several steps, from understanding the data requirements to implementing and testing the pipeline. The components to design are as follows:

- **Ingestion layer**: AI workflows often deal with massive amounts of data that must be processed efficiently. Pipeline design must account for batch vs. streaming data processing requirements, scalable architecture to handle growing data volumes, efficient data movement between pipeline stages, and efficient data movement between pipeline stages. Some standard data ingestion tools include:

  o **Apache Kafka**: An open source distributed streaming platform for real-time data ingestion.

  o **AWS Glue/Azure Data Factory**: A fully managed ETL service for batch data ingestion and an integration service for orchestrating data workflows.

  o **Databricks**: An Apache Spark-based platform that excels in both real-time and batch data ingestion at scale.

- **Processing layer**: Develop the data processing workflows to transform and clean the data. This involves writing data transformation scripts, setting up processing jobs, and configuring the processing framework. This layer should account for data validation checks and quality enforcement guidelines at multiple stages, automated data cleaning and standardization processes, anomaly detection mechanisms, applying aggregation and transformation (flattening, transposing, calculated columns, etc.) logics, scaling and standardization for subsequent AI models, and version control for datasets.

o　**ETL**: Traditional approach for batch processing.

o　**ELT**: Modern approach for leveraging the power of data warehouses for transformation.

o　**Stream processing**: Real-time processing of data streams using frameworks like Apache Flink.

We have gone through the aforesaid methodologies in *Chapter 4, Data Processing and Transformation for AI,* in detail.

- **Set up data storage**: Set up the data storage layer to store the processed data. This involves configuring databases, data lakes, or data warehouses and ensuring data is stored in an optimized format. Ensure data tiering policies to balance the cost of data retrieval and set appropriate IAM policies for access to the storage layer. Some common data storage types include:

- **Integrate with AI models**: Once the data is ready for consumption in the storage layer, integrate the pipeline with AI models to enable seamless data flow from storage to model training and inference. This involves setting up data connectors, configuring model training jobs, and deploying models.

A few commonly used AI integration tools include:

o　**TensorFlow Extended (TFX)**: An end-to-end platform for deploying production ML pipelines.

o　**MLflow**: An open-source platform for managing the ML lifecycle, including experimentation, reproducibility, and deployment.

o　**Kubeflow**: A Kubernetes-native platform for developing, orchestrating, and deploying scalable ML workflows.

- **Monitor and optimize**: Implement monitoring and optimization strategies to ensure the pipeline operates efficiently and meets performance requirements. This involves setting up monitoring tools, defining performance metrics, and optimizing the pipeline based on feedback. Comprehensive monitoring should include tracking pipeline performance metrics, logging data quality metrics at each stage, monitoring resource utilization, and setting up alerts for pipeline failures. Common pipeline monitoring and optimization tools include:

o　**Prometheus**: An open-source monitoring and alerting toolkit.

o　**Grafana**: A visualization tool for monitoring metrics and logs.

o　**Apache Airflow**: A platform for programmatically authoring, scheduling, and monitoring workflows.

Best practices for AI data pipeline design

Designing an effective data pipeline for AI workflows is as much about following best practices as it is about understanding the underlying principles. These best practices ensure that the pipeline is not only functional but also efficient, maintainable, and scalable. The following are some of the key best practices to consider:

- **Embrace modularity**: Modularity is the cornerstone of a flexible and maintainable data pipeline. By breaking down the pipeline into discrete, reusable components, you can easily update or replace individual parts without disrupting the entire system. Design each stage of the pipeline as an independent module with well-defined interfaces and develop components that can be reused across different pipelines, reducing redundancy and simplifying maintenance.

- **Implement robust data validation**: Data quality is paramount in AI workflows. Implementing robust data validation at various stages of the pipeline ensures that only clean, accurate data is used for training and inference. Validate incoming data against predefined schemas to catch errors early. Implement checks to ensure data consistency and integrity across different stages of the pipeline. Use statistical techniques or ML models to detect and handle anomalies in the data. For instance, in Databricks' medallion architecture, data validation and constraint checks are enforced when data is processed from the bronze (raw) to the silver layer.

- **Implement pub/sub architecture**: A **publish/subscribe (pub/sub)** architecture is an effective strategy for data ingestion in AI pipelines. In a pub/sub model, **data producers (publishers)** send messages to a topic, while **data consumers (subscribers)** receive messages from these topics. The **Message Broker** is an intermediary component that manages the routing of messages between publishers and subscribers. It receives messages from publishers and forwards them to subscribers based on their subscriptions. The Message Broker ensures that messages are delivered to the correct subscribers and can provide additional features such as message persistence, scalability, and reliability. A **subscription** represents a connection between a subscriber and a topic. Subscriptions define which messages a subscriber will receive based on the topics to which it is subscribed. Subscriptions can have different configurations, such as message delivery guarantees (for example, at-most-once, at-least-once) and acknowledgment mechanisms. This decouples the data producers from the consumers, enhancing scalability and flexibility. Publishers and subscribers are loosely coupled, allowing independent scaling and maintenance. *Figure 5.1* shows the flow of information in a basic pub/sub system:

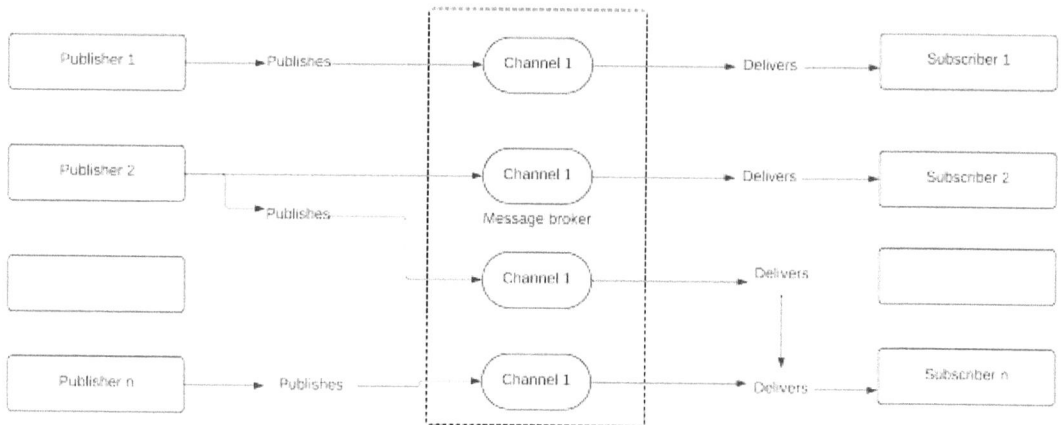

Figure 5.1: Pub/Sub system

Google Cloud Pub/Sub is a fully managed messaging service that allows you to send and receive messages between independent applications. Similarly, for AWS, **Simple Notification Service (SNS)** is used for message broadcasting, and **Simple Queue Service (SQS)** is used for message queuing. Apache Kafka also supports pub/sub architecture and is better suited for scenarios requiring high throughput, durable event streaming, and real-time data processing.

- **Prioritize scalability from the start**: Scalability should be a primary consideration from the outset. Design the pipeline to handle increasing data volumes and processing demands without requiring extensive rework. Design for horizontal scaling by distributing workloads across multiple nodes or clusters. Utilize cloud-native features like auto-scaling to dynamically adjust resources based on workload. Implement data partitioning strategies to distribute the processing load evenly. Some partitioning strategies include:

  o **Vertical partitioning**: Splits a table into multiple tables, each containing a subset of the original table's columns. A primary key links the tables together.

  o **Functional partitioning**: Groups data based on how it is used in a system's bounded contexts. For example, an e-commerce system might store invoice data in one partition and product inventory data in another.

  o **Hash partitioning**: Divides a table into smaller, independent pieces based on a hash function applied to a specific column. This method is useful for data that is not ordered.

  o **Range partitioning**: Divides large fact tables into smaller segments based on a key attribute, such as date, region, or product category.

  o **Hybrid partitioning**: Applies multiple partitioning methods to different subsets of the data. This approach can provide flexibility and optimize performance for complex datasets.

The choice of partitioning method depends on factors like data size, access patterns, processing requirements, and system architecture. A critical component of database partitioning is the partitioning key, which is used to identify the location of data in the partitioned table.

- **Ensure fault tolerance and reliability**: Reliability is crucial for maintaining the integrity of AI workflows. Design the pipeline to handle failures gracefully and ensure continuous operation. Implement redundancy at critical points to prevent single points of failure. Use checkpointing to save the state of the pipeline at regular intervals, enabling recovery from failures. Implement automatic retry mechanisms for transient errors and failures.

- **Implement caching and parallelism**: Caching is a technique used to store frequently accessed data in a temporary storage layer, reducing the time and resources required to retrieve it. In the context of data pipelines, caching can significantly enhance performance by minimizing redundant data processing and reducing latency. In-memory caching is used to store frequently accessed data in memory (for example, using Redis or Memcached) to provide rapid access. Caching query results is used to avoid re-executing complex queries on the underlying data store. For datasets that are heavily used for querying, it is a good idea to precompute and store aggregated or transformed data for quick retrieval using materialized views.

- **Implement idempotency**: Idempotency is essential in data pipeline design, ensuring consistent results when the same data is processed multiple times. In distributed systems, where retries or duplicate messages are common, idempotency maintains data integrity and simplifies error handling, allowing operations to be safely retried without causing data corruption. One way to achieve idempotency is through **unique identifiers** (**UUIDs** or hashes) to detect and ignore duplicates. Stateless operations, or carefully managed stateful ones using unique constraints, also support idempotency. Upsert operations (update if exists, insert otherwise) and deduplication techniques, like pub/sub brokers or Spark window functions, further reinforce idempotency throughout the pipeline

Pipeline design patterns for AI workflows

Designing data pipelines for AI workflows involves selecting appropriate architectural patterns that can handle the specific requirements of data volume, velocity, and variety. Two prominent design patterns that are often used in AI workflows are the Lambda architecture and the Kappa architecture. These architectures provide different approaches to processing large-scale data and have their own advantages and trade-offs.

Lambda architecture

The Lambda architecture is a robust and versatile design pattern that addresses the need for both real-time and batch data processing. It was introduced to handle the limitations of traditional batch processing systems by integrating a real-time layer. The architecture is divided into three main layers:

- **Batch layer**: The batch layer is responsible for processing large volumes of historical data in batches. It generates comprehensive, accurate views of the data by processing it in bulk. This layer is designed to handle high throughput, low-latency processing, and it typically uses distributed computing frameworks like Apache Hadoop or Apache Spark. Raw data is stored in a distributed file system, such as HDFS or Amazon S3. Periodic batch jobs are executed to process the raw data and generate batch views or precomputed aggregates. The data in the batch layer is immutable, ensuring consistency and simplifying data management.

- **Speed layer**: Designed to process data with low latency. It handles data that needs to be processed and made available immediately, complementing the batch layer by providing real-time updates. Real-time data streams are processed using stream processing frameworks like Apache Storm, Apache Flink, or Apache Kafka Streams. The speed layer generates incremental updates, which are merged with the batch views to provide a real-time view of the data.

- **Serving layer**: Responsible for merging the batch views from the batch layer and the real-time updates from the speed layer. It provides a unified view of the data that can be queried by end-users or downstream systems. The merged views are stored in a database or data store optimized for read performance, such as HBase, Cassandra, or Elasticsearch. The serving layer exposes an interface for querying the unified view, enabling quick and efficient data retrieval.

Kappa architecture

The Kappa architecture is a simpler alternative to the Lambda architecture, designed to address some of its complexities. It eliminates the need for a separate batch processing layer by relying solely on stream processing. The architecture is based on the idea that all data processing can be done in real-time using a single stream processing engine.

In the Kappa architecture, all data is ingested as streams and processed in real-time. The architecture leverages stream processing frameworks like Apache Kafka, Apache Flink, or Apache Kafka Streams to handle continuous data processing. Processed data is stored in a data store optimized for real-time access, such as a NoSQL database or a distributed file system. The storage system must support efficient read-and-write operations to handle the continuous influx of data. The architecture provides a query interface for accessing the processed data. This interface enables users and downstream systems to query the data in real-time, supporting various analytical and operational use cases.

Workflow management and orchestration tools

Effective workflow management and orchestration are crucial for building robust data pipelines that support AI workflows. These tools automate the scheduling, execution, and monitoring of complex data processes, ensuring that data flows smoothly from ingestion to analysis. Organizations can achieve greater efficiency, reliability, and scalability in their AI pipelines by leveraging workflow management and orchestration tools.

Key components of workflow management tools

Workflow management tools are essential for orchestrating the various stages of data pipelines, from data ingestion to model training and deployment. These tools provide several key capabilities that streamline the management of complex workflows.

The following are the key components of workflow management tools:

- **Scheduling**: Scheduling is at the heart of workflow management. It involves defining when and how tasks should be executed, whether on a fixed schedule, in response to specific events, or based on data availability. Time-based scheduling allows for tasks to be scheduled at specific times or intervals, like cron jobs. Event-driven scheduling triggers tasks based on specific events, such as the arrival of new data or the completion of a previous task. Dependency management ensures that tasks are executed in the correct order, respecting dependencies between tasks.

- **Resource management**: Efficient resource management ensures that workflows run smoothly and do not overwhelm the available computational resources. Resource allocation dynamically allocates resources, such as CPU, memory, and storage, to tasks based on their requirements, while auto-scaling automatically scales resources up or down based on workload, ensuring optimal performance and cost-efficiency. Load balancing: distributes workloads evenly across available resources to prevent bottlenecks and ensure high availability.

- **Monitoring and observability:** Provides visibility into the status and performance of workflows, enabling real-time tracking and troubleshooting. Real-time monitoring tracks the execution of tasks in real-time, providing insights into their status, progress, and performance. Logging and alerts capture logs and trigger alerts for errors, failures, or performance issues, enabling quick resolution. Dashboards offer visual dashboards that provide an overview of workflow health, metrics, and **key performance indicators** (**KPIs**). Examples of such KPIs would be the number of jobs failed, the average CPU utilization in percentage, the number of records parsed, and the number of records quarantined after the QA job.

Popular workflow management tools

Several workflow management tools have gained popularity for their ability to handle the complexities of data engineering and AI workflows. The following are some of the most widely used tools:

- **Apache Airflow**: Apache Airflow is an open-source platform for programmatically authoring, scheduling, and monitoring workflows. It uses DAGs to represent workflows, where each node represents a task and edges define dependencies. DAGs define workflows as DAGs, making it easy to visualize and manage task dependencies. It supports custom plugins and operators, allowing for integration with various data sources and processing frameworks. It provides a powerful scheduler to manage task execution, supporting cron-like scheduling and complex time-based triggers. It further offers a web-based user interface for monitoring workflows, viewing logs, and managing task execution. For example, a data pipeline that ingests data from multiple sources, processes it using Apache Spark, and stores the results in a data warehouse can be orchestrated using Airflow. The DAG can define tasks for data ingestion, transformation, and loading, with dependencies ensuring that each step is executed in the correct order.

- **Databricks Workflow**: It provides a comprehensive suite of workflow management tools designed specifically for AI and data pipelines. It provides Jupyter-style notebook workflows that allow for orchestrating notebook-based data processing with multi-language support in a single notebook and runtime. It provides a pipeline environment called DLT, which is a declarative framework for building reliable, maintainable, and testable data processing pipelines. You define the transformations to perform on your data, and DLT manages task orchestration, cluster management, monitoring, data quality, and error handling. It also provides end-to-end integration with MLflow to manage ML lifecycles.

- **Kubeflow**: Kubeflow is an open-source platform designed to facilitate the deployment, orchestration, and management of ML workflows on Kubernetes. It aims to make scaling ML models and workflows as simple, portable, and scalable as possible. Kubeflow leverages Kubernetes for container orchestration, ensuring that ML workflows can scale efficiently and reliably. It provides a robust pipeline management system that allows users to define, schedule, and monitor complex ML workflows. It also supports end-to-end ML workflows, from data preparation and model training to deployment and serving. Lastly, it integrates with various ML frameworks, such as TensorFlow, PyTorch, and scikit-learn, and supports custom components. For example, an ML workflow that involves data preprocessing, model training, hyperparameter tuning, and deployment in a Kubernetes environment can be managed using Kubeflow.

Future trends in workflow orchestration

The workflow management and orchestration field is continuously evolving, with emerging trends that promise to enhance these tools' capabilities and efficiency.

AI-driven optimization leverages ML algorithms to automatically optimize workflows, resource allocation, and task scheduling. This approach can significantly improve the performance and efficiency of data pipelines, reducing manual intervention and enabling more intelligent decision-making.

Low-code and **no-code** solutions are gaining popularity for their ability to simplify the development and management of workflows. These platforms provide visual interfaces and pre-built components, allowing users to design and deploy workflows without extensive coding knowledge. This trend democratizes workflow management, making it accessible to a broader range of users.

Workflow management and orchestration tools are essential for building efficient, reliable, and scalable data pipelines for AI workflows. By automating the scheduling, execution, and monitoring of tasks, these tools ensure that data flows smoothly through the pipeline, from ingestion to analysis. Selecting the right tool and following best practices is crucial for the success of AI initiatives. As the field continues to evolve, emerging trends like AI-driven optimization and low-code/no-code solutions promise to further enhance the capabilities and accessibility of workflow management tools.

Monitoring and error handling in data pipelines

Robust monitoring and error handling are critical components of successful AI data pipelines. As data pipelines grow in complexity and scale, effective monitoring becomes essential for ensuring reliability, performance, and data quality. These practices ensure that data pipelines operate smoothly, detect issues promptly, and recover gracefully from failures. This section explores key strategies and best practices for implementing comprehensive monitoring and error handling in AI data pipelines.

Monitoring data pipelines

Monitoring involves tracking the execution of data pipelines, capturing metrics, and generating alerts for anomalies or failures. The following are some key aspects of monitoring data pipelines:

- **Metrics collection**: Collecting metrics is the foundation of effective monitoring. Metrics provide quantitative data about the performance and health of data pipelines. Task execution metrics track the execution time, success rate, and failure rate of individual tasks within the pipeline. Resource utilization metrics monitor the usage of computational resources, such as CPU, memory, and storage, to identify potential bottlenecks. Data throughput metrics measure the volume of data processed by the pipeline over time, providing insights into the pipeline's capacity and performance. Tools like Grafana or Kibana can be used to create interactive and customizable dashboards. Alerts are set up to notify operators of anomalies, failures, or performance issues. Alerts can be configured based on predefined thresholds or conditions, ensuring that critical issues are addressed promptly.

- **Logging**: Captures detailed information about the execution of data pipelines, including error messages, warnings, and informational logs. Centralized logging is implemented to aggregate logs from different components of the pipeline. Tools like Elasticsearch and Logstash can be used to store and analyze logs. Use log analysis tools to search, filter, and analyze logs, helping to identify the root cause of issues and track the pipeline's behavior over time.

- **Distributed tracing**: Provides end-to-end visibility into the flow of data through the pipeline, capturing the execution path of individual requests or transactions. Traces are collected from different components of the pipeline, capturing information about task execution, dependencies, and latency. Use trace analysis tools to visualize the execution path, identify performance bottlenecks, and diagnose issues. Tools like Jaeger or Zipkin can be used for distributed tracing.

Error handling in data pipelines

Error handling involves detecting, managing, and recovering from errors that occur during the execution of data pipelines. The following are some key strategies for effective error handling:

- **Error detection**: Detecting errors promptly is essential for minimizing the impact of failures and ensuring the reliability of data pipelines. Implement validation checks at various pipeline stages to detect data quality issues, such as missing values, outliers, or schema violations.

- **Error logging**: Logging errors provides valuable information for diagnosing and resolving issues. Ensure that error logs capture detailed information about the nature and context of the error. Include descriptive error messages that provide insights into the cause of the error and potential solutions. Capture contextual information, such as the input data, task parameters, and execution environment, to facilitate troubleshooting.

- **Retry mechanisms**: Retry mechanisms enable data pipelines to recover from transient errors by automatically retrying failed tasks. Use exponential backoff to gradually increase the delay between retry attempts, reducing the load on the system and increasing the likelihood of success. Define retry policies that specify the conditions under which retries should be attempted, the maximum number of retries, and the delay between attempts.

- **Fault tolerance**: Ensures that data pipelines can operate smoothly even in the presence of failures. Implement checkpointing to save the state of the pipeline at regular intervals. In the event of a failure, the pipeline can resume from the last checkpoint, minimizing data loss and reprocessing. Use data replication to create redundant copies of critical data, ensuring that data is not lost in the event of a failure.

- **Graceful degradation**: Allows data pipelines to continue operating at reduced functionality in the event of a failure, ensuring that critical tasks are still completed. Implement fallback mechanisms that provide alternative solutions or degraded service levels when certain components of the pipeline are unavailable. Allow for partial processing of data, where non-critical tasks can be skipped or deferred in the event of a failure, ensuring that critical tasks are prioritized. Try-catch blocks with appropriate error classification and dead letter queues for handling problematic data are common examples of graceful degradation techniques.

Scalability and performance optimization

Ensuring that data pipelines can scale efficiently and perform optimally is essential for maintaining AI models' reliability, speed, and accuracy. Scalability and performance optimization are essential for several reasons. First, it helps gracefully handle data growth. As data volumes increase, scalable pipelines can accommodate the growth without compromising performance. Second, optimized performance ensures that data processing tasks are completed quickly and efficiently, reducing latency and resource consumption. Next, efficient use of resources helps manage costs, especially in cloud environments where resource usage directly impacts expenses. Lastly, scalable and optimized pipelines are more resilient to failures and can maintain consistent performance under varying workloads. This section will explore key strategies and best practices for achieving scalability and performance optimization in data pipelines.

Key strategies for scalability

Scalability involves designing data pipelines that can handle increasing data volumes and processing demands without significant rework.

Here are some key strategies for achieving scalability:

- **Horizontal scaling**: Horizontal scaling, also known as scaling out, involves adding more machines or nodes to distribute the workload. This approach is particularly effective for handling large-scale data processing tasks and offers several advantages in terms of flexibility, fault tolerance, and cost-efficiency. Common ways to achieve horizontal scaling are:

  o **Distributed computing frameworks**: Use distributed computing frameworks like Apache Spark, Hadoop, or Flink to parallelize data processing across multiple nodes.

  o **Cluster management**: Implement cluster management tools like Kubernetes or Apache Mesos to orchestrate and manage the resources in a distributed environment.

  o **Load balancing**: Evenly distributes network traffic equally across a pool of resources that support an application. Load balancers can be classified as application load balancers (run and scale your services behind an anycast IP address) and network load balancers (a transport layer-based balancer that uses TCP and UDP protocols to manage transaction traffic). We will look further into load balancing in *Chapters 8, Scalable Machine Learning Infrastructure* and *9, Real-time AI System and Stream Processing.*

o **Implementation considerations**: The following practices should be considered when implementing horizontal scaling:

- **Data partitioning**: Use sharding to divide the dataset into smaller, manageable shards that can be processed independently across different nodes. Use effective partition keys to distribute data evenly across partitions. Avoid keys that could lead to skewed distribution and hotspots.

- **Fault tolerance**: Design the system to be fault-tolerant by replicating data across multiple nodes. This ensures that data is not lost in the event of a node failure. Implement checkpointing to save the state of the pipeline at regular intervals, allowing for recovery from failures without significant data loss.

- **Stateless design**: Each request from client to server is treated as an independent transaction, and the server does not maintain any information about the previous interactions with the client. This lack of memory about past interactions makes stateless architectures highly scalable and efficient, as servers do not need to store or manage session data for individual clients.

- **Vertical scaling**: Vertical scaling, also known as scaling up, involves adding more resources (CPU, memory, storage) to existing machines. While this approach can provide immediate performance improvements, it has limitations compared to horizontal scaling, such as hardware constraints and diminishing returns. Common ways to implement vertical scaling are:

o **Resource upgrades**: Increase the number of CPU cores and the amount of RAM in existing machines to handle more intensive data processing tasks. Upgrade to faster storage solutions, such as SSDs, to improve data read/write speeds and reduce latency.

o **Optimized resource allocation**: Use resource management tools to dynamically allocate resources based on task requirements. Ensure that critical tasks receive the necessary resources to operate efficiently. Implement auto-scaling features in cloud environments to automatically adjust resources based on workload, providing flexibility and cost-efficiency. Choose cloud-native applications that support auto-scaling whenever possible.

o **Implementation considerations**: The following practices should be considered when implementing vertical scaling:

- **Resource monitoring**: Continuously monitor resource usage to identify bottlenecks and inefficiencies. Use monitoring tools like Prometheus or Datadog to track CPU, memory, and storage utilization. Set up alerts to notify operators of resource constraints or performance issues, enabling prompt resolution.

- **Performance tuning**: Optimize the performance of data processing tasks by fine-tuning algorithms, query execution plans, and data structures. Identify and address any performance bottlenecks. Be aware of the limitations of vertical scaling, such as hardware constraints and diminishing returns. As resources are added to a single machine, the performance gains may decrease over time.

Both horizontal and vertical scaling are essential strategies for building scalable and efficient data pipelines. By distributing workloads across multiple nodes, horizontal scaling offers flexibility, fault tolerance, and cost-efficiency. Vertical scaling provides immediate performance improvements by upgrading resources on existing machines. It is often a good idea to plan for a hybrid approach combining vertical and horizontal scaling to achieve optimal performance and scalability.

Caching

Caching is a powerful technique for improving the performance and efficiency of data pipelines. By storing frequently accessed data in a temporary storage layer, caching reduces the time and resources required to retrieve and process data. Caching is essential for several reasons, listed as follows:

- **Reduced latency**: By storing data closer to the processing layer, caching significantly reduces the time required to access data, leading to faster query execution and data processing.

- **Improved throughput**: Caching can handle a higher volume of data requests by offloading read operations from the primary data store, thereby improving overall throughput.

- **Cost efficiency**: By reducing the load on primary data stores and computational resources, caching can lead to cost savings, especially in cloud environments where resource usage is directly tied to expenses.

- **Enhanced user experience**: For applications that require real-time data access, such as dashboards and interactive analytics, caching ensures a smooth and responsive user experience.

There are several caching strategies that can be employed in data pipelines, each with its own set of use cases and benefits. The following are some of the most common caching strategies:

- **In-memory caching** stores data in the RAM of a server, providing extremely fast read and write access. This strategy is ideal for scenarios where low latency is critical. Redis is an open-source, in-memory data structure store that supports various data types, such as strings, hashes, lists, sets, and sorted sets. It is widely used for caching due to its high performance and rich feature set. Memcached is another popular in-memory caching system designed for simplicity and speed. It is particularly effective for caching small chunks of data, such as database query results, session data, and API responses.

- **Query caching** involves storing the results of frequently executed database queries. This reduces the need to re-execute complex queries on the primary data store, thereby improving query performance. Many relational databases, such as MySQL and PostgreSQL, offer built-in query caching mechanisms. These databases automatically cache the results of frequently executed queries, reducing the load on the database engine.

- **Distributed caching** involves spreading the cache across multiple nodes, providing scalability and fault tolerance. This strategy is particularly useful for large-scale applications that require high availability and performance. Apache Ignite is an in-memory computing platform that provides distributed caching capabilities. Amazon ElastiCache is a fully managed caching service that supports both Redis and Memcached. It provides the scalability and reliability needed for large-scale applications, with features like automatic failover and data replication.

- **CDN caching** involves storing static content, such as images, videos, and web pages, on servers distributed across multiple geographic locations. This reduces latency by serving content from the server closest to the user. Cloudflare is a widely used CDN that caches static content and provides global content delivery. It also offers features like DDoS protection and SSL/TLS encryption. Amazon CloudFront is a CDN service that integrates seamlessly with other AWS services. It caches static and dynamic content, providing low-latency access to users worldwide.

Performance optimization techniques

Optimizing the performance of data pipelines is crucial for ensuring efficient data processing and minimizing resource consumption. Effective performance optimization can be achieved at various levels, including the data level, the processing level, and the resource level. Some of the common optimization scenarios are as follows:

- **Data-level optimization**: It focuses on improving the efficiency of data storage, retrieval, and processing by selecting appropriate data formats, applying compression, and implementing indexing strategies.

  o **Data format selection**: Choosing the right data format is essential for optimizing storage and processing efficiency. Efficient data formats can significantly reduce storage requirements and improve read/write performance. Parquet is a columnar storage format optimized for analytical queries. It supports efficient data compression and encoding schemes, making it ideal for large-scale data processing tasks. **Optimized Row Columnar (ORC)** is another columnar storage format designed for high-performance data processing. It provides efficient compression and indexing, reducing the amount of data read from disk.

o **Compression**: It reduces the size of data, leading to lower storage costs and faster data transfer. However, it is essential to balance the compression ratio with the processing overhead. Use compression algorithms that offer a good balance between compression ratio and decompression speed. Apply compression selectively based on data characteristics. Compress large, repetitive datasets while avoiding compression for small or already compressed data.

o **Indexing**: Indexing improves data retrieval speed by creating data structures that allow for quick lookups. Implementing appropriate indexing strategies can significantly enhance query performance. Use primary indexes on key columns to speed up data retrieval for common queries. Implement secondary indexes on frequently queried columns to improve query performance without significantly impacting write performance.

- **Resource optimization**: Resource optimization focuses on efficient management and allocation of computational resources to balance performance and cost.

o **Resource pooling**: It involves sharing computational resources efficiently across multiple tasks and pipelines. Implement resource pooling mechanisms to ensure that resources are allocated dynamically based on task requirements. Use container orchestration tools like Kubernetes to manage resource allocation.

o **Autoscaling**: Automatic scaling dynamically adjusts resources based on workload, ensuring that resources are allocated efficiently and cost-effectively.

o **Cost optimization**: Balancing performance and resource costs is essential for managing expenses, especially in cloud environments. Use cost-effective resources, such as spot instances or reserved instances, to reduce costs while maintaining performance.

- **Pipeline architecture for scalability**: A scalable pipeline architecture is crucial for handling increasing data volumes and processing demands. Two key architectural patterns for achieving scalability are microservices architecture and event-driven architecture.

o **Microservices architecture**: It involves decomposing data pipelines into independent, loosely coupled services that can be developed, deployed, and scaled independently. Break down the pipeline into smaller, self-contained services, each responsible for a specific task. Scale individual services based on their specific resource requirements, ensuring efficient resource utilization and avoiding over-provisioning. Scale individual services based on their specific resource requirements, ensuring efficient resource utilization and avoiding over-provisioning. More importantly, update and maintain individual services without impacting the entire pipeline, reducing downtime and improving agility.

o **Event-driven architecture**: It leverages message queues and event streams to decouple pipeline components and enable asynchronous processing. Use message queues like Apache Kafka or RabbitMQ to facilitate asynchronous communication between pipeline components. Decouple pipeline components to reduce dependencies and improve scalability. Implement strategies to handle burst workloads efficiently, such as buffering events in message queues and scaling processing components dynamically.

- **Optimization for different workload types**: Different workload types require specific optimization strategies to achieve optimal performance and scalability.

o **Batch processing**: It involves processing large volumes of data in periodic batches. Optimization strategies for batch processing focus on efficiency and throughput. Implement efficient checkpointing strategies to save the state of the pipeline at regular intervals, allowing for recovery from failures without significant data loss. Use bulk operations to process large datasets in fewer steps, reducing overhead and improving performance.

o **Stream processing**: It involves real-time processing of continuous data streams. Optimize strategies for stream processing, focusing on minimizing latency and managing state efficiently. Aim for reducing data shuffling and leveraging in-memory processing. Use windowing strategies to group and process data within specific time intervals, enabling real-time analysis and aggregation. Optimize state management to ensure efficient handling of stateful operations.

o **ML workload optimization**: ML workloads involve data preparation, model training, and inference. Optimization strategies focus on efficient data processing and model management. Implement efficient feature engineering pipelines to preprocess and transform raw data into features suitable for model training. Balance preprocessing and model inference tasks to ensure efficient resource utilization and minimize overall processing time.

Common scalability challenges and solutions

Scalability challenges can arise due to uneven data distribution, resource contention, and other factors. The following are some common challenges and their solutions:

- **Data skew** occurs when data is unevenly distributed, leading to processing bottlenecks and inefficiencies. Implement salting techniques to distribute data more evenly across partitions. Add random or hash-based values to partition keys to avoid hotspots. Use adaptive query optimization techniques to dynamically adjust query execution plans based on data distribution and runtime statistics. Implement custom partitioning strategies to ensure balanced data distribution.

- **Resource contention** occurs when multiple components compete for limited resources, leading to performance degradation. Implement resource isolation techniques to allocate dedicated resources to critical tasks, reducing contention and ensuring consistent performance. Use appropriate scheduling strategies to prioritize tasks based on their resource requirements and importance. Leverage tools like Kubernetes to manage resource scheduling.

CI/CD for data pipelines

CI/CD are pivotal practices in modern software development, and their principles are equally valuable when applied to data pipelines. Implementing CI/CD for data pipelines ensures that changes are integrated and deployed in a reliable, automated, and repeatable manner. CI/CD for data pipelines involves automating data processing workflows' integration, testing, and deployment. The goal is to ensure that changes to the data pipeline, whether they involve code, configuration, or data schema, are consistently validated and deployed without manual intervention. This approach enhances the reliability, agility, and maintainability of data pipelines.

Key components of CI/CD for data pipelines

Implementing CI/CD for data pipelines involves several key components, each of which plays a crucial role in ensuring a smooth and reliable deployment process:

- **Version control**: **Version control systems** (**VCS**) like Git are the foundation of CI/CD. They track changes to the codebase, configuration files, and data schemas, enabling collaboration and ensuring that changes are documented and reversible. Often, a branching strategy, such as GitFlow or trunk-based development, is used to manage changes and integrate them into the main codebase. Commit hooks are often implemented to enforce coding standards and trigger automated tests upon each commit.

- **Automated testing**: This ensures that changes to the data pipeline are validated before they are deployed. This includes unit tests, integration tests, and data validation tests. Individual data pipeline components, such as data transformation functions, are tested to ensure they work as expected. Interactions between different components of the data pipeline are validated, ensuring that they work together seamlessly. The integrity and quality of the data being processed are checked, ensuring that it meets predefined criteria.

- **CI**: It involves automatically building and testing the data pipeline whenever changes are committed to the version control system. CI tools like Jenkins, GitLab CI, or CircleCI are used to automate the build and test process. These tools are configured to trigger builds and tests upon each commit or pull request. Build pipelines are defined as compiling code, running tests, and generating artifacts, such as deployment packages or Docker images.

- **CD**: It automates the deployment of changes to the data pipeline, ensuring that they are consistently and reliably moved from development to production environments. CD tools like Spinnaker, Argo CD, or Azure DevOps are used to automate the deployment process. These tools are configured to deploy changes automatically upon successful completion of CI pipelines. *Figure 5.2* shows the basic schematic overview of the CI/CD process:

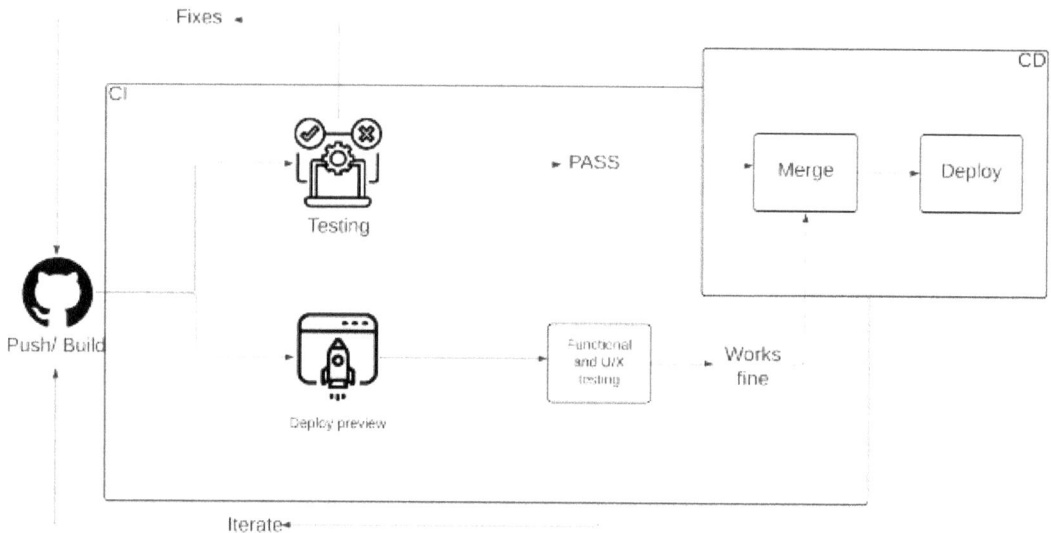

Figure 5.2: Basic overview of CI/CD

Strategies for implementing CI/CD for data pipelines

Implementing CI/CD for data pipelines requires careful planning and consideration of various factors. The following are some key strategies to ensure successful implementation:

- **Modular pipeline design**: Design the data pipeline as a collection of modular components, each responsible for a specific task. This approach simplifies testing, integration, and deployment. Ensure that each component is isolated and can be developed, tested, and deployed independently. Create reusable modules for common tasks, such as data ingestion, transformation, and validation, to promote consistency and reduce duplication.

- **Environment consistency**: Ensure that development, testing, and production environments are consistent to avoid discrepancies and ensure reliable deployments. Use IaC tools like Terraform or Ansible to define and provision environments consistently across different stages. Implement configuration management practices to manage environment-specific settings and ensure consistency.

- **Automated rollbacks**: Implement automated rollback mechanisms to revert changes in case of deployment failures, minimizing downtime and reducing the impact of errors. Define rollback scripts that can be triggered automatically upon deployment failures to revert to the previous stable state. Store versioned artifacts, such as deployment packages or Docker images, to facilitate easy rollbacks.

- **Monitoring and observability**: Incorporate monitoring and observability into the CI/CD process to track the performance and health of the data pipeline and detect issues promptly. Implement log aggregation solutions to collect and analyze logs from different data pipeline components, enabling quick diagnosis and resolution of issues.

Serverless architectures for data processing

Serverless architectures have revolutionized the way we design and deploy data processing pipelines. By abstracting away the underlying infrastructure, serverless computing allows developers to focus on writing code without worrying about server management, scaling, or maintenance. Serverless computing, often referred to as **function as a service (FaaS)**, is a cloud computing model where the cloud provider dynamically manages the allocation of machine resources. In a serverless architecture, developers write and deploy functions executed in response to events. These functions are stateless, ephemeral, and scale automatically based on demand. Cost efficiency, scalability, simplified operations, and rapid development are the hallmarks of serverless operations. *Table 5.1* summarizes the comparison between serverless and traditional architecture of the four key aspects:

Aspect	Serverless	Traditional
Scaling	Automatic	Manual. Pre-provisioned
Cost	Usage based	Fixed + Usage
Maintenance	Minimal	Significant
Cold start	Yes	No

Table 5.1: Serverless vs. traditional architecture

Key components of serverless data processing

Serverless data processing relies on several key components, each crucial in building and orchestrating data pipelines. They are as follows:

- **Serverless functions**: Serverless functions are the core building blocks of a serverless architecture. These functions are triggered by events and execute specific tasks, such as data transformation, aggregation, or enrichment.

  AWS Lambda is a popular serverless computing service that allows you to run code in response to various events, such as changes in data, HTTP requests, or scheduled tasks. **Azure Functions** is a serverless compute service provided by Microsoft Azure, offering similar capabilities to AWS Lambda with seamless integration into the Azure ecosystem. **Google Cloud Functions** is a lightweight, event-driven computing service that allows you to run code in response to events from Google Cloud services and other sources.

- **Event sources**: Event sources generate events that trigger serverless functions. These events can come from various sources, such as data storage services, message queues, or HTTP requests. Data storage services like Amazon S3, Azure Blob Storage, and Google Cloud Storage can trigger functions when new data is uploaded or modified. Message queues like Amazon SQS, Azure Queue Storage, and Google Cloud Pub/Sub can trigger functions to process messages asynchronously. HTTP Requests using API Gateway services, such as Amazon API Gateway or Azure API Management, can trigger tasks in response to HTTP requests.

- **Orchestration services**: Orchestration services coordinate the execution of multiple serverless functions, managing dependencies, retries, and error handling.

  AWS Step Functions is a serverless orchestration service that allows you to build complex workflows by chaining together Lambda functions and other AWS services. **Azure Durable Functions** is an extension of Azure Functions that enables the orchestration of stateful workflows, allowing for long running and complex processes. **Google Cloud Workflows** is a service for orchestrating and automating workflows across Google Cloud and HTTP-based APIs.

Figure 5.3 shows a generic AWS-based serverless architecture diagram:

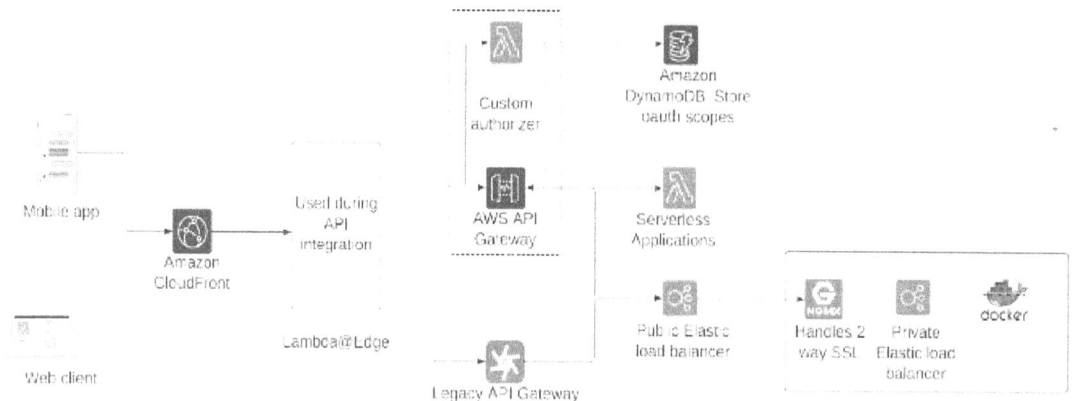

Figure 5.3: A sample AWS serverless architecture

Challenges and workarounds of serverless architectures

Serverless architectures offer numerous benefits, such as cost efficiency, scalability, and simplified operations. However, they also come with their own set of challenges. Understanding these challenges and their potential workarounds is crucial for successfully implementing serverless data processing pipelines. The following are some of the challenges with serverless architecture and their potential workaround:

- **Cold start latency**: Cold start latency refers to the delay that occurs when a serverless function is invoked for the first time or after a period of inactivity. This delay is caused by the time required to initialize the execution environment and load the function code. Cold starts can impact the performance of latency-sensitive applications, leading to slower response times.

  Workarounds:

  o **Warm-up strategies**: Implement warm-up strategies to keep functions warm and reduce cold start occurrences. For example, schedule periodic invocations of the function to prevent it from becoming idle.

  o **Provisioned concurrency**: Some serverless platforms, like AWS Lambda, offer provisioned concurrency, which ensures that a specified number of function instances are always warm and ready to handle requests.

  o **Language and runtime choice**: Choose languages and runtimes with faster initialization times, such as Node.js or Python, to minimize cold start latency.

- **Resource limits**: Serverless functions have resource limits on memory, CPU, and storage. These limits can constrain the function's processing capabilities and impact performance, especially for resource-intensive tasks.

  Workarounds:

  o **Optimize resource usage**: Optimize the code and data processing logic to reduce resource consumption. Use efficient algorithms, data structures, and libraries to improve performance.

  o **Appropriate memory allocation**: Allocate appropriate memory to the function based on its resource requirements. Higher memory allocations can lead to better performance but also higher costs. Find a balance that meets performance needs without excessive costs.

  o **External storage**: Offload large data storage to external services, such as Amazon S3 or Azure Blob Storage, to reduce the storage burden on the function.

- **Vendor lock-in**: Serverless architectures often rely on specific cloud provider services and APIs, leading to vendor lock-in. This can make it difficult to migrate to another cloud provider or adopt a multi-cloud strategy.

Workarounds:

- o **Abstraction layers**: Use abstract layers and frameworks, such as the Serverless Framework or Terraform, to define serverless functions and infrastructure in a cloud-agnostic manner. This makes it easier to port functions across different cloud providers.

- o **Standardized APIs**: Design your serverless functions to use standardized APIs and protocols, such as REST or GraphQL, to minimize dependencies on proprietary cloud services.

- o **Multi-cloud strategies**: Adopt a multi-cloud strategy by deploying serverless functions across multiple cloud providers. This provides flexibility and reduces dependence on a single provider.

- **Cold data and state management**: Serverless functions are stateless by design, meaning they do not retain any state between executions. Managing stateful workflows and handling cold data can be challenging in a serverless architecture.

Workarounds:

- o **External state stores**: Use external state stores, such as databases (for example, DynamoDB, Cosmos DB) or distributed caches (for example, Redis, Memcached), to manage state and persist data between function executions.

- o **Stateful workflow services**: Leverage stateful workflow services, such as AWS Step Functions or Azure Durable Functions, to manage complex, stateful workflows and maintain state across multiple function executions.

- o **Event sourcing**: Implement event sourcing patterns to capture and store state changes as a sequence of events. This allows you to reconstruct the state by replaying events when needed.

Testing and validation of data pipelines

Ensuring the accuracy, reliability, and robustness of data pipelines is critical for maintaining the integrity of data-driven applications. Testing and validation play a crucial role in achieving these objectives by identifying issues early and ensuring that data pipelines perform as expected.

Types of tests for data pipelines

Effective testing of data pipelines involves various types of tests, each targeting different aspects of the pipeline's functionality and performance:

- **Unit tests** focus on individual components or functions within the data pipeline, ensuring that they operate correctly in isolation. Test individual data transformation functions, ensuring they produce the expected output for given inputs. Validate that those functions handle edge cases and boundary conditions correctly, such as empty inputs or maximum data sizes.

- **Integration tests** validate the interactions between different components of the data pipeline, ensuring that they work together seamlessly. They also test the integration of data ingestion, transformation, and storage components, verifying that data flows correctly between them. Finally, integration tests ensure that data remains consistent and accurate as it passes through various stages of the pipeline.

- **End-to-end tests** validate the entire data pipeline from data ingestion to final output, ensuring that the pipeline meets functional and performance requirements. Test the complete data processing workflow, verifying that data is ingested, transformed, and stored correctly. Measure the pipeline's performance, such as processing time and resource utilization, under different workloads.

- **Data validation** tests focus on the quality and integrity of the data being processed, ensuring that it meets predefined criteria. Verify that the data conforms to the expected schema, including data types, field names, and required fields. Implement data quality checks, such as validating ranges, detecting duplicates, and ensuring completeness.

Cloud-native pipeline management

Cloud-native pipeline management has revolutionized the way organizations design, deploy, and manage data processing workflows. By leveraging cloud-native platforms, data engineers and scientists can build scalable, efficient, and resilient data pipelines that are tightly integrated with cloud services. Cloud-native pipeline management involves designing and managing data pipelines using cloud-native tools and services. These platforms provide a range of features, including automated scaling, integrated monitoring, and seamless integration with other cloud services. They offer a host of benefits like automatically scaling resources based on workload, ensuring efficient processing of large data volumes, providing a wide range of tools and services to build complex workflows, and ensuring high availability and fault tolerance through distributed architectures and built-in redundancy.

Key cloud platforms for pipeline management

Several cloud platforms offer robust tools and services for managing data pipelines. These platforms include AWS, Azure, Google Cloud, and Databricks, each providing unique features and capabilities:

- **AWS Data Pipeline and AWS Step Functions**: AWS offers a variety of services for building and managing data pipelines, including AWS Data Pipeline and AWS Step Functions. AWS Data Pipeline is a web service that helps you process and move data between different AWS compute and storage services. It allows you to define data-driven workflows and manage dependencies between tasks.

AWS Step Functions is a serverless orchestration service that lets you coordinate multiple AWS services into serverless workflows. It supports complex workflows with branching, parallel execution, and error handling.

- **Azure Data Factory**: A cloud-based data integration service that allows you to create, schedule, and orchestrate data workflows. It supports data integration from various sources, including on-premises and cloud-based data stores. It also provides a visual interface for designing and managing data pipelines, with support for scheduling, monitoring, and error handling.

- **Google Cloud**: It offers powerful tools for data pipeline management, including Google Cloud Dataflow and Cloud Composer. Google Cloud Dataflow is a fully managed service for stream and batch processing. It uses Apache Beam to define data processing workflows and provides automatic scaling and optimization. Cloud Composer is a managed workflow orchestration service built on Apache Airflow. It allows you to author, schedule, and monitor complex workflows across Google Cloud services.

- **Databricks Workflows**: It is a fully managed orchestration service built into the Databricks Lakehouse Platform. It simplifies the creation, scheduling, and monitoring of data and ML workflows, making it an ideal choice for cloud-native pipeline management. It is a unified platform that integrates seamlessly with the Databricks environment, allowing users to manage data, analytics, and ML workflows in one place. It provides a powerful scheduler to automate the execution of tasks, with support for time-based, event-driven, and dependency-based triggers. It allows for the creation of interactive workflows using Databricks notebooks, enabling collaborative development and debugging.

Creating and managing workflows

Creating and managing workflows in a cloud-native environment involves key steps listed as follows:

- **Defining the workflow**: Define tasks using cloud-native tools, such as AWS Lambda functions, Azure Functions, Google Cloud Functions, or Databricks notebooks. Each task can be configured with specific parameters, such as input data sources and output destinations. Specify dependencies between tasks to ensure they are executed in the correct order. Use orchestration services like AWS Step Functions, Azure Data Factory, Cloud Composer, or Databricks Workflows to manage task dependencies.

- **Scheduling the workflow**: Schedule the workflow to run at specific times or in response to specific events. Cloud platforms provide flexible scheduling options to meet various requirements. You can schedule workflows to run at regular intervals, such as daily, weekly, or monthly. You can use cron expressions to define complex schedules. Trigger workflows in response to specific events, such as data arrival in a storage service or the completion of another workflow.

- **Monitoring and managing workflows**: Monitor the performance and health of workflows using the built-in monitoring and alerting capabilities of cloud platforms. Track the status of running workflows, view logs, and monitor key metrics, such as task execution times and resource utilization. Set up alerts to notify users of workflow failures, performance issues, or other anomalies. Configure alert thresholds and notification channels, such as email or messaging apps. Execute individual tasks interactively to test and debug them before integrating them into the workflow.

Conclusion

This chapter comprehensively explored modern data pipeline management, highlighting the critical role of CI/CD, serverless architecture, and cloud-native platforms in building robust, scalable, and efficient data workflows. We began by examining the significance of CI/CD in automating the integration, testing, and deployment of data pipelines, ensuring consistency, reliability, and rapid iteration. The discussion on serverless architectures underscored the benefits of abstracting infrastructure management, enabling developers to focus on code while leveraging automatic scaling and cost-efficiency.

We also looked into the nuances of testing and validation, emphasizing the importance of maintaining data integrity, pipeline reliability, and performance assurance through various types of automated tests. The section on cloud-native pipeline management showcased how platforms like AWS, Azure, Google Cloud, and Databricks Workflows offer powerful tools for orchestrating complex workflows, with features such as job scheduling, real-time monitoring, and interactive debugging.

In the next chapter, we will transition from the technical intricacies of pipeline management to the strategic realm of data governance and security. This chapter will cover essential concepts such as data privacy, regulatory compliance, and data stewardship. We will explore best practices for implementing robust data governance frameworks, ensuring data quality, and safeguarding sensitive information. Additionally, we will discuss the importance of establishing clear data ownership and accountability, as well as strategies for managing data access and usage policies.

Join our Discord space

Join our Discord workspace for latest updates, offers, tech happenings around the world, new releases, and sessions with the authors:

https://discord.bpbonline.com

CHAPTER 6

Data Governance, Security, and Compliance in AI

Introduction

In this era of AI, data governance has become rapidly important. In this chapter, we will focus on how different data governance frameworks help companies to preserve data. Organizations make sure that with an increasing amount of data, they comply with data management regulations like GDPR and CCPA. Data governances involve various aspects that organizations must follow, like bias detection in datasets through data lineage in AI datasets. This chapter focuses on how organizations can remain within ethical considerations and integrate with modern AI platforms without breaching any of the data security rules. It has become paramount for organizations to follow regulations from the start of data collection and all the way through the deletion. Now, organizations that utilize AI frameworks make sure that they maintain data stewardship along with utilizing AI transformative tools. Moreover, in this chapter, we explore various data governance frameworks along with potential bias detection in AI datasets, and so on and so forth. Moreover, we will focus on practical approaches to implementing privacy-preserving techniques, establishing audit trails, and maintaining transparent data practices that build trust while fostering innovation.

Readers from all walks, like data scientists, policymakers, or organizations, will be able to implement robust data governance strategies that should be implemented in AI journeys.

Structure

The chapter covers the following topics:

- Data governance frameworks for AI
- Privacy-preserving AI techniques
- Regulatory compliance in AI data management
- Data encryption and access control mechanisms
- Audit trails and data lineage for AI systems
- Bias detection and mitigation in AI datasets
- Ethical considerations in AI data usage
- Integrated governance features in modern AI platforms

Objectives

This chapter provides a comprehensive exploration of data governance frameworks, highlighting their benefits and practical applications. It emphasizes the critical role of AI in maintaining data privacy and ensuring the development of high-quality, robust AI tools that adhere to regulatory compliance frameworks such as GDPR and CCPA. The chapter looks into defining and enforcing access controls, data encryption protocols, and establishing solid infrastructural foundations to ensure ethical use and secure management of datasets. It addresses the identification and prevention of potential security threats, including cyberattacks, and promotes best practices for data security and governance to foster success in AI-driven platforms. By the end, readers will gain a clear understanding of the essential steps for ensuring data security, compliance, and governance in organizational or AI-empowered initiatives.

Data governance frameworks for AI

AI data governance frameworks have become increasingly important in various sectors. Hence, it has become paramount to leverage data management for training, validation, and deployment of AI models in such a way that ethical standards, regulatory requirements, and organizational policies are not violated. Key elements included in these frameworks are assurance of data quality, security, privacy, transparency, and accountability.

They generally include how data should be collected, stored, and controlled for access. They also provide ways of mitigating bias in AI systems to avoid discriminatory outcomes. Active monitoring and auditing processes for continuity in artificial intelligence regarding data practices that are in concert with changing laws, among other ethical expectations, are also underlined within data governance frameworks, especially when handling sensitive or personal data. Similarly, the framework provides support for an organization with clearly defined structures in managing data across the data lifecycle. This, in turn, would be beneficial in building effective AI systems that are trusted and compliant with industry standards and regulations such as GDPR and CCPA, among many more.

Importance of data governance in AI

AI systems are working heavily on tremendous, complex datasets that, in turn, have elements of sensitive personal data and include significant societal implications. Without good governance, AI risks such as biased outcomes, data breaches, and regulatory violations could undermine trust and cause harm. Data governance provides the framework for managing these risks and ensuring responsible development and deployment of AI. The major objectives of data governance in AI include:

- **Data quality and integrity**: High-quality, accurate, and reliable data are the backbone of AI's effectiveness. Data governance ensures that information being fed into these models is clean, consistent, and error-free. Setting a standard for data quality and best practices will ensure that organizations will not be skewed into certain insights while reducing AI models that go out and make biased or incorrect decisions due to ill-constructed data.

- **Data security and privacy**: AI systems often handle sensitive personal data or enterprise confidential data, for which data security and privacy are paramount. A robust data governance framework will define how the data must be secured and protected against unauthorized access, including adherence to all related privacy laws, such as GDPR or CCPA. These steps help reduce the chances of data breach and breach of privacy rights of individuals.

- **Regulatory compliance**: While AI applications are becoming pervasive, the regulatory landscape for data utilization is getting increasingly intense. The structures of data governance ensure that the organizations meet the concerned laws, industry standards, and regulations governing the usage of data. This includes audit trails, consent, and adherence to binding legislation about storage, sharing, and processing that could save one from costly legal penalties.

- **Ethical AI practices**: AI has broader implications for society than just technical performance, and its development and deployment must, therefore, be done ethically. Data governance plays a key role in ensuring AI systems are based on ethical premises like fairness, transparency, and accountability. This includes ensuring algorithmic bias, the use of diverse and representative datasets, and providing mechanisms to hold algorithms accountable in cases where an AI system causes harm or acts in unintended ways.

Taken together, these goals underpin a comprehensive data governance approach to ensure that AI is effective and efficient, responsible and trustworthy, and consonant with societal values.

Key elements of AI data governance frameworks

A comprehensive data governance framework for AI is one that governs data through its lifecycle along multiple layers. Each element in this framework addresses a certain aspect of managing data in order for AI systems to be functional, ethical standards met, and live up to the standards related to it. These elements interactively work together to ensure the integrity, security, and value of information while mitigating such risks as bias, leakage of data, and non-conformity with regulatory requirements. Critical components comprising a robust AI data governance framework include, but are not limited to, the following:

- **Data governance policies**: The set of policies regarding data governance should be well-defined to guide data management and data stewardship within an organization. This will ensure the proper handling of data with responsibility and alignment with business objectives and regulatory requirements.

  o **Data ownership and stewardship**: Ownership and stewardship of data are the very basic parts of data governance. Data owners are supposed to ensure accuracy, availability, and adequate usage of data. A data steward plays a major role in maintaining the quality and integrity of data over time. Such an assignment of ownership helps clarify the responsibility for AI data management involved in training models and ensures that ethical guidelines are followed.

  o **Data classification and handling**: Classifying data according to the level of sensitivity, for instance, into public, internal, confidential, or sensitive classes, will provide the right ways of handling. AI systems require highly sensitive data, such as personal health records or even financial information; such data requires extra safeguards. Through classification, it will be possible to undertake access controls, encryption methods, and secure storage practices.

  o **Data access and usage**: Again, it provides the ability to define who shall have access to the data and under what conditions. Data governance frameworks determine the roles that are authorized to access and manipulate the data and set clear policies on access permissions. Also, the data usage policy defines for what purpose data can be used, thereby reducing the chances of data misuse or unethical applications of AI.

- **Data quality management**: Data quality is crucial for AI; low-quality data produces poor models and biased results and may lead to unexpected consequences. A well-constructed data governance framework gives guidelines on how to assess, maintain, and enhance data quality.

  o **Data profiling and assessment**: Data profiling provides a comprehensive analysis with respect to understanding the structure of information, the content, and the quality. In essence, it helps in ascertaining any gaps, inconsistencies, or other anomalies within data sets that may affect the reliability of AI models. It will also be regularly assessed for any omissions in terms of data that best fit the standards needed for accuracy, consistency, and completeness.

o **Data cleansing and enrichment**: It is the process of looking for and correcting errors or inconsistencies in the data. This can involve everything from the removal of duplicates and correction of typos to the filling in of missing values. Data enrichment involves adding more relevant data to a dataset to enhance its value. Both play an important role in ensuring AI models learn from clean and quality data.

o **Data quality metrics**: Second, metrics for data quality will ensure that organizations can always track and assess data used in AI systems. These metrics can include accuracy, completeness, consistency, timeliness, and relevance. Once there is regular tracking of data quality, it provides room for detecting issues in advance, which means timely intervention is possible.

- **Data security and privacy**: Data protection against breach, unauthorized access, and misuse is a key concern of data governance. Strong security and privacy measures are in place, especially for AI systems dealing with personally or confidentially sensitive information, not only to observe the due process of law but also to gain user confidence.

o **Data encryption**: Encryption of data is among the most important security measures for both data in transit and data at rest. In a situation where data may be intercepted or accessed without authority, encryption ensures that such data remains unreadable without appropriate keys for decryption. For AI handling large datasets, encryption becomes quite essential in protecting such sensitive information.

o **Access control**: Access control regulates the policy of who may be authorized to perceive, modify, and share data. By acting strictly within a **role-based access control** (**RBAC**), an organization can ensure that sensitive data access will be given to authorized users only and minimize the risk of data leakage, thereby acting in compliance with privacy regulations.

o **Data masking and anonymization**: Data masking and anonymization are key techniques for protecting **personally identifiable information** (**PII**) and other sensitive data. Masking replaces sensitive values with fictitious or scrambled data, while anonymization removes identifiable elements altogether. These techniques are crucial in AI, where datasets often need to be shared or analyzed without compromising privacy. Additionally, emerging cryptographic approaches like zero-knowledge proofs allow one party to prove the validity of information without revealing the data itself, offering a powerful complement to traditional privacy-preserving techniques in distributed AI systems.

- **Regulatory compliance**: With increased regulation both on AI and the use of data, compliance with the relevant laws and industry standards will become increasingly critical. A well-structured framework of data governance ensures that AI systems operate within the limits of the law and specific industry regulations.

  o **Compliance audits**: Regular audits are very important in ascertaining whether or not data governance practices actually match exactly what is provided for by regulatory requirements. Audits assist an organization in ascertaining whether or not they are in compliance with the legislation on data protection, industry standards, or internal policies. Audits, in regard to AI, are able to consider whether or not the models of AI use data in a legal and ethical way.

  o **Data protection impact assessments (DPIAs)**: DPIAs also provide a very important tool in the identification and mitigation of privacy risks with regard to activities involving the processing of data. When deploying AI systems, especially those that involve large volumes of personal data, a DPIA becomes very instrumental in supporting organizations' efforts toward assessing any likely impacts on privacy and introducing necessary safeguards.

  o **Record keeping and documentation**: This is highly important for compliance reasons, especially when regulators come knocking. Proper documentation will also help demonstrate that the handling of data and AI models has been ethical in nature and hence allow for transparency in decision-making processes.

- **Metadata management**: Metadata management deals with how one manages data that describes other data; hence, it gives context, structure, and meaning to information. The essence of metadata management is to make data semantics available for interpretation by AI systems, thereby making it easier to better organize the data or reuse it when appropriate.

  o **Metadata repositories**: Centralized metadata repositories house metadata on the structure, usage, and inter-relations of an organization's data assets. These repositories facilitate both the discovery and accessibility of data by AI systems and may enforce consistency in the definition across data.

  o **Metadata standards**: Metadata standards ensure consistency, interoperability, and machine readability. Well-defined standards enable collaboration both among people and systems since integrations are easy, hence permitting data to be used for training AI models.

  o **Automated capture of metadata**: Capture of metadata through automation reduces the manual effort involved in keeping the metadata updated concerning the data assets. Through automation, an AI system can track the lineage of data as it captures metadata of data from its origin and how it is transformed over time. This plays a critical role in areas of transparency and accountability, more so in regulated industries.

- **Ethical AI practices**: Ethical consideration is central to the responsible building and deployment of AI. Data governance frameworks need guidelines for alignment with basic ethical tenets such as fairness, accountability, and transparency of AI systems.

  o **Bias detection and mitigation**: Bias in AI models can further promote discrimination and injury towards marginalized groups. Data governance frameworks must, therefore, provide procedures for the detection and mitigation of bias in training data, algorithms, and model outcomes through the diversification of sources, fairness algorithms, and routine audits for bias.

  o **Transparency and explainability**: AI systems should be transparent in their decision-making processes, especially when they involve individual lives. Explainability refers to the degree to which one can explain how an AI model reached a particular decision. Governance frameworks should demand the interpretability of AI models to such an extent that it would enable the stakeholders to understand and believe in the decision-making process.

  o **Accountability and responsibility**: Mechanisms of accountability are essential to the proper functioning of responsible AI. Clear lines of accountability must be drawn for organizations that develop, manufacture, produce, disseminate, implement, or use AI systems. Mechanisms of accountability ensure possible redress when AI systems cause harm or otherwise act in ways inconsistent with ethical standards.

Data governance frameworks implementation for AI

A complete data governance framework for AI should be implemented through a strategic multi-step approach. In general, it encompasses stakeholder engagement, establishment of governance structures, integration of technology, and continuous improvement. Key stages in the effective deployment of data governance frameworks within AI include:

- **Stakeholder engagement**: It is impossible to have effective data governance in AI in isolation. In-depth engagement with various stakeholders, from data scientists and IT staff to legal, compliance, and business leaders, will be of paramount importance, making sure that the endeavor aligns with both the organizational goals and the requirements of regulators. Second, stakeholder involvement will ensure that these stakeholders endorse and apply the policies that they participate in defining, setting priorities, and providing guidelines with respect to ethical AI development. In this manner, ongoing engagement will ensure that the data governance frameworks remain relevant as AI technologies evolve.

- **Committees of governance**: This makes the governance committees or cross-functional teams very important to make the data governance practices consistent throughout the organization. They should include representatives from IT, data management, legal, compliance, and ethics. They will be responsible for ensuring that governance policies are implemented accordingly and that governance practices are monitored, with issues proactively identified and resolved. Governance committees also need to make sure AI development is well within ethical bounds and regulatory requirements are catered to in its making.

- **Training and awareness**: In sum, investment in training and awareness programs for all employees associated with AI development and data management is a critical component that ensures that the performance of an organization's data governance frameworks is successful. Key areas that should be covered by the training programs encompass data privacy, security, ethical AI practices, and compliance with applicable laws. Awareness creates a culture of responsible data stewardship where employees understand the need for governance protocols and their contributions to data quality and ethics within AI systems.

- **Technology and tools**: Appropriate technology and tools can also automate and simplify data governance processes. A strong AI requires an advanced data management platform to perform activities on data profiling, quality monitoring, encryption, access control, and metadata management. Data anomaly detection, compliance monitoring, and bias detection can also be ensured with various state-of-the-art technologies using artificial intelligence and machine learning. Investment in the right tools ensures that the governance practices are efficient as well as scalable.

- **Continuous improvement**: Data governance is a process, not an event. The core competencies of AI technologies and their regulatory landscapes are continuing to evolve. Organizations need to periodically reassess and work toward the betterment of their data governance frameworks. This includes periodic reviews of the data governance policies, audits, and changes to keep pace with new technologies, emerging threats, and changing regulations. These continuous feedback loops will allow organizations to stay agile and responsive to maintain the integrity, security, and ethical standards of their AI systems.

These are the key steps that can guarantee a full, holistic data governance framework complying with legal requirements and security, including trust and accountability in AI projects for any organization.

Privacy-preserving AI techniques

With the ever-increasing integration of AI systems into daily life and business processes, ensuring the privacy of the data they handle has become a critical challenge. Privacy-preserving AI techniques are designed to enable AI models to function effectively while protecting sensitive information, thereby assuring compliance with regulations and ensuring trustworthiness.

Importance of privacy in AI

Privacy in AI is important for several reasons:

- **Regulatory compliance**: Governments and other regulatory bodies around the world have promulgated strict data protection laws, such as GDPR and CCPA, which place a burden of responsibility on organizations for the protection of user data. Non-compliance can result in severe legal and financial penalties.

- **User trust**: Living in a world where people are concerned about data misuse, privacy-preserving AI engenders trust. People are more likely to use AI systems when they feel confident their information is secure.

- **Ethical considerations**: Preserving privacy is an ethical responsibility, ensuring data subjects maintain autonomy over their personal information, and mitigating risks of misuse or harm.

Key privacy-preserving AI techniques

Several techniques are instrumental in ensuring privacy in AI workflows:

- **Differential privacy**: Introduces mathematical noise into data processing to obscure individual data points while preserving overall insights. Useful for anonymized statistical analysis.

- **Federated learning**: Provides the capability to AI models to learn from data across devices or organizations without aggregating data. Suitable for edge devices, including smartphones.

- **Homomorphic encryption**: Allows computations to be directly performed on encrypted data with the assurance that the raw data will not be accessed even while processing. Suitable for sensitive data in financial or healthcare industries.

- **Secure multi-party computation (SMPC)**: Distributes computations among multiple parties such that no single party gains access to the full dataset. It is ideal for collaborative AI training across organizations.

- **Data anonymization and pseudonymization**: Transforms personal identifiers into non-identifiable formats. This is useful in data sharing or transfer, with its main use case following privacy laws.

Effectively implementing privacy-preserving AI techniques

To implement privacy-preserving AI techniques effectively, the following steps are required:

- **Assess privacy requirements**: Identify the nature of the data, its sensitivity, and regulations to establish privacy requirements.

- **Techniques to choose**: Employ differential privacy in the case of statistical datasets for which public reporting is needed. Apply federated learning in the case of decentralized data, such as personalized recommendations on devices. Leverage homomorphic encryption for computation on encrypted data in highly sensitive industries. Employ SMPC for collaboration across organizations. Share anonymized datasets when sharing for analytics or development.

- **Embed techniques in the AI workflow**: Embed techniques of privacy at model development, training, and deployment to ensure consistent compliance with the set privacy regulations.

- **Monitor and evaluate**: Continuously monitor the AI systems to find privacy vulnerabilities and update their privacy-preserving measures to address emerging risks.

These techniques of privacy-preserving AI protect sensitive data while fostering innovation by ensuring secure data usage, encouraging collaboration, and building trust in the AI system.

Regulatory compliance in AI data management

With the rampant adoption of AI technologies, the way data management and analysis are performed by organizations has completely changed. Considering this, AI systems are in possession of massive amounts of sensitive information and personal data; hence, regulatory compliance is a key concern to avoid associated legal risks, ensure end-user trust, and, most importantly, maintain ethics. Established regulations need to be followed, and proactive compliance measures have to be taken by businesses reaping the benefits of AI.

Importance of regulatory compliance in AI

The importance of regulatory compliance is as follows:

- **Legal obligations**: Compliance with data protection and privacy laws is a basic requirement for organizations using AI. Failure to comply leads to legal penalties, financial losses, and reputational damage. Legal adherence ensures AI systems operate within the boundaries of current laws, such as GDPR, CCPA, and HIPAA.

- **User trust and confidence**: Regulatory compliance builds trust by ensuring that personal data is handled in a secure and transparent manner. Users are more likely to engage with AI-driven services when they believe their privacy and rights are respected.

- **Ethical AI practices**: Regulatory compliance promotes ethics in AI development and application. Fairness, accountability, and transparency embedded in AI systems help organizations reduce biases, avoid harm, and hence contribute to socially responsible applications of AI.

Key regulations impacting AI data management

The key regulations are as follows:

- **GDPR**: The GDPR in the European Union imposes rigid controls on data protection, consent, data minimization, and the right to erasure. It demands that businesses establish a legal and transparent processing of personal information.

- **CCPA**: CCPA provides a set of rights to California residents regarding their personal information, including the right to access, erase, and opt out. Any organization that uses AI will have to adhere to the provisions of the CCPA or risk facing substantial fines and losing customer confidence.

- **HIPAA**: Where AI systems handle healthcare data, HIPAA imposes strict privacy and security requirements. The organizations should ensure protection for **Protected Health Information** (**PHI**) and maintain the requirements for confidentiality.

Good practices to ensure regulatory compliance

Some of the good practices to ensure regulatory compliance in AI are as follows:

- **Periodic DPIAs**: DPIAs help an organization identify and mitigate privacy risks associated with AI systems. Conducting such assessments assures compliance with regulations like GDPR and encourages good behavior in the handling of data.

- **Enact robust data governance policies**: It helps an organization establish a complete data governance framework with defined roles, responsibilities, and processes regarding data management. This encompasses data quality, access controls, and compliance tracking.

- **Ensure transparency and accountability**: Organizations must document the processes of AI, maintain records of the use of data, and make the process understandable to users regarding how their data is processed and protected.

- **Implement technical and organizational safeguards**: Technical measures like encryption, anonymization, and access controls should complement organizational practices in training employees and conducting compliance audits. Together, these safeguards create a robust framework for regulatory adherence.

This structured approach to regulatory compliance in AI data management will enable organizations to move through the changing landscape of data privacy laws while engendering user trust and fostering ethical behavior.

Data encryption and access control mechanisms

Data encryption and access control mechanisms are fundamental to safeguarding sensitive information from unauthorized access and breaches. These tools and techniques are critical in ensuring that data remains confidential, intact, and available only to those with appropriate permissions. This section explores the principles and techniques of data encryption and access control, emphasizing their importance in AI data management and offering practical insights for implementation.

Importance of data encryption and access control

The importance of data encryption and access control is as follows:

- **Data security**: Encryption and access controls provide the first layer of protection against cyber threats. It secures sensitive data in such a manner that unauthorized access to information is prevented, and, in cases of interception, such data becomes unreadable to any attacker.

- **Regulatory compliance**: Laws such as GDPR, CCPA, and HIPAA impose strict use of encryption and access controls for protecting personal and sensitive data. Compliance will save one from legal penalties, improving the credibility of the organization.

- **Data integrity**: Encryption prevents unauthorized modification of data, while access controls prevent alteration of information by everyone except the authorized ones. This keeps the datasets accurate and reliable.

Data encryption

The types of encryptions are as follows:

- **Symmetric encryption**:
  - **What it is**: This is a technique that utilizes the same key for both encryption and decryption.
  - **When to use**: Good for large data encryption because of its speed, such as encrypting database files.
  - **Challenges**: The distribution of keys securely is complex.
  - **Advantages**: Fast and computationally efficient.
- **Asymmetric encryption**:
  - **What it is**: Makes use of a pair of keys: public and private. The public key will encrypt data, while the private key decrypts.

- o **When to use**: Ideal for secure key exchanges and scenarios requiring authentication.

- o **Challenges**: Slower compared to symmetric encryption.

- **Implementing encryption**:

  - o **Selection of correct algorithm**: Based on use cases, evaluate either AES for symmetric encryption or RSA for asymmetric encryption.

  - o **Key management**: Make use of secure key management systems that are centralized in nature for key generation, storage, and revocation.

  - o **Data encryption in transit and rest**: Use HTTPS/TLS protocols for data in transit and AES for encryption of data at rest.

  - o **Regularly update encryption protocols**: Replace outdated protocols with newer, more secure standards.

Access control mechanisms

The following are some of the access control mechanisms:

- **RBAC**: Assigns access permissions based on user roles within the organization, for instance, admin and analyst.

  - o **Advantage**: Simplifies management because permissions are grouped together.

- **Attribute-based access control (ABAC)**: This allows access based on the attributes of the user, like job title and location.

  - o **Advantage**: It is flexible and adaptive to complex policies.

- **Discretionary access control (DAC)**: Owners define policies for data access.

  - o **Advantage**: Granular control, although inconsistent permissions may occur.

The access control mechanisms implementation includes the following:

- **Access policy definition**: Identify and document policies related to who shall have access to what data and under what circumstances.

- **Identity and access management**: Avail of IAM systems for efficient authentication and authorization. Use multi-factor authentication.

- **Audit and monitor activities around access**: Regularly perform log reviews to identify attempts at unauthorized access and further ensure compliance with set policies.

By implementing strong encryption and access controls, organizations can ensure that sensitive data is kept safe, especially in AI-powered workflows. These strategies not only prevent data breaches but also guarantee the integrity and credibility of the information.

Audit trails and data lineage for AI systems

Today's artificial intelligence is complex, with data passing through layers and processes. The integrity and compliance across the AI systems demand complete transparency of these processes. Audit trails and data lineage provide the fundamental frames through which the flow of data can be tracked and traced back in these systems. Audit trails record in great detail the activity with data in an AI system, a verifiable record of who accessed the data, what changed within the data, and when the movement occurred. Data lineage allows for the mapping of data from its origin to its final result. Both provide the foundation for creating an accountability framework necessary for regulatory requirements, security, and the sustenance of trust in AI activities.

Audit trails and data lineage in governance

The functions of audit trails and data lineage extend beyond technical necessity; they are central components in creating transparent, reliable, and resilient AI systems that meet both ethical and regulatory standards.

- **Transparency and accountability**: The basis of confidence building among all stakeholders, regulators, users, and even internal governance bodies lies in transparency. Offering full insight into the data processing procedures, storage protocols, and practices of handling facilitates accountability. Thus, audit trails and data lineage, while allowing visibility and traceability, make the actions of an organization both more intelligible and ethically correct, considering increased scrutiny for the manner in which organizations use data and the decisions thereby derived.

- **Regulatory compliance**: Most global regulatory frameworks, including Europe's GDPR and the HIPAA in the United States, require tight controls regarding data traceability and documentation. As a practical matter, audit trails and data lineage create accessible, reviewable records that solve these requirements. These records provide evidence of compliance and supply an organization with defensible documentation to present when an incident may prompt a regulatory audit.

- **Data quality and integrity**: The quality of the data used directly impacts the precision and efficiency of model outputs in AI applications. Even one inconsistency can lead to biased predictions or AI decisions. Audit trails and data lineage provide data integrity through error and inconsistency detection and correction in data pathways. This practice will promote better model performance with enhanced credibility in AI systems.

- **Operational efficiency and troubleshooting**: Audit trails and data lineage ensure operational efficiency by enabling rapid identification and resolution of issues. In the event of data discrepancies, unauthorized access, or even a security breach, having a detailed record of the activities involving data can handily expedite troubleshooting. These systems reduce on-site resources and the overall shutdown time used to work around data issues.

Audit trails

Audit trails provide a comprehensive log of all actions taken within an AI system. It may be in the form of user identity, timestamp, what was done, and where it came from, coming together to constitute a very valuable asset in reconstructing past events.

The key elements of audit trails are as follows:

- **User identification**: Records users' identities associated with events of data access or modification.

- **Action details**: Defines the kind of action taken, whether it is an access, modification, or deletion.

- **Timestamp**: Records the date and time of every action so that accuracy within chronological order is maintained.

- **Location**: Establishes the origin of the action, like a device or network, helping in forensic analysis.

The benefits of audit trails are as follows:

- **Enhanced security**: Logging each action serves as a deterrent to unauthorized access and provides evidence for identifying security vulnerabilities.

- **Forensic analysis**: Audit trails, if security incidents occur, present a series of events that can be parsed by forensic experts to understand how a breach occurred.

- **Compliance verification**: Audit trails by logging the handling practices of data and facilitating compliance audits and reporting.

Data lineage

Data lineage records the journey of data across the AI system, capturing each transformation and movement from source to output. This documentation provides a transparent overview of data flow and serves as a diagnostic tool to monitor data dependencies and impacts.

The components of data lineage are as follows:

- **Data source**: It defines the source from which the data initially originates; this gives a baseline for traceability.

- **Transformation**: Records all the changes affected on the data to provide visibility into the data processing.

- **Data flow**: It maps the journey of data across system components and workflows.

- **Data destination**: It shows where the data will finally reside, at rest in storage or actively in use, and enables end-to-end traceability.

The benefits of data lineage are as follows:

- **Traceability**: It is a mechanism of tracing backward the organization of information. It concerns data origin, data transformation, and data destination. This is really important for validation.

- **Error detection and correction**: It locates points in data flow where problems may occur; hence, troubleshooting is easier and more accurate.

- **Impact assessment**: This provides insight into how changes to data or processes affect the results, as organizations can head off and minimize risk.

Implementing audit trails and data lineage

To maximize the various benefits of audit trails and lineage, there are certain best practices that need to be performed by an organization. These are as follows:

- **Define objectives**: Establish clear goals for why audit trails and data lineage are necessary, whether for regulatory, security, or operational purposes.

- **Adopt automation**: Avail the benefit of automated technology that can capture real-time logs of data activity and its lineage to reduce the chances of human error.

- **Comprehensive coverage**: Ensure that all critical data processes, from initial ingestion to storage, are accounted for in audit and lineage records.

- **Protect data integrity**: Implement security measures to prevent unauthorized access or alterations to audit and lineage records.

- **Regular reviews and updates**: Periodically assess audit trail and data lineage practices to adapt to evolving regulations and technological advancements.

Bias detection and mitigation in AI datasets

The increasing prevalence of AI across various industries brings both opportunities and challenges, particularly around the issue of bias. Bias within AI can have significant implications for fairness, accuracy, and reliability, especially as these systems increasingly influence critical decisions in fields ranging from healthcare to criminal justice. Bias could emanate from many quarters: data collection methods, historical and societal inequities, and even algorithmic construction. If biases in AI are not attended to, then preexisting prejudices will be reinforced, which will result in neither fair nor just outcomes. Thus, detecting and addressing bias in AI datasets is crucial to ensure ethical, unbiased, and equitable decision-making. This chapter provides a structured examination of the origins of bias in AI, methods for its detection, and strategies for effective mitigation.

Types of bias in AI systems

To mitigate bias effectively, it is essential to understand the different forms it can take. This section categorizes and explains four primary types of bias that are common in AI systems:

- **Selection bias**: Selection bias describes when the data used for training does not adequately represent the larger population or area to which it will be applied. A skewed dataset leads to prejudicial outcomes that disproportionately and adversely impact certain groups. For example, a medical AI application trained more heavily on only one class of demographics will find reductions in effectiveness for other groups, thus ensuring an inequitable outcome.

- **Measurement bias**: Measurement bias occurs when irregularities or inaccuracies in data capture lead to errors in feature or group representation. Most often, this type of bias develops from the reliance on proxy variables or subjective judgments that will not accurately capture the intended characteristics. A typical example could be using socioeconomic status as a proxy for access to health, where errors can come in and, therefore, the model may be biased.

- **Label bias**: Label bias in supervised learning happens when human annotators inadvertently embed subjective judgment or societal biases in the data labels. Since these biases become encoded into the training data, they then become part of the model, where they will influence its predictions and perhaps amplify pre-existing stereotypes. Label bias is most common in applications where human perceptions and interpretations form data, for instance, sentiment analysis.

- **Algorithmic bias**: This bias is due to the design and operation of the algorithm. Even a balanced dataset, because of the ways in which certain algorithms process data, giving importance to certain features over others, amplifies biases. Algorithmic bias underlines that it will become necessary to question not only data quality but also the structure and behavior of algorithms, at least in high-impact domains such as hiring or lending.

Techniques for detecting bias in AI datasets

Detecting bias in AI datasets is a systematic process involving quantitative analysis, visualization tools, and comprehensive audits. By using these methods, organizations can reveal hidden biases and disparities in model performance across demographic groups. Common techniques include:

- **Statistical analysis**: Statistical metrics are probably the most common approach for analyzing fairness across demographic groups, from disparate impact ratio and demographic parity to equalized odds and predictive parity. These metrics compare the prediction rate and error distributions across different demographic groups in quite extensive detail.

- **Visualization techniques**: Visualization techniques include confusion matrices and distribution plots, which make the performance of models across different groups visually appealing by showing disparities between predicted and actual outcomes. For instance, a confusion matrix might indicate that some demographic groups are more likely to be mislabeled than others, hence biased.

- **Bias audits**: Bias audits are the formal procedures for analyzing fairness in AI systems, where one must deeply analyze data sources and model outputs. In fact, organizations do conduct audits, which enable them to systematically detect biases and decrease their impact, particularly those related to demographic groups with common characteristics. Most of the audits will be reviewing changes to the data sources or model parameters for their impact on fairness.

- **Counterfactual fairness testing**: This generates what-if or counterfactual scenarios to alter just one demographic feature, gender. All the rest remain the same. Through observation of the model's performance across these varied scenarios, analysts will be able to gauge whether diverse individuals are treated equitably regardless of demographic attributes. The counterfactual testing method is effective in unearthing and eliminating sensitive features-based biases.

Strategies for bias mitigation in AI

Once the bias is detected, various strategies can be implemented to mitigate its impact. Effective bias mitigation often involves a combination of data preprocessing, algorithmic fairness techniques, and post-processing adjustments. Key strategies include:

- **Data preprocessing**:
    - **Resampling**: This can be done by resampling techniques like oversampling the underrepresented group or under-sampling over-represented groups to balance out the data for fair representation across different demographics.

    - **Reweighting**: It is a process in which samples from underrepresented groups have higher weights. By re-weighting, the model considers those samples during training. It makes the model sensitive to various data points.

    - **Data augmentation**: Techniques like the generation of synthetic data could artificially increase the representation of underrepresented groups to make a training dataset more balanced. Examples include the generation of synthetic images to supplement data in medical AI systems for conditions that are rarely experienced.

    - **Data transformation**: Data normalization and scaling go a long way in having features uniformly distributed across groups, hence reducing measurement bias. For instance, the transformation of income data to comparable scales can reduce measurement disparities in socioeconomic backgrounds.

- **Algorithmic fairness techniques**:
    - **Fair representation learning**: It reduces reliance on biased features during training by forcing models to depend more on neutral representations. Such methods are subsequently adopted very much in applications where the predictions might be influenced by demographic features.

- o **Adversarial debiasing**: Introduce an adversarial model that is designed to counteract biased predictions from the main model. Adversarial debiasing works best in complex neural networks where feature interactions may introduce unintended biases.

- o **Fairness constraints**: Constraints imposed, such as demographic parity or equal opportunity, during model training can ensure that the outcomes are balanced across groups. These encode ethical considerations into the architecture of the model itself to elicit fair predictions.

- **Post-processing adjustments**:

  - o **Calibration of models**: Adjusting prediction probabilities post-training helps align outcomes across demographic groups, ensuring that the model treats all groups equitably.

  - o **Threshold adjustment**: One other way threshold adjustment can help in fairness across demographic segments is by setting prediction thresholds based on group-specific error rates-for example, false positives and false negatives. This reduces biased outcomes when it comes to, for instance, loan approvals or hiring.

- **Explainability tools**: The use of explainability tools such as **SHapley Additive exPlanations** (**SHAP**) and **Local Interpretable Model-Agnostic Explanations** (**LIME**) may help derive insight into how the model makes a certain prediction based on every feature. These tools identify the sources of bias in features, mitigating the bias of model predictions.

Best practices for bias mitigation in AI systems

Best practices in bias mitigation ensure that AI systems operate ethically and responsibly. The following guidelines support organizations in building equitable AI systems:

- **Diverse data collection**: Data collection from several sources allows for a wide array of representations about perspectives and groups to be included, hence avoiding selection biases. In general, the more diverse datasets normally support the most accurate and inclusive AI.

- **Reverse bias audits**: Conducting reverse audits, which search for potential biases within assumptions, has the effect of uncovering problems at an early stage during development. These reverse audits provide proactive mitigation of bias in deployment.

- **Inclusive AI development**: Involving interdisciplinary teams with diverse perspectives in AI development promotes fairness by reducing the influence of unconscious biases. This approach ensures that AI models are more likely to reflect an array of perspectives and needs.

- **Transparency and accountability**: Documenting sources of data, choices about model development, and bias mitigation strategies increase transparency. Providing insights into the model's development process to the stakeholders builds trust by showing an organization's commitment to ethical AI practices.

- **Continuous monitoring and iterative improvement**: Bias mitigation is an ongoing process requiring continuous monitoring, evaluation, and model retraining. By adapting models in response to new data and societal expectations, organizations can ensure that their AI systems remain fair, reliable, and aligned with evolving ethical standards.

Ethical considerations in AI data usage

As AI continues to permeate critical sectors such as healthcare, finance, and law enforcement, the ethical management of data has become a pressing concern. How data is used within AI systems significantly influences both the integrity of these technologies and their societal impact. Ethical data usage is essential for ensuring AI systems are fair, transparent, accountable, and respectful of privacy. This section examines the core ethical principles guiding AI data usage, the specific challenges that arise, and best practices for fostering ethical AI development and deployment.

Core ethical principles in AI data usage

The ethical use of data in AI is guided by fundamental principles that aim to establish public trust and ensure AI systems operate within socially acceptable boundaries. Four primary principles underpin ethical data practices in AI:

- **Fairness**: Fairness in AI requires preventing discriminatory practices and ensuring equitable outcomes across diverse demographic groups. Ensuring fairness involves analyzing both the data and algorithms in depth to avoid generating biased or prejudicial outcomes that are unfavorable to a particular group due to characteristics related to race, gender, age, and socio-economic status, among others. This principle is vital in applications where decisions by AI directly affect people's lives.

- **Transparency**: Transparency entails open communication about how AI systems function, including the data they utilize and the processes behind their decision-making. Transparency AI system gives the users and other stakeholders an insight into the input, workings, and outputs of the model, which in turn develops trust and accountability. Being transparent also involves the exposition of limitations, assumptions, or any other potential biases that are presumptively contained within the AI system, especially in domains involving healthcare and criminal justice.

- **Accountability**: This means responsibility by developers, organizations, and stakeholders for the results of the AI systems. In other words, accountability would require mechanisms through which errors, biases, or unethical outcomes are identified and addressed for correction. It requires organizations to be prepared to accept responsibility for the actions of their AI systems, provide avenues for oversight, and take remedial action when problems arise. This principle provides a framework for redress, therefore reinforcing public trust in AI technology.

- **Privacy**: Privacy is an important concern in AI data use, as AI applications invariably deal with volumes of personal or sensitive information. Observance of privacy involves recognizing users' rights to their information and ensuring that collection, storage, and use are well-guarded to protect individuals against exposure to, or harm from, unwarranted access. The primary ways for ethical management of data in AI to ensure data privacy involve anonymization, encryption, and data minimization.

Ethical challenges in AI data usage

Despite the principles of fairness, transparency, accountability, and privacy, organizations often encounter ethical challenges in managing data within AI systems. These challenges, if unaddressed, can undermine the ethical integrity of AI operations:

- **Bias and discrimination**: AI can inadvertently reinforce or amplify social prejudices through their training data, hence leading to discriminatory decisions. Many of those biases flow from the historical inequities captured in the data or from choices about how an algorithm is designed that inherently favor certain groups. The identification of bias is complex, a continuous challenge that needs a lot of attention regarding data sources, model training, and validation practices. Left unmitigated, such biases could very well propagate inequality and further erode public trust in AI systems.

- **Lack of transparency**: Most AI models are black boxes, completely uninterpretable by their end-users or other stakeholders. This may lead to a lack of confidence in the models since users cannot understand through what methods a model came up with certain results. The concern is very critical in high-stakes contexts where decision-making without transparency can compromise fairness and accountability. For example, in criminal justice, non-transparent AI predictions might influence sentencing without allowing any exposition into the reasons why that prediction was made.

- **Privacy concerns**: The increasing utilization of personal data by AI raises serious and disturbing questions about privacy. Very often, users have no idea when, how, or for what purpose their information is gathered, shared, or processed, which might lead to misuse or unauthorized disclosure of sensitive data. To be privacy-sensitive, AI systems should be designed within the data protection regulatory framework, including GDPR and CCPA, using specific privacy-enhancing technologies, including data anonymization, differential privacy, and secure data-sharing protocols. Poor data privacy results in the violation of principles of ethics, legal complications for the organizations concerned, and even reputation threats.

Best practices for ethical AI data usage

The effective mitigation of these ethical challenges, brought about by using AI data, requires an upfront and holistic approach to integrating ethics throughout all phases of the AI development lifecycle. The following best practices will help an organization build ethical AI:

- **Development of ethical AI guidelines**: An enterprise-wide ethical framework is a crucial gateway toward fairness, transparency, accountability, and respect for privacy in AI. It provides context for where a specific set of guidelines might fit into how various ethical challenges data acquisition to the development, deployment, and ongoing monitoring of the model be addressed throughout its life cycle and need to be periodically reviewed and updated as norms and standards evolve.

- **Building diverse and inclusive teams**: Building teams with diverse backgrounds and perspectives will help in the better oversight of ethics for artificial intelligence projects. With different viewpoints, such teams can recognize gaps and blind spots that may relate to ethics without much effort. Participation in the representation of diversity in the setting up of AI systems includes ethicists, sociologists, and domain experts to help ensure the AI reflects a diverse set of users and reduces exclusionary or biased outcomes.

- **Continuous monitoring and evaluation**: AI systems intrinsically require long-term monitoring and assessment in building their ethical implications. Regular audits regarding model effectiveness with respect to bias, privacy, and transparency place an organization in a good position to address potential problems before they become significant. In this respect, the iterative approach will ensure AI systems meet ethical standards constantly to evolve with new data and changing social norms over time.

- **Stakeholder engagement and involvement**: Engaging various stakeholders early on-especially users, regulators, and community representatives in the development process, enhances transparency and accountability. Such stakeholder involvement offers insights into ethical considerations that need to be included while ensuring the AI system remains within the bounds of social acceptance and user expectations. Similarly, informed consent and clear user agreements will give users control over their information in the use of the AI system and engender trust and integrity for ethics.

Integrated governance features in modern AI platforms

It is critical that, as AI systems start to be increasingly sophisticated and impactful, robust mechanisms in regard to governance become established to guarantee integrity in the data, conformance to regulations, and ethics. It furnishes modern AI and public cloud platforms with the relevant governance instruments that would empower an organization to manage data cataloging, monitor its quality and access, and ensure compliance. These features contribute to improving not only operational efficiency but also enhancing the accountability, security, and ethical resilience of artificial intelligence systems. The chapter describes the most important features of governance in state-of-the-art AI platforms and explains their application and benefits.

Key integrated governance features

Modern AI platforms contain a host of critical tools that advance holistic data governance, helping an organization stay reliable and compliant with regulations. Core governance features include data cataloging, automated quality assessment, role-based access management, compliance oversight, data lineage tracking, and ethical AI tools. The following are explanations of the features along with their importance for the development of reliable and ethically correct AI systems:

- **Data cataloging and metadata management**: Data cataloging and metadata management tools empower these needs through a unified store for the purpose of storage, organization, and governance of data assets. These make datasets discoverable, linked with sources, structure, and history of usage for data lineage and quality control. Metadata management is a key component in data cataloging; adding context to data through descriptions, ownership, and tags for classification makes the process of organizing or finding particular data very easy.

  o **Example**: Azure Data Catalog and Google Cloud Data Catalog, which both provide features for finding and accessing data assets from multiple cloud environments in ways that ensure consistency in metadata standards for efficient data discovery, enhancement of data quality, and governance.

- **Automated data quality monitoring**: Different toolings for automated data quality monitoring ensure that the data meets the set standard for quality and, hence, is usable for AI models. These consistently monitor the data against anomalies, missing values, and inconsistencies to alert the teams about potential issues that might affect model performance or lead to incorrect results. This proactive identification, and hence treatment, of data quality issues underlines dependable data pipelines via these tools.

  o **Example**: IBM Watson Knowledge Catalog and AWS Glue Data Quality bake in automated quality assessments that will help an organization find and fix data issues before they impact model reliability and provide high-quality results in AI.

- **RBAC**: RBAC allows an organization to restrict access to data based on the role of a user. In other words, it ensures that only those users receive access for whom it is authorized. RBAC helps in reducing any chance of leakage and thus provides better privacy protection, which becomes very important in some cases.

- o **Example**: Azure Active Directory and Google IAM, these are advanced RBAC systems that afford an organization granular control over the access entitlements of data, hence affording them a better way of ensuring the security of data and compliance with regulations.

- **Compliance management and reporting**: Compliance management tools let an organization meet the regulatory standards of GDPR, HIPAA, and CCPA through automated compliance checks to find out, manage, and provide audit trails for data protection measures. Compliance reporting may allow an organization to document its compliance with relevant regulations and prove such compliance to any regulatory body or stakeholder.

  - o **Example**: Azure Purview and Compliance Dashboard by Google Cloud allow the creation of means to check regulatory requirements and generate compliance reports, thus automating compliance monitoring, but with sufficient documentation in support of audits.

- **Data lineage and provenance tracking**: Data lineage and provenance tracking record the lifecycle of the data, right from its origin through to the final output. They map all transformations thereof. This will let organizations trace the source, transformation, and destination of data within an AI pipeline for accountability, error detection, and regulatory reporting.

  - o **Example**: Databricks and AWS Glue provide lineage tracking tools to visualize the flow of data with their respective dependencies and transformations. Such tools are supposed to enable transparency in how data flows, which is critical to auditing, debugging, and ensuring data integrity.

- **Ethical AI and bias mitigation tools**: These tools for ethical AI are designed to identify, assess, and mitigate the different biases within AI models. This helps organizations to check on model fairness, determine the source of discrimination, and apply remedies. Since these tools help mitigate bias, it furthers the ethical standing of AI systems, ensuring models provide fair and unbiased outcomes.

  - o **Example**: IBM AI Fairness 360 and Google's What-If Tool allow the detection of bias and its mitigation by allowing simulations of different kinds of scenarios, analyzing model behavior, and comparing different parameters to optimize for fairness. These kinds of tools support efforts to align AI models built within an organization with ethical standards for fairness and inclusion.

Conclusion

This chapter has provided a complete discussion of data governance, security, and compliance in relation to AI creation and management. We first addressed the discussion by emphasizing that proper data governance mechanisms are essential to overcome the special obstacles that come with the complexity and sensitivity of data used in AI systems.

Such frameworks should ensure that data quality, security, privacy, and compliance standards are maintained throughout the AI lifecycle, with responsibly operating AI-driven systems. Among others, it underlined some of the most valuable techniques that can help maintain user privacy: differential privacy, federated learning, and secure multi-party computation. We also explored compliance requirements in great detail and mainly focused on the legal and ethical considerations of AI-driven organizations under laws such as GDPR and CCPA.

From a security standpoint, the chapter addressed essential protective measures, encompassing data encryption and access control mechanisms, which are critical in preventing unauthorized access and mitigating potential breaches. The significance of audit trails and data lineage was highlighted for their contributions to monitoring data transformations, fostering transparency, and upholding accountability within artificial intelligence systems. It also ranged towards the detection and mitigation strategies of bias, showing that facing up to bias is crucial in the development of appropriate and decent outcomes through artificial intelligence applications. In this chapter, ethical issues were presented in relation to data usage, based on key concepts like fairness, transparency, accountability, and privacy. Further, we discussed the ethical dilemmas commonly occurring in AI systems and pointed out some of the major challenges: discrimination and a lack of clarity about AI operations.

The wide array of governance capabilities comprising data cataloging, quality control, role-based access control, and compliance monitoring functionalities can be widely seen in next-generation AI and cloud platforms. Each of these capabilities adds to the array of AI governance practices and forms essential competencies for any organization willing to implement and sustain ethical and compliant AI frameworks. Aggregated, these elements provide a structured backbone that fosters responsible AI development, one that encourages transparency, equity, and consideration for user rights and regulatory requirements.

Join our Discord space

Join our Discord workspace for latest updates, offers, tech happenings around the world, new releases, and sessions with the authors:

https://discord.bpbonline.com

CHAPTER 7

AI Algorithms and Their Impact on Data Architecture

Introduction

AI has completely changed the way organizations make use of data, thus challenging traditional boundaries in data architecture. At the heart of AI is a set of algorithms that have been developed to process, analyze, and provide insights from large volumes of data. These algorithms have special requirements, changing the way data is stored, accessed, and used across industries. This book examines the complex interplay between AI algorithms and data architecture to provide a holistic view of technologies and strategies driving contemporary innovation.

From deep learning architectures requiring immense data storage to the computational demands of large language models, AI systems are forcing organizations to rethink scalability. Generative AI, which can create new content, necessitates novel storage and processing frameworks. Federated learning introduces privacy-centric decentralization by enabling model training across distributed data sources without sharing raw data, while edge AI emphasizes local inference to optimize latency and bandwidth efficiency. Reinforcement learning, relying on simulated environments, presents unique challenges in dynamic data processing. Meanwhile, **automated machine learning (AutoML)** streamlines AI model development but increases the need for robust and scalable data preprocessing pipelines.

This chapter also explores scaling strategies specific to different AI paradigms, enabling practitioners to overcome the challenges of integrating AI into their data ecosystems. Such a guide will bridge the gap between algorithmic innovation and data architecture, serving as a crucial enabler for anyone looking to responsibly and effectively harness the power of AI.

Structure

The chapter covers the following topics:

- Overview of AI algorithms data requirements

- Deep learning architectures and impact on storage

- Large language models and data-intensive AI

- Generative AI and its architectural requirements

- Federated learning and edge AI considerations

- Reinforcement learning and data simulation

- AutoML and its impact on data preprocessing

- Scaling strategies for different AI paradigms

Objectives

By the end of this chapter, the reader will explore this critical juncture where AI algorithms and data architecture meet, clearly understanding the design and implementation of an AI system that directly impacts and is impacted by the underlying data infrastructure. It outlines the different unique data requirements and architectural demands imposed by various paradigms of AI, thus setting up the reader to embark on the road of building optimized data ecosystems for applications of advanced AI.

Readers will look at the fundamental basis on which AI algorithms operate, their consumption of data, and how deep learning architectures require high throughput, scalable storage solutions. The chapter also explores how large language models and generative AI affect data-intensive operations and strategies to control these power-consuming systems. Federated learning and edge AI will be discussed in the context of decentralized data storage, while reinforcement learning will introduce readers to the simulation-driven data demands of these systems. Furthermore, this chapter will shed light on the AutoML frameworks, how they affect data pre-processing pipelines, and make the reader ready to accommodate the automation of modeling tasks. Practical strategies for scaling the different paradigms of AI to prepare the reader for resiliency by design toward future-proof architectures will follow. This chapter is devoted to providing concrete actions about how to embrace AI while keeping a keen alignment with sound principles of data architecture.

Overview of AI algorithms data requirements

AI models are as good as the data architecture on which they stand. The success of these models calls for an architecture that must support volumes of data, quality, and efficient preprocessing and transformation. Scalability, diversity in data types, strong pipelines, and mechanisms to maintain privacy and security remain the most important checkpoints while designing a data architecture. Each of these AI paradigms has different data requirements and, therefore, dictates different data structures, access, and processing. We present in the next section several data considerations across various types of AI algorithms.

Classic machine learning algorithms

Traditional machine learning algorithms comprise methods such as linear regression, decision trees, and SVM. These generally require structured data represented in tabular formats, with rows usually representing instances and columns usually representing features. The following are the factors that dictate the data requirements for classic ML models:

- **Data volume**: Standard traditional machine learning algorithms can handle up to a moderate volume of data. However, with increasing volumes of data, computational and training time grow linearly. Scalable data partitioning strategies like **reservoir sampling** enable uniform sampling from streaming or large datasets without loading all data into memory, making them ideal for real-time ML pipelines. **Distributed stratification** ensures class balance across partitions in distributed systems, preserving label distribution for model training and validation. These approaches enhance scalability, efficiency, and model robustness in traditional ML pipelines handling massive, imbalanced, or continuously generated data. Other applied techniques in this regard that work pretty well on handling high dimensionality include dimensionality reduction techniques such as PCA and feature selection.

- **Data quality**: Traditional ML algorithms require high-quality, clean, and preprocessed data. Missing values, outliers, and noisy data are common problems that may degrade model performance. The techniques for improving data quality include:

  o **Imputation**: Imputation of missing values by mean, median, or predictive methods.

  o **Outlier detection**: It may be done using statistical methods (like Z-scores) or algorithms such as isolation forest.

  o **Normalization**: Scaling of data for a particular range, for example, min-max scaling.

○ **Feature engineering**: Most of the traditional machine learning algorithms achieve success based on feature selection and feature engineering, which requires domain expertise. The domain expert identifies appropriate features and transforms raw data into a format that can be modeled. Some of the major techniques include:

○ **Categorical encoding**: One-hot encoding or label encoding for non-numeric data.

○ **Interaction terms**: Feature creation using the interaction of existing features.

○ **Feature scaling**: Standardization to improve model convergence.

Table 7.1 summarizes the impact of data on various classic ML models:

Algorithm	Data quality sensitivity	Outlier sensitivity	Normalization	Feature scaling needed	Categorical encoding	Feature engineering importance	Interaction terms
Linear regression	High	High	Often	Yes	One-hot/ Ordinal	High	Often beneficial
Logistic regression	High	High	Often	Yes	One-hot/ Ordinal	High	Often beneficial
Decision trees	Moderate	Low	Not needed	No	Label encoding works	Moderate	Captured implicitly
Random forests	Moderate	Low	Not needed	No	Label encoding works	Moderate	Captured implicitly
Gradient boosting (e.g., XGBoost, LightGBM)	Moderate to high	Moderate	Not needed	No (but helps)	Label/ One-hot	High	Captured implicitly
Support vector machines (SVM)	High	High	Often	Yes	One-hot/ Ordinal	Moderate	Beneficial
k-nearest neighbors (knn)	High	High	Yes	Yes	One-hot	Low to moderate	Beneficial
Naïve Bayes	Moderate	Moderate	Sometimes	Sometimes	One-hot	Moderate	Not needed

Algorithm	Data quality sensitivity	Outlier sensitivity	Normali zation	Feature scaling needed	Categorical encoding	Feature engineering importance	Interaction terms
K-means clustering	High	High	Yes	Yes	One-hot	Moderate	Not appli-cable
PCA (for dimen-sionality reduction)	High	High	Yes	Yes	One-hot	High	Not appli-cable

Table 7.1: *Summary of the impact of data on classic ML models*

Ensemble learning models

The general idea of ensemble learning methods, such as random forests and gradient boosting machines, is to combine several models to achieve better predictive accuracy by reducing both variance and bias. Often, these methods outperform single models. The following shows how ensemble methods are impacted by data volume, quality, and other factors:

- **Data volume**: Ensembles can support volumes greater than those of individual models. However, they lead to increased computational and memory requirements. In the scenario of large-scale data processing, efficient techniques may involve utilizing distributed computing frameworks, including Hadoop or Spark, among others.

- **Data quality**: Ensemble methods are generally more robust to noisy data and outliers than traditional algorithms; high-quality data is still crucial. Preprocessing techniques, such as the use of robust scalers for numerical data or methods of outlier detection, improve performance.

- **Feature engineering**: While feature engineering is still helpful, the ensemble methods, especially tree-based algorithms, can automatically learn higher-order interactions between features with much less need for complex manual feature engineering. Yet, even in those cases, binning of numerical features or encoding of categorical data can result in significant improvements.

Deep learning algorithms

Deep learning models, including CNNs, RNNs, and transformer architectures, are designed to learn from data in raw formats. These models demand a well-designed data pipeline and infrastructure. The following shows how deep learning algorithms are impacted by data volume, quality, and other factors:

- **Data volume**: Deep learning algorithms require massive data to perform well. As such, training a neural network often requires hundreds of thousands to millions of labeled examples. Distributed data storage solutions like HDFS or cloud storage and parallel processing capabilities are necessary to manage such a data volume.

- **Data quality**: Deep learning models can take a bit of noise in data, but better quality data usually ensures good generalization. Improvement techniques in datasets include:

  o **Data augmentation**: Increasing the size of image datasets by applying rotations, flips, and other transformations.

  o **Synthetic data generation**: Generating more data points through techniques such as **Synthetic Minority Oversampling Technique (SMOTE)** or **generative adversarial network (GANs)**.

  o **Label quality**: Accurately and consistently annotated data is especially important in supervised learning applications.

- **Data types**: Deep learning models can accept a wide range of data types:

  o **Images**: CNNs are great at extracting spatial features.

  o **Sequential data**: RNNs or LSTMs are suitable for time-series and text data.

  o **Text**: Transformers, such as BERT or GPT, handle complex NLP tasks.

- **Architecture**: The architecture depends on the type of data and the problem domain.

- **Computational requirements**: Deep learning models demand huge computational resources such as GPUs or TPUs. Efficient data pipelines using frameworks like TensorFlow or PyTorch ensure smooth data flow during training.

Reinforcement learning algorithms

Reinforcement learning algorithms include Q-learning and deep RL, which model decision-making problems in which the agent learns through trial and error to optimize its actions. The following shows how RL methods are impacted by data volume, quality, and other factors:

- **Data volume**: RL algorithms rely heavily on interaction data. Simulations are often used to generate the required data volume. Techniques like experience replay allow efficient utilization of stored interaction data, enabling models to learn from past experiences.

- **Data quality**: The quality of the reward signal and the environment model directly influences policy learning. Sparse or noisy rewards easily impede the learning process. Techniques such as reward shaping and noise filtering improve the quality of learning.

- **Data structure**: RL algorithms make use of complex data structures, including state-action pairs and reward signals. To manage this data, there is a need for specialized storage systems, such as in-memory databases, and retrieval mechanisms for efficient access.

Generative AI models

Generative AI models, including large language models and GANs, are designed to generate new content based on patterns they learn:

- **Volume of data**: Generative models are supposed to learn data distribution by being trained on massive datasets. For example, training a GPT model requires text data in terabytes. For such volumes, effective data preprocessing and sampling methods become necessary.

- **Data quality**: The quality of generated outputs is highly related to the quality of training data. High-quality and diversified datasets reduce artifacts or unrealistic generations. Cleaning and preparing training datasets are crucial steps.

- **Data types**: Generative models fit various data types:

  o **Images**: GANs work well for generating realistic visuals.

  o **Text**: Transformers, such as GPT, are good at text generation.

  o **Audio**: Models such as WaveNet generate high-quality audio.

Preprocessing steps must be tailored to the type of data to enhance the model's performance.

Federated learning

Federated learning allows the training of a model in a decentralized manner with the collaboration of several devices without sharing raw data:

- **Volume of data**: Federated learning runs data processing on millions of devices. Scalable aggregation algorithms like **federated averaging** (**FedAvg**) reduce communication overhead. Adaptive sampling and prioritizing updates from high-quality data sources further optimize resource utilization.

- **Data quality**: Variability in the quality of device data affects the overall performance of the model. To handle this variability, techniques such as clustering devices based on data similarity, weighted updates based on device performance, and incorporating quality-control metrics into the aggregation process are used. Besides that, anomaly detection methods help in identifying and excluding poorly performing devices from the training process.

- **Data privacy**: Federated learning is privacy-first, keeping data on local devices. Advanced privacy-preserving techniques include:

- o **Differential privacy**: Ensures that individual data points cannot be inferred from model updates.

- o **Secure multi-party computation**: Enables encrypted computations across multiple devices.

- o **Homomorphic encryption**: Allows computations on encrypted data without decryption.

These techniques enhance data security and make regulatory standards such as GDPR and HIPAA binding. Regular audits added to secure aggregation protocols enhance robustness against adversarial attacks.

Deep learning architectures and impact on storage

Deep learning architectures have fundamentally transformed the landscape of artificial intelligence, enabling significant advancements in domains such as computer vision, natural language processing, and speech recognition. These architectures present unique challenges and considerations for data storage due to their substantial data requirements, extensive preprocessing needs, and computational complexities. This section looks into the storage implications of two prominent deep learning architectures: **convolutional neural networks** (**CNNs**) and **recurrent neural networks** (**RNNs**), including their variant **long short-term memory** (**LSTM**) networks. We also discuss general considerations for deep learning storage solutions.

Convolutional neural networks

CNNs are a class of deep learning models that excel in processing data with a grid-like topology, such as images. The success of CNNs in tasks like image classification, object detection, and segmentation is largely attributed to their ability to learn spatial hierarchies of features through convolutional layers automatically. However, this capability comes with significant data storage demands. CNNs require large datasets to achieve high accuracy, often involving millions of high-resolution images. Such datasets can rapidly consume storage resources, necessitating the use of efficient storage formats.

Image data is typically stored in compressed formats such as JPEG or PNG to reduce storage space while maintaining quality. For deep learning frameworks like TensorFlow, specialized data formats such as TFRecord are employed to optimize data input pipelines, enabling efficient reading and processing during training. These formats allow for streamlined data handling, minimizing the overhead associated with large-scale image datasets.

Data augmentation and storage implications

Data augmentation techniques are widely used in training CNNs to enhance model robustness and generalization. Techniques such as rotation, scaling, and flipping artificially expand the training dataset by creating modified versions of existing images. While data augmentation improves model performance, it also increases storage requirements, as augmented data may need to be stored or generated on the fly during training. On-the-fly augmentation is often preferred to avoid excessive storage consumption, leveraging computational resources to dynamically generate augmented samples.

Computational needs and cloud integration

The computational demands of CNNs are particularly high, especially when dealing with high-resolution images. These demands are often met by scaling up compute resources to include GPUs and TPUs, which significantly accelerate the training process. In cloud environments, object storage solutions such as AWS S3 or Google Cloud Storage are commonly used to handle large datasets, providing scalable and cost-effective storage options. The integration of cloud-based storage and compute resources facilitates seamless scaling and efficient management of CNN workloads.

Recurrent neural networks and long short-term memory networks

Data requirements and storage solutions: RNNs and their variants, such as LSTM networks, are designed to process sequential data, making them well-suited for applications in **natural language processing** (**NLP**), time-series analysis, and speech recognition. These architectures have distinct data storage needs due to the nature of sequential data, which is often extensive and complex.

In NLP tasks, sequence data such as text corpora is typically stored in plain text or binary formats like JSON or CSV. Time-series data, on the other hand, may require specialized databases such as InfluxDB or TimeScaleDB, which are optimized for handling temporal data and allow for efficient querying and retrieval. These storage solutions are crucial for managing the large volumes of data required for training RNNs and LSTMs.

Preprocessing needs and ETL pipelines

Text data often undergoes extensive preprocessing before being fed into RNNs and LSTMs. Preprocessing steps may include tokenization, stemming, and lemmatization, which transform raw text into structured formats suitable for sequence modeling. These processes can generate additional intermediate data that needs to be stored, further increasing storage demands.

Effective ETL pipelines are essential for managing these preprocessing tasks, ensuring that data is efficiently transformed and stored in formats compatible with deep learning frameworks. ETL pipelines automate the preprocessing workflow, reducing manual intervention and enhancing data consistency across large-scale training datasets.

Scalability and performance considerations

Deep learning models, particularly RNNs and LSTMs, impose high demands on data volume and computational resources. Scalable storage systems and high-performance storage solutions, such as **solid state drives** (**SSDs**), are critical for meeting these demands. SSDs offer faster data access and retrieval, which is essential for high-performance training and inference tasks.

The computational load of training RNNs and LSTMs is often managed through the use of GPUs, which provide the necessary processing power to handle sequential data efficiently. The combination of scalable storage and advanced hardware accelerators ensures that deep learning models can be trained and deployed effectively, even in resource-intensive scenarios.

General considerations for deep learning storage

The demanding nature of deep learning models necessitates robust and scalable data architectures capable of supporting extreme data and computational requirements. Effective storage solutions must ensure fast access and retrieval of data, facilitating efficient preprocessing and preparation for training and inference tasks. Advanced hardware support, including GPUs and TPUs, plays a pivotal role in managing the computational load associated with deep learning.

Public cloud platforms offer scalable and cost-effective solutions for deep learning storage and computing needs. Cloud services provide integrated solutions for data pipelines, enabling seamless management of data storage, preprocessing, and model training. By leveraging cloud resources, organizations can scale their deep learning workloads dynamically, optimizing costs and performance.

In conclusion, the impact of deep learning architectures on data storage is profound, influencing the design and implementation of data systems across various AI applications. As deep learning continues to evolve, the development of innovative storage solutions and infrastructure will be essential to support the growing complexity and scale of AI models.

Large language models and data-intensive AI

Large language models (**LLMs**) have fundamentally transformed the field of NLP, enabling machines to process, understand, and generate human-like text with unprecedented accuracy and fluency. These models, exemplified by architectures such as **Bidirectional Encoder Representations from Transformers (BERT)** and **Generative Pre-trained Transformer (GPT)**, represent significant advancements in AI, often described as quantum leaps in technology. Their applications span a wide array of tasks across various industries, from machine translation and summarization to conversational AI and beyond. The power of LLMs lies in their ability to learn context from vast datasets and generalize across diverse applications, making them versatile tools in the AI toolkit.

Understanding LLMs

LLMs are sophisticated neural network architectures designed to generate coherent and contextually relevant text based on patterns learned from extensive datasets. At their core, LLMs rely on transformers, a model architecture that employs self-attention mechanisms to capture relationships and dependencies within text sequences. This architectural innovation allows LLMs to understand context and meaning at a granular level, distinguishing them from traditional NLP models that often rely on fixed word embeddings and lack contextual awareness.

Key characteristics of LLMs

The scale of LLMs is one of their defining features. These models are trained on datasets containing billions of words, often sourced from web-scale corpora, making them capable of understanding subtle linguistic nuances. The sheer volume of parameters in LLMs, often numbering in the billions or even trillions, enables them to model complex language patterns and generate text that closely resembles human language. This scale, however, presents significant challenges in terms of computational resources and data management.

Contextual understanding is another hallmark of LLMs. Unlike traditional models, LLMs interpret words based on their surrounding context, leveraging attention mechanisms to weigh the importance of each word in relation to others within a sequence. This capability allows LLMs to grasp the meaning and intent behind the text, facilitating more accurate and nuanced language processing.

Versatility is a key advantage of LLMs, as they can perform a wide range of NLP tasks without being explicitly trained for each one. Through fine-tuning or prompt engineering, LLMs can be adapted to specific applications such as question-answering, sentiment analysis, and creative writing. This adaptability makes LLMs invaluable in scenarios requiring rapid deployment and application across multiple domains.

Data requirements for LLMs

The performance of LLMs is intrinsically linked to the quality and diversity of the data they are trained on. High-quality, diverse datasets are crucial to ensure that LLMs generalize well across tasks and avoid biases that could compromise their effectiveness.

Volume and diversity

LLMs require enormous datasets to capture the intricacies of human language. These datasets often include sources like *Common Crawl, Wikipedia,* and curated collections from books and articles. The volume of data is essential not only for training the models but also for enabling them to understand complex language structures and generate coherent text.

Diversity in datasets is equally important. To ensure inclusivity and mitigate biases, datasets should encompass a wide variety of topics, languages, and styles. This diversity helps LLMs develop a more comprehensive understanding of language and enhances their ability to perform well across different contexts and applications.

Quality and preprocessing

Data quality is paramount in training LLMs. Noisy or biased data can lead to poor model performance and undesirable outputs. Preprocessing steps are critical in preparing datasets for training. These steps include deduplication to remove redundant data, normalization to ensure consistent formatting, tokenization to break text into manageable units, and filtering to eliminate irrelevant or harmful content. Effective preprocessing enhances model reliability and contributes to the overall success of LLMs.

Impact on data storage and management

The extensive data requirements and computational complexity of LLMs necessitate advanced storage systems capable of managing large-scale training datasets and model artifacts. Distributed storage systems are integral to supporting the scale and fault tolerance needed for LLMs.

Distributed storage systems

Systems like the HDFS have been widely used to store and manage large datasets. However, cloud-based object storage solutions, such as AWS S3 and Google Cloud Storage, offer greater scalability and flexibility. These platforms provide the infrastructure needed to handle the vast amounts of data required for training LLMs, ensuring that storage resources can be dynamically allocated and managed.

Effective data management

Effective data management is critical for the successful deployment of LLMs. Key aspects include versioning, metadata management, and lineage tracking. Versioning ensures that datasets are consistently tracked for changes, facilitating reproducibility and transparency. Metadata management involves cataloging data properties such as origin, format, and purpose, enabling efficient data retrieval and organization. Lineage tracking provides visibility into the data flow across the AI pipeline, aiding in debugging and ensuring data integrity.

Integration with AI architecture

The integration of LLMs into AI architectures spans the entire AI lifecycle, from training to deployment and beyond. This integration requires substantial infrastructure and well-defined process flows to ensure seamless operation and scalability.

Training and distributed frameworks

Training LLMs involves distributed frameworks like TensorFlow and PyTorch, which enable parallel computations across multiple CPUs and GPUs. For large-scale LLMs, **Tensor Processing Units (TPUs)** or custom accelerators are often employed to expedite training. Mixed precision training techniques are used to reduce memory requirements and accelerate computations, optimizing resource utilization and training efficiency.

Inference and deployment

Efficient inference and deployment of LLMs are facilitated by scalable cloud services such as AWS SageMaker and Azure ML. These platforms offer various deployment options, allowing LLMs to be scaled according to demand. AutoML solutions further simplify the deployment process by automating model selection and tuning. For real-time applications, such as virtual assistants or personalized recommendations, low-latency solutions are achieved through edge computing and **content delivery networks (CDNs)**, minimizing response times and enhancing user experience.

Integration with AI pipelines

The integration of LLMs with AI pipelines involves several critical steps, including preprocessing, model training, evaluation, and continuous deployment. Preprocessing is managed through tool-managed pipelines like Apache Airflow, ensuring efficiency and reliability. MLOps best practices are leveraged to automate training, testing, and evaluation, maintaining consistent model performance, and facilitating rapid iteration. Continuous deployment is enabled by full-cycle CI/CD pipelines, allowing for seamless updates and safe deployment of models into production environments.

LLMs represent a transformative force in the field of AI, unlocking new frontiers in data-driven innovation. Their ability to process and generate human-like text has revolutionized NLP and expanded the possibilities for AI applications across industries. The successful deployment of LLMs hinges on robust data storage and management systems, advanced computational infrastructure, and seamless integration into AI architectures. As LLMs continue to evolve, ongoing advancements in data management, computational resources, and AI integration will be essential to harnessing their full potential and driving further breakthroughs in AI technology.

Generative AI and its architecture requirements

Generative AI (GenAI), happens to be one of the fastest-evolving areas under artificial intelligence. It creates new instances of data that would look like the data on which it was trained. By learning the underlying distribution of input data, generative models can generate images, text, audio, or videos. These models go beyond simple prediction and classification of data. As such, they have been enacting revolutionary applications in areas like creating content, designing, and simulations.

The typical use cases of GenAI are as follows:

- **Creative industry**: Creating artwork, making music, and video generation.

- **Synthetic data generation**: Creation of additional data for better training of discriminative models.

- **Text-to-image generation**: The potential of translating words into real or imaginative visuals, for example, DALL-E.

- **Personalization**: The art of making each user's experience different and unique, or giving personalized recommendations.

Understanding GenAI

Unlike traditional discriminative models, generative models aim to model the data distribution themselves, which enables them to generate new, unseen data points that align in characteristics with the original dataset. Further, we explore the very foundational type of generative models:

- **Generative adversarial networks (GANs)**: These consist of two competing neural networks:

   o **Generator**: It learns to generate realistic data samples.

   o **Discriminator**: It evaluates any given sample as real from the training data or fake, generated.

   o Over the rounds of adversarial training, GANs become proficient in generating good-quality outputs. GANs usually find broad applications in:

      ▪ **Image generation**: Generating realistic faces, paintings, or medical images.

      ▪ **Style transfer**: Changing the style of an image to adopt the style of another image.

      ▪ **Super-resolution**: Enhancement of the resolution of poor-quality images.

- **Variational autoencoders**: VAEs involve a probabilistic framework that maps the input data to a latent space to reconstruct it into the original domain.
  - o **Encoder**: This compresses the input to a latent vector.
  - o **Decoder**: The decoder generates output data from the latent vector.
  - o VAE learns the probability distribution within data explicitly, making VAE particularly good at:
    - ▪ Generating variations of existing data.
    - ▪ Interpolation between the points in the latent space.
    - ▪ Semi-supervised learning tasks.
- **Transformer-based models**: Transformers have become a kind of backbone in most of the GenAI since transformers are capable of handling sequential data and capturing long-range relations using self-attention mechanisms.
  - o **BERT**: Though primarily developed for language understanding, the architecture of BERT has also inspired variations in generation tasks.
  - o **DALL-E**: An unconditional state-of-the-art generative model using transformers to generate high-quality visuals from natural language descriptions.
  - o **GPT models**: Generative models like GPT-3 are built with the explicit purpose of coherent and contextually relevant text output, making such models the heart of so many applications in conversational AI and content creation.

Data and processing needs of GenAI

The data and processing requirements for generative models mirror many of the needs outlined above for the discriminative models. These would include:

- **High computing resource needs**: For transformer-based generative tasks, very expensive, large-scale cloud computing resources such as GPUs or TPUs are needed.
- **Large and diverse data**: Amounts of high-quality data needed to be fed into generative models to enable them to produce realistic output.
- **Cloud-based deployment**: Typically involves containerized environments such as Docker and orchestration tools such as Kubernetes to ensure scalability and reliability.

Generative models will fit into mainstream AI cloud architectures with not very different ingestion workflows for data, model training, and inference. It is the additional layers of output validation and quality controls often placed on top, however, that deal with the unique challenges that generative tasks bring with them.

Federated learning and edge AI considerations

The most groundbreaking advancements in addressing critical challenges with artificial intelligence revolve around **federation learning** (**FL**) and edge AI. These approaches prioritize data privacy, reduce latency, and enable decentralized processing. By handling data locally, either independently or through collaboration across multiple devices, they ensure both scalability and efficiency.

Understanding federated learning

Federated learning involves training machine learning models directly on multiple devices or nodes without the need to send raw data to a central server. Instead, only model updates, like gradients, are shared and combined centrally to create a global model.

The key features of federated learning are as follows:

- **Privacy preservation**: Since FL keeps the data local on the devices, hence addressing privacy issues; it also adheres to regulations such as GDPR.

- **Decentralized**: Training happens on distributed devices, reducing reliance on centralized infrastructure.

- **Scalable**: FL scales up to millions of devices, hence suitable for mobile and IoT ecosystems.

In particular, it becomes very useful in applications such as personalized services, for instance, mobile keyboard suggestions, and sensitive information industries like healthcare and finance.

Data characteristics for federated learning

The decentralized nature of federated learning presents distinct challenges in managing data across various devices:

- **Heterogeneity of data**:

  o **Quality variance**: Different devices produce data of varying quality due to differences in hardware capabilities or environmental factors.

  o **Non-IID data**: The data may not be identically and independently distributed among devices, leading to biases that can impact model convergence.

  o **Volume disparities**: Devices generate different amounts of data, which requires training algorithms to be adaptable.

- **Privacy and security**: Federated learning employs advanced techniques to maintain data security during the training process:

- o **Differential privacy**: Introduces noise to model updates to safeguard against the reverse engineering of original data.

- o **Secure multi-party computation**: Facilitates secure collaboration among devices by encrypting the computations.

- o **Homomorphic encryption**: Enables computations to be carried out directly on encrypted data, thus preserving privacy.

- **Efficient communication**: Due to bandwidth and latency limitations, communication-optimized protocols are essential to reduce the overhead associated with transmitting model updates. Techniques such as compression and sparsification are frequently utilized to minimize the size of updates.

Understanding edge AI

Edge AI refers to deploying AI models directly on devices like smartphones, IoT gadgets, or sensors, enabling them to process data and make decisions locally. Unlike traditional cloud-based AI, it handles information right where it is generated, at the source.

Salient features of edge AI are as follows:

- **Real-time processing**: It saves the transmission of data to a central server and hence ensures real-time responses in applications requiring instantaneous output, such as autonomous vehicles and industrial automation.

- **Bandwidth efficiency**: It reduces bandwidth by greatly minimizing the amount of data sent to the cloud and hence reduces their associated costs.

- **Improved privacy**: Since the data stays on the device, the risk of data breaches is significantly reduced.

- **Scalability**: Processing is spread across multiple edge devices, making it easier to scale AI systems efficiently.

Edge AI is used in various applications, including real-time video analytics, smart home automation, and predictive maintenance for industrial systems.

Integration into AI architecture

Robust tools, frameworks, and platforms make the successful implementation of federated learning and edge AI viable:

- **Federated learning frameworks**: Frameworks like TensorFlow Federated and PySyft ease the implementation of FL by providing tools that handle distributed model training and aggregation in the following ways:

- o **TensorFlow Federated**: Supports research and development in FL with a library that allows customization and scaling.

o **PySyft**: An open-source framework allowing for privacy-preserving ML workflows and supporting various techniques such as secure computation and differential privacy.

These frameworks handle all the hassle of data heterogeneity, communication, and security issues, allowing the developer to build an effective model.

- **Edge computing platforms**: Edge computing platforms will provide the required infrastructure to deploy and manage AI models on edge devices:

    o **AWS IoT Greengrass**: It extends AWS capability to edge devices, allowing local inference, data processing, and integration with the cloud.

    o **Azure IoT Edge**: It is Microsoft's platform for the deployment of AI models on IoT devices, ensuring seamless integration with analytics in the cloud.

    o **Google Edge TPU**: The hardware accelerator is designed for low-power, high-performance AI inference at the edge.

These would enable organizations to realize the benefits of edge AI in the form of real-time analytics, scalability, and enhanced security, integrated into a general AI architecture.

Combining federated learning with edge AI allows the creation of systems that are privacy-preserving, efficient, scalable, and address unique challenges introduced by distributed and local processing. Both of these forms of approaches represent ways toward new generations of AI technologies.

Reinforcement learning and data simulation

Reinforcement learning is a fascinating branch of machine learning where the systems, called **agents**, learn by doing. The RL agents operate in an environment, trying different things and learning from the feedback they get. The goal is to maximize rewards over time. It is an approach that makes RL quite ideal for solving complex decision-making problems, from teaching robots to move or training self-driving cars to navigate, to mastering chess or Go.

Understanding reinforcement learning

In a nutshell, reinforcement learning provides a means that allows learning from experience. An agent does some exploration, gets some reward vs. penalty feedback for certain actions, and then refines that strategy over time in order to determine the best achievable outcome.

Here is a quick look at the major pieces of an RL system:

- **Agent**: Consider this as an entity that makes decisions, such as a robot or a video game character.

- **Environment**: The world that the agent interacts with could be a physical space, a virtual game, or a simulated scenario.

- **State**: A snapshot of the current situation in the environment, like a chessboard's layout or a car's position on a road.

- **Actions**: Any of the choices available to the agent-something like moving a piece in chess or turning left in the car.

- **Feedback**: The reward the agent receives for its action, positive for good choices, negative for bad ones.

- **Policy**: A strategy the agent follows to decide on its next action.

- **Value function**: A kind of crystal ball that predicts the long-term return for any given state.

These elements interact in the agent's learning process to make better decisions over time.

Role of simulation data in RL

That is another thing that makes RL so powerful; its ability to learn using simulations. Think about it: trying to teach a self-driving car by taking it on the road straight from scratch is highly impractical, too expensive, and simply not safe. Now, this is when a simulation comes in. Simulations are safe environments for agents to make mistakes and experiments while learning, avoiding real-world negative consequences.

Why simulations matter:

- **Safety**: Mistakes made in a simulation do not cost lives or damage equipment.

- **Scalability**: You can run thousands of simulations in parallel, thereby gaining speed in learning.

- **Control**: Want to test a robot in the rain, or a car on icy roads? Simulation allows the creation of any scenario you might need.

Types of simulation data

Different types of simulations serve to suit different purposes, depending on the problem one is trying to solve:

- **Physics-based simulations**: These are realistic simulations that mimic physical systems. Such scenarios are created with the help of tools like Gazebo or PyBullet.

- **Game simulations**: Some of them include virtual dynamics through game engines like Unity and Unreal, where agents play out skills, including navigation, strategy, and cooperation, among others-for example, virtually training a drone for navigation within virtual video game worlds.

- **Virtual environments**: These are higher-level abstractions of simulations, specialized to specific industries-for example, emulation of a hospital environment when training an AI that is to be used for healthcare applications, or simulation of a stock market for the training of trading algorithms.

- **Synthetic data**: Sometimes, we will generate fake data-synthetic data-to train RL agents, which is especially useful when it is hard to get or costly to collect real data.

Integration into AI architecture

For RL systems to function in the real world, they have to be part of a robust AI pipeline that masterfully handles everything from training of the agent in simulations to deployment in real-world applications. Here is how it all comes together:

- **Types of data and training requirements**: RL agents require massive data for training, and simulations have just that in plenty. The training requires high-performance hardware such as GPUs or TPUs to handle computational demands.

- **Inference and deployment**: Once trained, RL models need to be lightweight and fast in order to make real-time decisions. For instance, for an autonomous robot navigating the floor of a factory, delays with decision making are not at all acceptable.

- **AI pipeline requirement**: A strong AI pipeline means continuous improvement of the agent. This covers:

   o   Data collection from simulations.

   o   Training to fine-tune the agent's policy.

   o   Evaluation to test how well the agent performs in both simulated and real-world environments.

- **Common cloud services involved**: Cloud Services, on the other hand, cloud platforms are playing an important role in making RL systems practical:

   o   AWS RoboMaker lets you simulate and train robots in the cloud.

   o   Azure Machine Learning provides tools for training RL models.

   o   Physics-based simulation by integrating the solution with other services, like MuJoCo on the Google Cloud AI Platform. Coupled with powerful simulations and scalable AI architectures, RL is unleashing smarter systems that can learn, adapt, and make decisions on their own in the most complex environments.

AutoML and its impact on data preprocessing

Basically, AutoML is going to disrupt how we build machine learning models. With the automation of the most difficult and cumbersome tasks, AutoML will be able to empower anyone, from a greenhorn novice to an accomplished data scientist, to craft effective machine learning solutions without sweating over technical details. It accelerates development, simplifies workflows, and brings machine learning to people who might not have such a deep technical background, which is a real game-changer.

Understanding AutoML

Fundamentally, AutoML is the automation of the most important steps in machine learning. It saves you from having to clean the data for hours, tune models, or select the best algorithm yourself.

What AutoML does: Here is a simple rundown of the most important things that AutoML looks after:

- **Data preprocessing**: It prepares messy raw data through cleaning and organization for analysis.

- **Feature engineering**: This is the process of identifying and transforming the most important parts of the data to make it more accurate.

- **Model selection**: It chooses the best algorithm for you without having to test dozens manually.

- **Hyperparameter tuning**: This is a configuration of all settings in the model for the best performance.

- **Model evaluation**: The model is evaluated against the test data to ensure it is accurate enough for practical use.

By automating these steps, AutoML makes a user focus more on the problem at hand and less on tussling with technical details. The real value of AutoML lies in the fact that machine learning has now become accessible to anyone who has a dataset and a goal, even if one does not have a technical background.

Impact of AutoML on data preprocessing

Data preprocessing is one important step toward machine learning. If your data is not nice, clean, and prepared, even the most modern model will fail to perform properly. On this front, AutoML does a tremendous job by automating many of these tedious tasks that come forward to prepare it for modeling. Here is how it does its work:

- **Automated data cleaning**:

  o **Missing value imputation**: AutoML can automatically detect gaps in your data and fill them in using simple averages or even smarter predictions.

  o **Finding outliers**: It identifies odd data points that do not fit the pattern and decides whether to keep or remove them.

  o **Noise filtering**: It cleans up irrelevant or wrong data to make sure the model performs better.

- **Transformation and encoding of data**:

  o **Normalization and scaling**: AutoML normalizes the numeric data so features like age or income do not end up dominating the model just because their values are larger.

  o **Category handling**: If it is a text-based category, such as color or product type, then AutoML will change it into a one-hot encoding or embeddings format that the model can understand.

- **Feature engineering and selection**:

  o **Feature ranking**: AutoML automatically selects which part of the data is most relevant, termed as features most useful to the model.

  o **Data simplification**: It eliminates irrelevant features or combines them in ways that improve accuracy.

  o **Feature generation**: AutoML is able to generate completely new features from those already present, thus helping to find hidden patterns you may never have thought of.

- **Data augmentation**: When the tasks at hand are related to image classification or any form of text processing, AutoML can create new data by making slight changes to the already existing samples. That helps the model learn from more examples and improves performance without requiring additional real-world data.

Integration into AI architecture

AutoML is not a tool that exists in isolation; it integrates very well into the current workflows of modern AI, especially when extended with cloud services. These platforms handle everything from data preprocessing to deployment, making the entire process more efficient and scalable.

Popular AutoML platforms

Here are some big names offering AutoML as part of their services:

- **Google AutoML**: The platform developed by *Google* makes everything, from cleaning your data to deploying models, particularly for vision, language, and structured data, easier.

- **Amazon SageMaker Autopilot**: As part of AWS, the full pipeline-creation process, from picking the best models for one's purposes down to tuning, is automatic.

- **Azure AutoML**: Microsoft has made it extremely easy to run AutoML experiments, even at the enterprise scale.

- **H2O.ai**: It is open-source software that, through all its tools combined, allows AutoML for everything from data cleaning to model interpretability.

With these platforms, companies can take up AutoML with minimal or no investment in specialized infrastructure and talent.

AutoML has become a game changer by making machine learning faster, easier, and more accessible, from cleaning up dirty data to finding the best model and manufacturing brand-new features. AutoML automates the hard work while you focus on solving the problems. With cloud services making adoption seamless, AutoML is set to be critical in AI development for everyone, from small startups to corporations.

Scaling strategies for different AI paradigms

The rapid evolution of AI has led to the development of diverse paradigms, each with unique requirements and challenges. As AI systems continue to grow in complexity and scale, effective scaling strategies have become crucial to harness their full potential. This section looks into the scaling strategies applicable to various AI paradigms, including traditional machine learning, deep learning, and emerging approaches such as federated learning and edge AI. The discussion focuses on the architectural and infrastructural considerations necessary to support scalable AI systems, while also addressing the trade-offs and challenges associated with each paradigm.

Traditional machine learning

Traditional **machine learning** (**ML**) encompasses a range of algorithms, from linear regression to ensemble methods like random forests and gradient boosting. These algorithms often rely on structured data and require careful feature engineering. Scaling traditional ML involves both data and model considerations:

- **Data scaling**: Data scaling in traditional ML primarily involves managing large datasets efficiently. Techniques such as data partitioning and distributed computing frameworks are employed to handle vast amounts of data. Apache Hadoop and Apache Spark are popular platforms that facilitate distributed data processing, enabling parallel execution of ML tasks. Additionally, data sampling and dimensionality reduction techniques, such as PCA, are used to reduce the computational burden while preserving essential information.

- **Model scaling**: Model scaling in traditional ML focuses on optimizing algorithm performance and resource utilization. Ensemble methods are a common approach to enhance model accuracy and robustness. Techniques like bagging and boosting combine multiple models to improve predictions, leveraging parallel and distributed computing environments to manage computational demands. Furthermore, hyperparameter optimization and model tuning are critical for scaling traditional ML models, often requiring automated tools and grid search strategies to efficiently explore the parameter space.

Deep learning

Deep learning has revolutionized AI by enabling the development of models capable of learning complex patterns from unstructured data. However, the scalability of deep learning models poses significant challenges due to their computational and data-intensive nature:

- **Distributed training**: Distributed training is a fundamental strategy for scaling deep learning models. Techniques such as data parallelism and model parallelism are employed to distribute the training workload across multiple GPUs or nodes. Data parallelism involves splitting the dataset into smaller batches and training multiple copies of the model simultaneously, while model parallelism divides the model itself across different devices. Frameworks like TensorFlow and PyTorch provide robust support for distributed training, enabling efficient utilization of hardware resources and reducing training times.

- **Efficient model architectures**: Designing efficient model architectures is another crucial aspect of scaling deep learning. Techniques such as model pruning, quantization, and knowledge distillation are employed to reduce model size and computational requirements without sacrificing performance. Pruning involves removing redundant parameters, while quantization reduces the precision of model weights. Knowledge distillation transfers the knowledge from a larger model to a smaller one, maintaining accuracy while improving efficiency. These techniques are particularly important for deploying deep learning models in resource-constrained environments.

Federated learning

Federated learning represents a decentralized approach to training AI models, where data remains on local devices and only model updates are shared. This paradigm addresses privacy and data sovereignty concerns but introduces unique scaling challenges.

Communication efficiency

Scaling federated learning requires efficient communication protocols to minimize the overhead of transmitting model updates. Techniques such as model compression and update aggregation are employed to reduce the amount of data exchanged between devices and the central server. Compression techniques include quantization and sparsification, while aggregation methods, like federated averaging, combine updates from multiple devices to form a global model. These strategies are essential for scaling federated learning across large networks of devices.

Heterogeneity management

Federated learning environments often involve heterogeneous devices with varying computational capabilities and data distributions. Scaling federated learning necessitates strategies to handle this heterogeneity, such as adaptive learning rates and personalized models. Adaptive learning rates adjust the update frequency based on device capabilities, while personalized models tailor the global model to individual device characteristics. These approaches enhance the scalability and robustness of federated learning systems.

Edge AI

Edge AI involves deploying AI models directly on edge devices, enabling real-time processing and decision-making. Scaling edge AI presents unique challenges due to resource constraints and the need for low-latency operations.

Model optimization

Optimizing models for edge deployment is critical for scaling edge AI. Techniques such as model compression, pruning, and quantization are employed to reduce model size and computational requirements, enabling deployment on devices with limited resources. Additionally, **neural architecture search** (**NAS**) can be used to automatically design efficient model architectures tailored for edge devices. These strategies ensure that edge AI models can operate efficiently within the constraints of edge environments.

Distributed inference

Distributed inference is a strategy for scaling edge AI by distributing the inference workload across multiple devices. This approach leverages the collective computational power of edge devices to perform complex tasks, reducing the burden on individual devices and enhancing scalability. Techniques such as collaborative inference and model partitioning enable efficient utilization of edge resources, ensuring that AI applications can scale across diverse edge environments.

Scaling strategies for different AI paradigms are essential for unlocking the full potential of AI technologies. Traditional machine learning, deep learning, federated learning, and edge AI each present unique scaling challenges, requiring tailored approaches to address their specific requirements. Distributed computing frameworks, efficient model architectures, communication protocols, and optimization techniques play a pivotal role in enhancing the scalability of AI systems. As AI continues to evolve, ongoing advancements in scaling strategies will be crucial for enabling the deployment of AI applications across diverse and complex environments.

Conclusion

In this chapter, we have explored the intricate relationship between AI algorithms and data architecture, underscoring how various AI paradigms influence the design and scalability of data systems. The discussion began with an overview of traditional machine learning, highlighting the need for efficient data and model scaling strategies to handle large datasets and complex algorithms. We then looked into deep learning, emphasizing the critical role of distributed training and efficient model architectures in managing the computational and data demands of these models. The chapter also examined federated learning and edge AI, both of which present unique scaling challenges due to their decentralized and resource-constrained nature. Strategies such as communication efficiency, heterogeneity management, and model optimization were discussed as essential components for scaling these emerging paradigms.

The insights gained from this chapter highlight the evolving nature of AI systems and the necessity for adaptive data architectures that can accommodate diverse and dynamic AI workloads. As AI technologies continue to advance, the interplay between algorithms and data infrastructure will remain a focal point for researchers and practitioners aiming to optimize performance and scalability.

In the next chapter, we will transition from the algorithmic considerations of AI to the infrastructural aspects of building scalable machine learning systems. *Chapter 8, Scalable Machine Learning Infrastructure*, will focus on the construction and management of scalable machine learning infrastructure, exploring distributed training architectures, model serving strategies, and MLOps practices. We will look into the technical intricacies of containerization, orchestration, and lifecycle management, providing a comprehensive understanding of how to effectively scale machine learning workflows. Additionally, the chapter will address the unique challenges and solutions associated with edge AI and federated learning infrastructures, offering practical insights for deploying AI applications at scale.

Join our Discord space

Join our Discord workspace for latest updates, offers, tech happenings around the world, new releases, and sessions with the authors:

https://discord.bpbonline.com

CHAPTER 8
Scalable Machine Learning Infrastructure

Introduction

The advancement of **machine learning** (**ML**) has ushered in a transformative era across various sectors, driven by the deployment of increasingly sophisticated models. As the complexity and scale of these models expand, the demand for robust and scalable infrastructure becomes critical. This chapter looks into the multifaceted domain of scalable ML infrastructure, examining the innovations and methodologies essential for managing large-scale ML workloads effectively. Central to scalable ML infrastructure is the challenge of addressing the substantial computational demands inherent in training and deploying advanced models. Traditional single-node computation approaches quickly become inadequate as data volumes surge and model architectures grow more intricate. To overcome these limitations, distributed training architectures have emerged, leveraging data and model parallelism to distribute workloads efficiently across multiple nodes. This approach enhances computational efficiency and reduces training durations.

The transition of ML models from research to production environments underscores the necessity for efficient model serving and inference strategies. The capability to deliver real-time predictions with minimal latency is paramount, necessitating the development of robust serving methodologies that ensure high throughput and reliability. The chapter also explores the role of **automated machine learning** (**AutoML**) and hyperparameter optimization in democratizing access to ML. By automating model selection and tuning, AutoML allows practitioners to concentrate on strategic problem-solving rather than detailed configuration tasks. Furthermore, the integration of MLOps practices, which apply DevOps principles to the ML lifecycle, facilitates continuous integration, deployment, and monitoring of models. MLOps ensures the reliability and compliance of ML applications with evolving business and regulatory standards.

This chapter provides a comprehensive exploration of these themes, equipping readers with the knowledge to build and maintain scalable, efficient, and reliable machine learning systems.

Structure

The chapter covers the following topics:

- Distributed training architectures for large-scale ML
- Model serving and inference at scale
- Strategies for AutoML and hyperparameter optimization
- ML experiment and artifact management
- Introduction to experiment management
- Containerization and orchestration for ML workloads
- MLOps practices and tools for lifecycle management
- Edge AI and federated learning infrastructures
- Scaling deep learning systems and frameworks

Objectives

By the end of this chapter, readers will have developed a comprehensive understanding of the key components and strategies essential for building and maintaining scalable machine learning infrastructure. This chapter aims to equip practitioners, researchers, and students with the knowledge required to effectively address the challenges associated with deploying and managing large-scale machine learning systems.

The chapter begins by exploring distributed training architectures, providing insights into how data and model parallelism can be leveraged to optimize computational efficiency. Readers will gain an understanding of the techniques and frameworks that enable the distribution of ML workloads across multiple nodes, thereby reducing training times and enhancing scalability.

In addition, the chapter looks into model serving and inference strategies, emphasizing the importance of real-time processing capabilities in production environments. Readers will learn about the methodologies employed to achieve high throughput and low latency, ensuring that ML models can deliver timely predictions and insights. The exploration of AutoML and hyperparameter optimization strategies will further enhance the reader's ability to streamline model development processes. By understanding these automated techniques, readers will be able to focus on high-level problem-solving and innovation rather than the intricacies of model configuration.

Moreover, the chapter introduces MLOps practices, highlighting their role in facilitating continuous integration, deployment, and monitoring. Readers will gain insights into how MLOps enhances the reliability and efficiency of ML applications, ensuring that models remain performant and compliant with evolving requirements. Finally, the chapter examines the emerging paradigms of edge AI and federated learning, as well as the scaling of deep learning systems and frameworks. By understanding these cutting-edge approaches, readers will be prepared to tackle the challenges of data privacy, real-time processing, and model complexity, paving the way for the deployment of scalable and efficient machine learning solutions across diverse industries.

Distributed training architectures for large-scale ML

The rapid growth in data and the increasing complexity of machine learning models further demand scalable training architectures that can handle large-scale ML tasks. Distributed training architectures have emerged as a critical component in enabling efficient processing and learning from massive datasets. This section will cover the basics, methodologies, and technologies that form the backbone of distributed training architectures; it will focus on large-scale ML applications. It will provide an overview of major concepts and components involved in distributed training and lay the ground for further exploration of scalable ML infrastructure.

Introduction to distributed training

Distributed training refers to the distribution of the workload of training a machine learning model among multiple resources such as CPUs, GPUs, or even clusters of machines. It is one of the primary ways to handle the computational load arising from big models on big datasets because it is not feasible on a single machine due to limitations in memory, processing power, and time. By applying distributed systems, ML practitioners can significantly speed up the training process and improve model performance. The key principles of distributed training are to divide the workload, ensure efficient communication between computational units, and maintain synchronization to achieve the desired model accuracy.

Types of distributed training

The types of distributed training are as follows:

- **Data parallelism**: Data parallelism typically works by dividing the dataset into smaller subsets, each distributed across different computation nodes. Each node independently computes gradients on its portion of the data, after which the gradients are aggregated to collectively update the model parameters. Data parallelism scales efficiently when the model parameters fit within the memory of each node. However, overall throughput can also be constrained by factors such as interconnect bandwidth and per-node batch sizing, which influence synchronization efficiency and resource utilization.

- **Model parallelism**: Model parallelism splits the model across many nodes itself. Different nodes execute different parts of the model, running it on the same input in parallel. This type of approach helps in those scenarios where one single node cannot accommodate larger models; hence, very extensive neural networks could easily be spread across different nodes. In any case, this is tricky since heavy coordination would need to be developed in managing interdependence among its many parts, thus adding to its overall intricacy.

Architectures and frameworks for distributed training

Predominantly, these are the two architectures for distributed training:

- **Parameter server architecture**: The parameter server architecture is among the most adopted architectures for performing distributed training. This architecture designates a central parameter server for managing global model parameters, whereas the worker nodes execute actual computation. Gradients computed by worker nodes are sent to the parameter server, which updates the model parameters and sends them back to the workers. The architecture supports synchronous and asynchronous training paradigms, therefore, providing flexibility while handling various kinds of machine learning tasks. Synchronous training ensures updates will be consistent in all nodes; that is, each node has finished computing before updating the parameters. Meanwhile, asynchronous training allows flexibility but could come with a little inconsistency and faster iteration.

- **All-reduce architecture**: The all-reduce architecture is another paradigm to the parameter server model; it was designed to prevent a single bottleneck due to a centralized parameter server. In this architecture, each worker node directly communicates with other nodes to perform a collective reduction operation, such as summing over gradients across all nodes. This design evenly distributes the communication load across nodes for better scalability with less communication overhead. All-reduce is particularly well-suited for tightly coupled systems where low latency and high bandwidth are available.

Challenges and considerations in distributed training

The challenges and considerations in distributed training are as follows:

- **Communication overhead**: One of the biggest challenges in training a model in a distributed manner is communication overhead. With frequent communications between nodes, it results in significant delay and reduced throughput, especially under synchronous training. In order to fight these, techniques such as gradient compression, communication scheduling, and efficient network protocols are put in place. Gradient compression reduces the size of data exchanged by nodes, while in communication scheduling, the timing is optimized to avoid contention.

- **Fault tolerance**: The higher the number of nodes involved in the process, the higher the possibility of node failures in distributed systems. Ensuring fault tolerance is thus crucial to maintaining the integrity of the training process. This can be ensured by techniques like checkpointing, redundancy, and dynamic resource allocation that can help mitigate node failures and ensure continuous training.

- **Checkpointing**: Periodically save the state of the model and training progress so that, in case something goes wrong, recovery can be made from the most recent checkpoint.

- **Redundancy**: Ensure that there are always backup nodes available to take over tasks from failed nodes.

- **Load balancing**: Good load balancing among the nodes is highly essential for the efficient use of the resources and reduction of idle times. The imbalance in the distribution of data or model fragments will result in bottlenecks and reduced efficiency. Dynamic workload allocation, data sharding, and adaptive scheduling are some of the strategies to ensure even distribution of computational workloads. These approaches dynamically adjust the allocation of tasks with respect to the current state of the system and prevent the overloading of individual nodes.

Distributed training architectures are indispensable for scaling up machine learning to meet the challenges of constantly increasing data volume and model complexity. By using techniques ranging from data and model parallelism to parameter server architectures and all-reduce, combined with the issue of communication overhead, fault tolerance, and load balancing, ML practitioners will be able to build robust and scalable training systems. That continuous evolution in the methodologies and technologies for distributed training is eventually to play a considerable role in enabling big-scale ML applications. It will bring many unprecedented breakthroughs for the field, from natural language processing to computer vision and more.

Model serving and inference at scale

Model serving is the process of deploying machine learning models into production so that they can input data and return predictions in real time or near-real time. This step is critical in transforming machine learning models from experimental artifacts into actionable tools that unlock value in applications such as recommendation systems, fraud detection, and natural language processing. The efficiency and reliability of the model directly influence the performance and user experience of AI-driven systems.

Model serving basics

Model serving spans the gap between model development and its practical application. In other words, it allows the machine learning model to interact with the real-world system. Model serving essentially covers how to take these trained models and make them serve data, do computation, and send back predictions or decisions without delays. A model serving would be considered effective depending on:

- **Real-time processing**: Most applications, from fraud detection to autonomous cars, require real-time responses where latency directly impacts the outcome.

- **Scalability**: As the user base grows, along with the volume of data, the serving infrastructure needs to scale to meet increased demand without degradation in performance.

- **Reliability**: Continuous availability and fault tolerance ensure consistent service delivery, even under high load or unexpected failures.

By addressing these considerations, serving models transform them into robust, scalable, and high-performance blocks of much larger applications.

Challenges in model serving at scale

The following are the challenges in model serving at scale:

- **High throughput and low latency**: Whereas high throughput ensures a serving system can handle many requests simultaneously, low latency keeps the time to return predictions minimal. Achieving both together, however, is challenging for several reasons:

  o **Resource contention**: The scarcity of computational and network resources may cause bottlenecks.

  o **Model complexity**: Larger, more complex models take longer to compute, which increases the response time.

  o **Dynamic workloads**: Variable request patterns require elastic scaling to maintain performance.

- **Reliability and fault tolerance**: Reliability guarantees continuous service, while fault tolerance minimizes the impact of failures. Challenges include:

  o **Node failures**: Hardware or software failures in nodes are common in distributed systems and may disrupt service.

- o **Network issues**: High dependency on network communication increases the risk of latency spikes or connectivity loss.

- o **State management**: Maintaining consistency in stateful systems during failures requires robust mechanisms like checkpointing and redundancy.

- **Resource management**: Efficient resource management balances performance and cost. Key considerations include:

- o **Dynamic allocation**: Allocating resources based on real-time demand prevents over-provisioning or resource starvation.

- o **Model-specific requirements**: Different models may require varying computational, memory, or storage resources, complicating resource scheduling.

- o **Cost optimization**: using minimum infrastructure while serving the models efficiently, at the lowest cost, towards sustainable operation.

Architecture for scalable model serving

Several architectural paradigms have been developed to support scalable model serving, each offering unique advantages and trade-offs. These architectures are designed to handle the diverse requirements of different machine learning applications.

Microservices architecture

Microservices architecture is a popular approach to model serving, where each model or component of a machine learning system is deployed as an independent service. This architecture allows for modularity, scalability, and ease of maintenance. By decoupling services, organizations can deploy, update, and scale models independently, reducing the risk of system-wide failures. Microservices can be orchestrated using platforms like Kubernetes, which provide robust tools for managing service discovery, load balancing, and scaling.

The microservices architecture organizes a machine learning system into a collection of independent, loosely coupled services, each encapsulating a specific functionality or model and exposing its functionality via APIs. Key advantages include:

- **Modularity**: Individual services can be developed, deployed, and scaled independently, reducing the risk of cascading failures.

- **Scalability**: The services scale horizontally depending on demand, using resources efficiently.

- **Resilience**: The fault isolation prevents cascading failures, thus increasing reliability.

Orchestration platforms like Kubernetes extend the power of microservices architecture by automating the deployment, scaling, and management of containerized services.

Moreover, load balancing, service discovery, and rolling updates further smooth the operations.

Figure 8.1 illustrates the basic architecture of microservices:

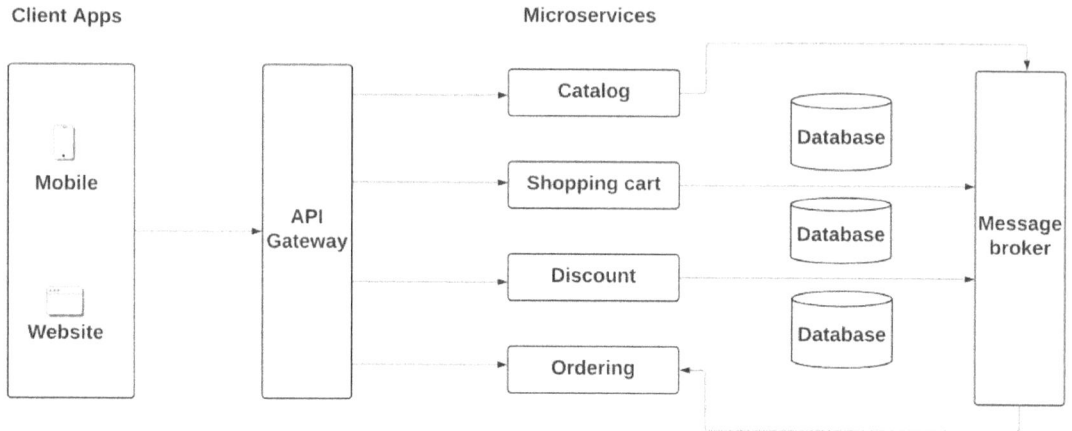

Figure 8.1: Microservices architecture

Serverless architecture

Serverless computing abstracts infrastructure management, freeing up the developer to deploy the code. The following are features of serverless architecture:

- **Event-driven execution**: Deployed models exposed as functions get triggered in the event of an incoming request.

- **Automatic scaling**: Functions scale based on incoming request rate, doing so elastically and cost-efficiently.

- **Minimum overhead**: A developer does not have to manage servers, storage, or networking, which makes deployment faster.

Services such as AWS Lambda, Google Cloud Functions, and Azure Functions provide serverless model-serving environments integrated with other services on the same cloud.

Inference optimization techniques

Optimizing inference performance is essential for achieving scalability in model serving. Various techniques can be applied to enhance the efficiency of inference processes, which we will discuss in this section.

Model compression and quantization

Model compression and quantization optimize the models by speeding up inference, along with lower usage of resources. Some key techniques include pruning, reducing a model's size along with its computation complexity, weight sharing in the model that groups some similar values with minimal storage required, and quantization that lowers precision on both weights and activation that allows a fast run on several hardware, including CPU, GPU, or edge devices.

These techniques are especially useful in the deployment of models to resource-constrained environments, such as mobile devices or IoT systems.

Batch processing and parallelization

Batch processing and parallelization increase inference throughput by the following:

- **Batching requests**: It groups multiple input requests into a single processing batch, reducing per-request overhead and improving computational efficiency.

- **Parallel computation**: It distributes the workload across multiple processors, leveraging hardware capabilities for faster processing.

The techniques that are done in these areas are implemented in frameworks like TensorFlow Serving and NVIDIA Triton Inference Server. Both provide tooling to accomplish high-performance inference in production environments.

Model serving and inference at scale are important to get the full benefit of machine learning into production. This is achieved by high throughput, low latency, reliability, and efficient resource management. Scalable architectures, including microservices and serverless computing, combined with optimization techniques such as model compression and parallelization, ensure that models meet real-world demands. Further, as technology evolves, the next wave of AI adoption in industries and improvement of user experiences will be driven by innovation in model serving and inference.

Strategies for AutoML and hyperparameter optimization

The increasing complexity and diversity of machine learning models have necessitated the development of automated approaches to model selection and hyperparameter tuning. AutoML and hyperparameter optimization strategies have emerged as pivotal tools in the quest to democratize machine learning and enhance its scalability. This section looks into the principles and methodologies underpinning AutoML and hyperparameter optimization, examining their roles in streamlining the development of scalable machine learning infrastructure.

Introduction to AutoML

AutoML refers to a paradigm shift in the field of machine learning; it deals with the automation of an end-to-end process of applying machine learning to real-world problems.

The different auto-machine learning frameworks are designed to handle tasks like data preprocessing, feature selection, model selection, and hyperparameter tuning, hence reducing the need for extensive human intervention. This can accelerate the development cycle and make machine learning accessible to nonspecialists, which is a great advantage for many users of advanced analytics techniques.

AutoML democratizes these technologies across different industries by abstracting the complexities of machine learning pipelines. The salient features of AutoML are the automation of data cleansing, generation of synthetic features, selection of algorithms, and tuning of hyperparameters for maximum performance of the models. Hence, this enables enterprises to achieve quicker time-to-insight without requiring specialized data science knowledge and skills, therefore assuring better scalability of machine learning solutions.

Hyperparameter optimization

Hyperparameters are a very important part of machine learning models, and their impact on the performance of such models is huge. Such parameters, which determine the behavior of the learning algorithm, should be chosen with care to achieve good results. Examples include the learning rate in gradient-based methods, the number of estimators in ensemble models, and regularization terms in linear models.

Several strategies have been developed for hyperparameter optimization, each offering distinct advantages and trade-offs:

- **Grid search**: This is a brute-force, exhaustive search over a set of predefined hyperparameters. Although it may be thorough, it is computationally expensive and hence impractical for high-dimensional spaces.

- **Random search**: A stochastic process in which the hyperparameters are randomly sampled from predefined distributions. This normally outperforms grid search in computational efficiency, especially in cases where only a few hyperparameters have the most influence over the performance of a model.

- **Bayesian optimization**: This is an advanced method involving a probabilistic model for guiding the search process. Bayesian optimization learns a surrogate model of the objective function that predicts performance for unexplored hyperparameter configurations and targets areas that are most likely to yield high-performing models. It iteratively refines the current strategy on which its search should lie and decreases the computational costs compared to either grid or random search.

- **Evolutionary algorithms**: These algorithms work, inspired by natural selection, by iteratively evolving a population of candidate solutions in view of optimizing hyperparameters. They employ mutation, crossover, and selection processes to explore the hyperparameter space.

- **Gradient-based optimization**: Recent work allows direct gradient-based optimization of hyperparameters. While very promising, this technique requires differentiable objectives and can be sensitive to initialization.

AutoML frameworks and tools

Some of them were designed and implemented as AutoML frameworks and tools to make model development and hyperparameter tuning automatic. These frameworks are built to offer user-friendly interfaces while seamlessly integrating with popular machine learning libraries, thus making them accessible to a wide swath of practitioners. Key frameworks include:

- **Google AutoML**: Part of Google Cloud's AI offerings, it is a full-stack platform that supports end-to-end machine learning workflows and integrates advanced neural architecture search.

- **H2O.ai's AutoML**: An open-source framework that supports regression, classification, and time-series modeling. It provides automatic model ensembling, hyperparameter tuning, and explainability features.

- **Auto-sklearn**: Built on the scikit-learn ecosystem, auto-sklearn automates tasks such as preprocessing, feature selection, and model tuning. It employs meta-learning to recommend configurations based on prior experiments.

- **Microsoft's Azure AutoML**: This is a cloud-based service to train, deploy, and monitor models. It focuses on explainability and compliance, which are crucial for enterprise applications.

- **Tree-based Pipeline Optimization Tool (TPOT)**: A genetic algorithm-based framework that automates machine learning pipelines along with hyperparameter tuning.

- **OpenML**: It is a collaborative platform for sharing datasets, algorithms, and experiments. It supports AutoML tasks by enabling benchmarking and reproducibility across different tools.

Challenges in hyperparameter tuning with AutoML

Some of the challenges of AutoML frameworks regarding hyperparameter tuning are as follows:

- **Computational complexity**: Hyperparameter tuning is a computationally expensive process, especially when it concerns high-dimensional spaces. It gets worse with complex models such as deep neural networks.

- **Resource allocation**: Poor resource allocation methods can lead to potential suboptimal outcomes, resulting in wasted resources. The distribution of computational resources across different configurations is important.

- **Scaling**: While AutoML frameworks work fine on small to medium-scale problems, scaling to large datasets or high-dimensional feature spaces is challenging.

- **Interpretability of models**: The complex model pipelines resulting from AutoML generally result in models that are hard to understand. This seriously affects their acceptance in domains such as healthcare and finance, where explainability is crucial.

- **Overfitting**: The automation of hyperparameter tuning increases the risk of overfitting, especially when cross-validation is not performed effectively. In this regard, generalizable models need robust validation strategies.

- **Limitation of customization**: Although there is a shift toward general-purpose solutions in current AutoML frameworks, they are rigid for certain domain-specific customizations, which negatively impacts the results in specialized applications.

- **Bias in search strategy**: An optimization strategy adopted by AutoML may subsequently be biased in giving preferences to configurations and may even lose some innovative solutions.

Meeting these challenges will ultimately make AutoML frameworks robust and reliable, and hence find wider diffusion in industries.

ML experiment and artifact management

Success in building good machine learning models seldom happens in a straight line. It is iterative, full of experimentation: configuration tweaks, testing of ideas, and making sense of what works. These various experiments and their many outputs can be hard to manage. This is where experiments and artifact management help in systematically keeping track of everything for reproducibility and improvement in collaboration within teams. That is why the usage of solid experiment tracking and artifact management tools can make life so easy by keeping everything organized and helping teams move faster and work better together.

Introduction to experiment management

Experiment management is, at its core, about staying organized. When building ML models, you are juggling a plethora of moving parts: model configurations, datasets, code, and metrics. If you have no system set up to track it all, it gets quite hard to understand what was different when something finally worked and what was better about one model than another. Having a good system in place keeps the chaos under control and makes it so much easier to learn from each experiment and keep building on what works.

Experiment management helps in tracking everything you tried, for example:

- Hyper-parameters
- Datasets
- Code
- Log its performance of accuracy, loss, varied F1-scores, etc.

- Provide you with the ability to compare results to make informed decisions on the next steps.

- Makes it easier to reproduce results by keeping a clear record of everything you have done, so you can pick up where you left off or build on past experiments without starting from scratch.

This is not only for neatness but also to give teams the power to learn from every experiment and quickly iterate, avoiding past mistakes.

Experiment tracking and versioning

Imagine you train some model; it goes amazingly well, but then in a few weeks, you cannot remember exactly the settings or code version that was used. That is where experiment tracking saves the day. Without experiment tracking, you would end up spending hours trying to piece together what you did, instead of using that time to improve and keep moving forward.

Tracking keeps a record of:

- **Input parameters**: The hyper parameters or model settings you have used.

- **Code versions**: What version of code you ran, tracked through Git or some other versioning tool?

- **Dataset versions**: The exact dataset (or its version) you used, including any preprocessing steps.

- **Performance metrics**: How the model performed (e.g., accuracy, precision, recall).

- **Experiment logs**: A detailed record of how the training went, things like runtime behavior, errors, and system settings, so you can easily troubleshoot and improve future experiments

Besides that, versioning allows you to reproduce past experiments when required. Tools like MLflow, DVC, and Weights and Biases make that easier by logging all the details by default. Tracking at this level makes it easy to understand how models evolve over time and what exactly is driving their performance.

Artifact management

When you build ML models, you create a lot of stuff. This includes trained models, datasets, feature sets, evaluation reports, and more. These are called artifacts, and managing them properly is crucial for keeping your ML workflow running smoothly. Managing artifacts properly also means you can easily go back to reuse or revisit your previous work, saving you tons of time when scaling projects or figuring out what went wrong.

Artifact management involves the following:

- **Storing**: Keep everything in one place, whether that is a local drive, cloud storage, or a dedicated tool.

- **Organizing**: Naming and categorizing artifacts so they are easy to find.

- **Retrieval**: Effortless recovery of artifacts when you need to reuse a model, analyze results, or try out new ideas.

For instance, consider that you have done the training of a model that works perfectly for some tasks. Some years later, this model might be needed for some similar projects. In this case, without any artifact management, you might have to retrain the model. Proper management of artifacts avoids that headache at all costs, making sure everything is accessible and reusable.

It becomes so much easier to track, store, and manage artifacts with the help of platforms such as MLflow and Neptune.ai, so that you will never lose track of anything.

Reproducibility and collaboration

Reproducibility might sound technical, but it is just this: Can you, or anybody else for that matter, reproduce your results? It is a big thing in machine learning. Without reproducibility, teams cannot trust the results, and collaboration turns chaotic. Reproducibility also makes it way easier to troubleshoot and improve your models since you can track exactly what changed between experiments and see how those changes affected the results.

Here is how experiment and artifact management make reproducibility easier:

- **Detailed records**: The fact that everything is tracked in an experiment (parameters, code, data, results) provides the ability to reproduce it later.

- **Version control**: Keeping versions of code and datasets ensures consistency between experiments.

- **Shared artifacts**: Models, datasets, and results are easily shared and reused by a team when they are stored in one place.

Reproducibility does not just validate your results, but it also allows collaboration. When people know what has been tried, what worked, and what did not, they can build on top of other people's work by not duplicating effort. It is about working smarter, not harder.

Containerization and orchestration for ML workloads

Deploying machine learning models into production is no cakewalk. From various hardware setups to fluctuating workloads, there are enough stumbling blocks that may just trip you up. That is where containerization and orchestration come in. Containerization and orchestration have indeed changed how one packages, deploys, and manages ML models, they can be easily scaled, run much more efficiently, and are a lot less stressful to maintain. It also makes it simpler to ensure consistency across environments, so the model runs the same way in production as it did during testing, reducing unexpected surprises.

Understanding containerization

You have just built an amazing ML model on your laptop; it works great. You tried to run it on the company server, and poof. Nothing works. Some dependency issues, mismatches in libraries, missing frameworks, you know the drill. That is when containerization comes to the rescue.

Well, it is just putting your ML model, along with all the libraries and frameworks and settings it needs, into one neat little box called a container. These are lightweight, portable, and self-contained, carrying everything the model will need to run without you ever having to consider what is there on hardware or at an operating system level. Run it on your laptop, on the cloud, or on some high-performance server; it does not matter. It will all behave the same.

The reason it is a game changer is:

- **Lightweight and fast**: Unlike virtual machines, containers do not need a full operating system to work with, so they are fast to spin up and lightweight on resources.

- **Portable**: Build once, run anywhere. Containers eliminate those annoying *it worked on my machine* problems.

- **Isolated**: Each container operates in its own bubble, so one model's mess will not impact others.

- **Reproducible**: You get the same results no matter where you deploy it. No surprises.

- **Scalable**: Need to handle a few requests or a million? Containers make it super easy to scale up or down without breaking a sweat.

In other words, containerization makes ML development and deployment predictable, reliable, and painless, enabling seamless scaling and integration across various environments. So, you can focus on building models instead of fighting environmental issues.

Risks with containers for ML workloads

When you are dealing with the chaos of machine learning projects, containerization steps in as a lifesaver, making it so much easier to manage, deploy, and scale your work without the usual headaches. Here is why it is such a big deal:

- **Portability**: ML workflows often transition from one environment to another-your local machine, on-prem servers, and cloud platforms. Containers make these transitions smooth and hassle-free.

- **Scalability**: Got an ML model that is seeing a spike in traffic? Spin up more containers and handle them like a pro.

- **Consistency**: The same containerized model runs the same way every time, regardless of where you deploy it.

- **Efficient resource use**: Containers are lightweight, so you can run more of them on the same hardware, making them ideal for resource-hungry ML tasks like training or inference.

- **Simplified dependency management**: The ML models, most of the time, rely on very specific libraries or versions. Containers package it all up so that you never have to worry about conflicts.

If you are serious about deploying ML models in production, containers are your best friend.

Understanding orchestration

Now, let us take it to the next level. There is this great containerization for a single ML model or application, but when there are many, what happens then? You are running several models, pre-processing data, handling inferences, and probably retraining models in real-time. You just cannot keep track of all those moving parts manually; that way lies chaos.

That is where orchestration comes in. Consider orchestrating the traffic controller for your containers, where everything flows, will scale automatically, and stay online regardless of everything. The most popular orchestration tools include Kubernetes, though other popular ones are Docker Swarm and Apache Mesos.

You need orchestration for the following reasons:

- **Automation**: No more babysitting. It automatically provides deployment, scaling, and monitoring.

- **Resilience**: Orchestration tools will automatically restart the containers in case a component breaks.

- **Scaling**: If lots of users arrive, the orchestration is also capable of scaling ML workloads in real time or vice versa.

- **Resource management**: This does, with greater efficiency, save money by not wastefully allocating your CPUs, Memory, and GPUs to your containers.

Orchestration forms the backbone for running complex distributed systems with regard to ML and without losing your head.

Importance of orchestration for ML

It is easy to feel while trying to manage a machine learning workload, like trying to juggle a dozen spinning plates and not drop any: managing infrastructure, scale models, and about a million little things that could go wrong. Everything spirals out of control way too easily. That is where orchestration comes in; it is like having an autopilot for your ML workflow that takes care of deployments, scaling, and resource management for you. Focus on what really matters, like building awesome models and creating true value, rather than being worried about servers, unexpected crashes, or resource underutilization.

Add orchestration to your ML workflow, and it finally feels complete. Here is what you get with it:

- **Auto-scaling**: When the going gets tough, as when there is an unexpected spiking of traffic or perhaps an out-of-band rush of requests for inferences, your ML models smoothly scale without intervention from you or any other person.

- **Wiser resource utilization**: Orchestration tools ensure that each container utilizes just about the right amount of resources, either CPU, memory, or GPU power, so that nothing is wasted.

- **High availability**: Sometimes, containers crash, but orchestration can ensure that the new ones will be up and running in no time, keeping your ML applications online.

- **Easy updates**: Rolling out a new version of your model? Orchestration lets you do it without taking the system offline.

- **Multi-cloud and hybrid setup**: Orchestration makes your containers run across different environments, prem, cloud, or both.

- **End-to-end workflow management**: Orchestration streamlines everything in the ML lifecycle, from data preprocessing to training, deployment, and monitoring.

Containerization and orchestration have really changed the paradigm of how ML workloads are deployed and managed. Containers bring portability and consistency, while orchestrations make everything run seamlessly, irrespective of how complex your setup is. Jointly, they enable you to focus on the most important thing: building great ML models and abstracting most pains from deployment to scaling.

MLOps practices and tools for lifecycle management

If you have worked on machine learning projects, you know that is not where the real challenge lies; it is what happens afterward that counts. How to get a model into production, how to keep it running smoothly, and how to make sure it stays relevant over time can be quite different ball games. That is where MLOps comes in. Think of it as the glue that connects building ML models with using them in the real world.

Understanding MLOps

In essence, MLOps is about easing and accelerating the deployment, management, and improvement of ML models. It is a collaboration that brings data scientists, ML engineers, and IT operations together. If DevOps changed the way software is developed and deployed, MLOps is doing that for machine learning.

The idea is simple: automate the repetitive tasks, such as testing or deployment, and standardize processes so teams are not reinventing the wheel for each new project. When done right, MLOps helps you:

- Deploy faster your models.
- Keep them running reliably.
- Scale with the growth of your business.

Why it matters: Without an appropriate MLOps setup, the deployment of an ML model can be awfully slow, messy, and unpredictable. Things break, fixes take forever, and it is hard to keep up with changes in data or business needs. MLOps will fix this by building systems that:

- **Speed up deployments**: Models move to production in weeks, not months.
- **Reliability**: You can trust your models to work, even as things change.
- **Scalability**: This allows more data or big workloads to be handled with ease, without much stress.

Key MLOps practices

Keeping the machine learning models up and running means not only getting them up once but also keeping them reliable, adaptive to changes, and abiding by the rules over time. That is where the best practices for MLOps come in, to take the guesswork out of the whole ML development to deployment and beyond for sustained accuracy, efficiency, and manageability. Version control, continuous integration and deployment, automated testing, monitoring, and governance; this means teams avoid expensive mistakes and can move quicker while keeping things very transparent. Fewer headaches, smoother workflows, and with it, a much easier time managing ML projects.

- **Version control**: Think of how difficult it would be to explain how your ML model arrived at its results several months after building it with no proper documentation. Version control keeps tabs on each modification you make to code, data, or models. This is made possible and easy with versioning utilities like Git and DVC, making documentation and reproduction at any moment effortless.

- **Continuous integration and deployment (CI/CD)**: CI/CD is the game-changer for ML projects. It will automate the testing and deployment process so that new models or updates can go live on time. Think of it like a conveyor belt for your ML workflows; everything flows well and fast.

- **Automated testing**: Testing ML models goes beyond just looking at code; it also involves checking data and performance. Automating tests catches issues, such as:

  o Code that does not work.

  o Models are not as accurate as they can be.

  o Data validation to ensure there are no problems, even in data formatting or missing values.

  This helps you identify and fix problems early, so they do not derail your project later.

- **Monitoring and feedback**: The best ML models will not stay perfect over time. Data changes, user behavior shifts, and trends evolve, which pretty much causes models to degrade over time. That is why monitoring is so important: it will help track the performance of a model, detect problems, such as model drift, and give feedback for improvements

- **Governance and compliance**: With regulations such as GDPR and increasing concerns about ethics in AI, governance is not an option. MLOps ensures you can explain how your models work, document your workflows, and stay compliant without scrambling at the last minute.

This best practice integration in your ML workflows is not only a time-saver but also a game-changer: it makes your models more reliable, easier to scale, and ready for the future. MLOps is not just about automation; it is about creating a smart, flexible system that evolves with your data, adapts to business needs, and keeps you from scrambling at the last minute when things go wrong.

Figure 8.2 shows a typical MLOps workflow showing the different components and how they control the various aspects of deploying and monitoring an ML artifact:

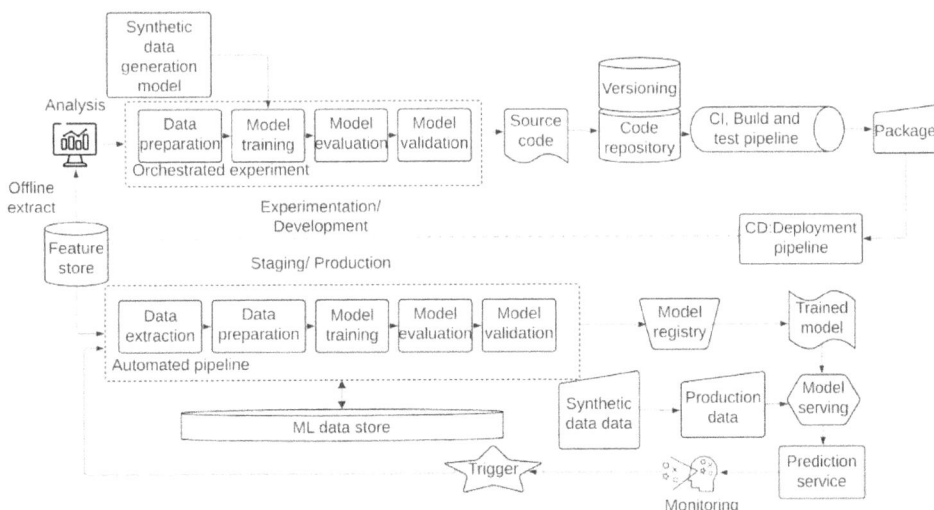

Figure 8.2: *Architecture of MLOps*

Tools for MLOps lifecycle management

Getting started with MLOps requires the right set of tools to streamline workflows and manage ML models effectively. Fortunately, there are plenty of powerful platforms designed to simplify the process, making it easier to track experiments, automate workflows, and deploy models seamlessly. These tools help teams handle everything from versioning and monitoring to scaling and optimization, ensuring that machine learning projects transition smoothly from research to real-world impact. Here are some of the most popular and widely used MLOps platforms that can make managing ML models significantly easier.

MLflow

MLflow is a one-stop shop for tracking your ML experiments. It allows you to:

- Log parameters, metrics, and results.
- Store and version your models.
- Deploy models into production with ease.
- It is open-source, easy to use, and works with all the major ML frameworks.

Kubeflow

Kubeflow is a versatile platform built on Kubernetes that is perfect for large, complex ML workflows. It can:

- Automate processes like data preparation and model deployment.
- Scale workflows across different environments (on-premises or clouds).
- Handle distributed ML projects with ease.

TensorFlow Extended

If you are working with TensorFlow, **TensorFlow Extended** (**TFX**) is a natural choice. It provides tools for:

- Validating the data to avoid bad input.
- Analyzing your models so you know they are performing as they should be.
- Deploying at scale using TensorFlow Serving.

Amazon SageMaker

Amazon SageMaker is an all-in-one ML platform that takes you from building to deploying models. It is fully managed, meaning you do not need to worry about infrastructure. Key features include:

- Prebuilt algorithms for faster development.

- Automated training and tuning for better models.

- Built-in monitoring to catch issues early.

MLOps connects ML projects from an interesting concept to where something generates actual value. It is not about finding the right set of tools and processes, but about building a system to let teams become smarter, not work harder. You can bring the best practices for version control, continuous integration/continuous deployment, monitoring, and MLflow, KFP, TFX, and SageMaker to drive in fast, reliable, and scalable machine learning pipelines.

After all, MLOps is what eventually converts an ML prototype into a real-world solution. It connects the gap between research and creating an impact that allows the organization to unlock a wide range of possibilities with machine learning.

Edge AI and federated learning infrastructures

The proliferation of connected devices and the exponential growth of data have catalyzed the emergence of edge AI and federated learning as pivotal components of modern machine learning infrastructure. These technologies address the limitations of traditional centralized approaches by enabling distributed computation and learning directly at the edge of networks, where data is generated. This section explores the principles, architectures, and challenges of implementing edge AI and federated learning infrastructures, emphasizing their transformative impact on scalable machine learning systems.

Introduction to edge AI

Edge AI refers to the deployment of artificial intelligence models on edge devices, such as smartphones, IoT sensors, and autonomous vehicles, allowing for real-time data processing and decision-making closer to the data source. This paradigm shift from centralized cloud computing to decentralized edge computing addresses several critical challenges, including latency, bandwidth consumption, privacy, and reliability. By processing data locally, edge AI reduces the need for data transmission to centralized data centers, thereby minimizing latency and conserving network bandwidth. This capability is particularly beneficial for applications requiring immediate responses, such as autonomous driving, industrial automation, and smart healthcare.

Moreover, edge AI enhances data privacy and security by keeping sensitive information on local devices rather than transmitting it to external servers. This approach aligns with growing regulatory demands for data protection and privacy, such as the GDPR. Additionally, edge AI improves system reliability by ensuring that critical functionalities remain operational even in the absence of network connectivity, a crucial feature for remote or mobile applications.

Figure 8.3 is an architecture diagram of edge AI computing:

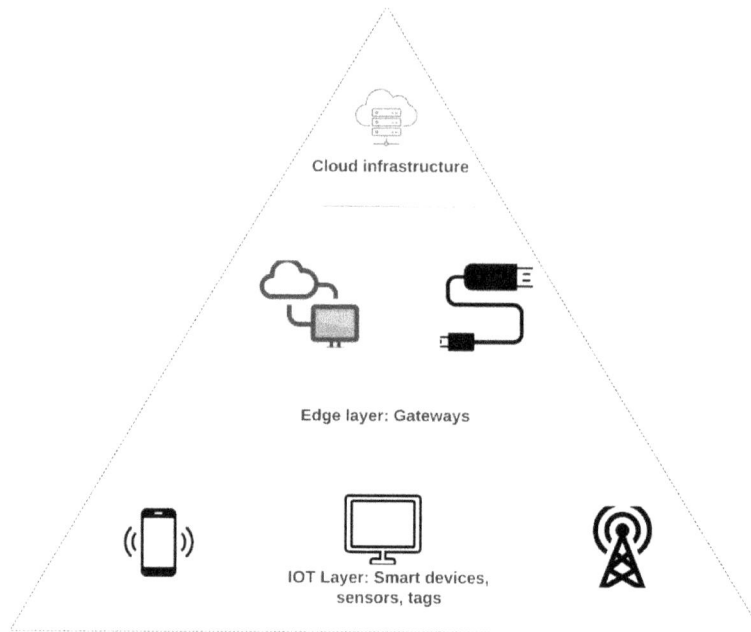

Figure 8.3: Edge AI computing architecture

Architecture for edge AI

Implementing edge AI requires specialized architecture that accommodates the computational constraints and resource limitations of edge devices. These architectures typically involve lightweight models optimized for efficient inference on resource-constrained hardware. Techniques such as model compression, quantization, and pruning are employed to reduce model size and computational complexity, enabling deployment on devices with limited processing power and memory capacity.

Hardware accelerators, such as GPUs, TPUs, and dedicated AI chips, play a crucial role in enhancing the performance of edge AI applications. These accelerators are designed to execute AI workloads efficiently, providing the necessary computational capabilities to support real-time inference. Additionally, edge computing frameworks, such as TensorFlow Lite, PyTorch Mobile, and Apache MXNet, offer tools and libraries for developing and deploying AI models on edge devices, facilitating the integration of AI capabilities into diverse application domains.

Introduction to federated learning

Federated learning is a distributed machine learning approach that enables model training across multiple decentralized devices or servers while keeping the training data localized.

This paradigm addresses the challenges of data privacy and security by ensuring that sensitive data remains on the devices where it is generated, with only model updates being shared and aggregated. Federated learning is particularly relevant in scenarios where data is distributed across numerous edge devices, such as smartphones, wearables, and IoT sensors.

The federated learning process involves multiple rounds of local model training on individual devices, followed by the aggregation of model updates on a central server. This server computes a global model by averaging the updates received from participating devices, which is then redistributed to the devices for further training. This iterative process continues until the global model converges to a satisfactory level of performance.

Architecture for federated learning

The implementation of federated learning infrastructures requires a robust architecture that supports secure communication, efficient model aggregation, and fault tolerance. Communication efficiency is a critical consideration, as federated learning involves frequent exchanges of model updates between devices and the central server. Techniques such as model compression, update frequency reduction, and differential privacy are employed to minimize communication overhead and enhance data privacy.

Security and privacy are paramount in federated learning, necessitating the use of encryption protocols and secure aggregation techniques to protect model updates during transmission. Differential privacy mechanisms can be integrated to ensure that individual data points cannot be inferred from the aggregated updates, further enhancing privacy protection.

Fault tolerance is another essential aspect of federated learning architectures, as devices may experience connectivity issues or drop out of the training process. Federated learning systems must be designed to handle such disruptions gracefully, ensuring that the global model continues to improve even in the presence of device failures or intermittent connectivity.

Challenges and future directions

While edge AI and federated learning offer significant advantages in terms of scalability, privacy, and efficiency, several challenges remain in their widespread adoption and implementation. One major challenge is the heterogeneity of edge devices, which vary widely in terms of computational capabilities, network connectivity, and power availability. Developing models and algorithms that can adapt to this diversity is crucial for the success of edge AI and federated learning initiatives.

Another challenge is the management of non-**independently and identically distributed (IID)** data across devices in federated learning. Data generated by edge devices often exhibit significant variability and bias, complicating the process of achieving a globally optimal model. Advanced algorithms and techniques are needed to address these issues and ensure robust model performance across diverse data distributions.

Looking forward, the integration of edge AI and federated learning with other emerging technologies, such as 5G networks and blockchain, presents exciting opportunities for enhancing the scalability and security of distributed AI systems. By leveraging the high-speed connectivity of 5G and the decentralized trust mechanisms of blockchain, practitioners can develop more resilient and efficient AI infrastructures that meet the demands of next-generation applications.

Edge AI and federated learning represent transformative advancements in the field of scalable machine learning infrastructure, enabling real-time data processing and privacy-preserving model training at the network's edge. By addressing the limitations of traditional centralized approaches, these technologies offer significant benefits in terms of latency reduction, bandwidth conservation, and data privacy. As the field continues to evolve, ongoing research and innovation in edge AI and federated learning will be essential to unlocking their full potential, driving the next wave of AI-driven transformation across industries.

Scaling deep learning systems and frameworks

The advent of deep learning has significantly transformed various domains, including computer vision, NLP, and robotics. The ability of deep learning models to learn complex patterns from vast amounts of data has driven their widespread adoption. However, this success is accompanied by substantial computational demands, often beyond the capacity of a single machine. As the scale of data and model complexity continues to grow, the need for scalable deep learning systems and frameworks becomes increasingly critical. This paper explores the methodologies and innovations necessary for scaling deep learning systems, addressing both hardware and software challenges and highlighting the latest advancements in this field.

Hardware acceleration and optimization

The scalability of deep learning systems is inextricably linked to the capabilities of the underlying hardware infrastructure. GPUs have become the cornerstone of deep learning acceleration due to their ability to perform parallel computations efficiently. Unlike traditional CPUs, which are optimized for sequential processing, GPUs are designed to handle thousands of operations simultaneously, making them ideal for the matrix and vector operations prevalent in deep learning.

In addition to GPUs, specialized hardware accelerators such as TPUs and **field programmable gate arrays (FPGAs)** have been developed to further enhance performance. TPUs, designed by Google, are tailored specifically for tensor operations, providing significant speedups for large-scale deep learning tasks. Their architecture allows for high throughput and efficiency, particularly in environments where power consumption and computational density are critical considerations. FPGAs, on the other hand, offer a reconfigurable architecture that can be customized to suit specific computational needs. This flexibility makes FPGAs suitable for a variety of applications, including those requiring low latency and high throughput.

Optimizing the use of hardware resources is crucial for achieving scalability in deep learning systems. Techniques such as mixed-precision training have been widely adopted to improve computational efficiency. Mixed-precision training involves using lower-precision arithmetic for certain operations, reducing memory consumption and increasing computational speed without significantly compromising model accuracy. This approach allows for larger models to be trained within the same hardware constraints, facilitating scalability.

Software frameworks and distributed training

While hardware provides the necessary computational power, software frameworks play an equally important role in scaling deep learning systems. Modern frameworks such as TensorFlow and PyTorch have been optimized to leverage the parallelism offered by GPUs and other accelerators, enabling efficient training and inference. These frameworks provide abstractions that simplify the implementation of complex neural networks, allowing researchers and practitioners to focus on model design and experimentation.

Distributed training is a key strategy for scaling deep learning systems across multiple nodes. This approach is essential for handling large datasets and models that exceed the capacity of a single machine. Two primary strategies are employed in distributed training: data parallelism and model parallelism. Data parallelism involves partitioning the dataset across multiple nodes, each of which processes a subset of the data and computes gradients independently. These gradients are then aggregated to update the global model parameters. This strategy is effective when the dataset size is the primary bottleneck.

Model parallelism, in contrast, involves distributing different parts of the model across multiple nodes. This approach allows for the training of extremely large models that cannot fit into the memory of a single node. Model parallelism requires careful coordination to ensure efficient communication and synchronization between nodes, as the dependencies between different parts of the model must be managed effectively.

Frameworks such as Horovod and NVIDIA's NCCL provide robust support for distributed training, implementing efficient communication protocols to minimize the overhead associated with gradient aggregation and synchronization. These frameworks enable seamless scaling across multiple GPUs and nodes, enhancing the scalability of deep learning systems.

Challenges in scaling deep learning systems

Despite significant advancements, several challenges remain in scaling deep learning systems. One major challenge is the communication overhead associated with distributed training. As the number of nodes increases, the volume of data exchanged between nodes can become a bottleneck, limiting the scalability of the system. Techniques such as gradient compression, which reduces the size of gradient updates, and asynchronous training, which relaxes synchronization constraints, are employed to mitigate communication overhead.

The efficient utilization of resources in heterogeneous environments is another challenge. Different nodes may have varying computational capabilities, and it is crucial to ensure that all nodes are effectively utilized to prevent bottlenecks and maximize throughput. Load balancing and dynamic resource allocation strategies are essential to address these challenges, enabling the efficient distribution of workloads across available resources.

The complexity of model architecture also constrains the scalability of deep learning systems. As models become deeper and more intricate, the computational demands increase, necessitating innovative approaches to model design and optimization. Techniques such as **neural architecture search** (**NAS**) and automated hyperparameter tuning are employed to identify efficient model architectures that balance performance and scalability. NAS involves the use of machine learning algorithms to explore the space of possible model architectures, identifying configurations that optimize performance while minimizing computational requirements.

Innovations and future directions

Recent innovations have focused on addressing the challenges of scaling deep learning systems, with a particular emphasis on optimizing both hardware and software components. One promising area of research is the development of new hardware architectures that provide greater computational efficiency and flexibility. For example, neuromorphic computing, which mimics the architecture of the human brain, offers the potential for significant improvements in energy efficiency and parallel processing capabilities. These advancements could enable the deployment of deep learning models in resource-constrained environments, such as edge devices and mobile platforms.

On the software side, advancements in distributed computing frameworks and algorithms continue to drive improvements in scalability. The integration of machine learning with **high-performance computing** (**HPC**) environments offers new opportunities for scaling deep learning systems. HPC platforms provide the infrastructure necessary for large-scale simulations and data processing, and their integration with deep learning frameworks can significantly enhance the scalability and efficiency of ML applications.

Additionally, the use of transfer learning and pre-trained models has become a popular strategy for scaling deep learning systems. By leveraging models that have been pre-trained on large datasets, practitioners can reduce the computational burden associated with training from scratch, enabling faster deployment and iteration. This approach is particularly beneficial in domains where data is scarce or expensive to collect.

Scaling deep learning systems and frameworks is a multifaceted challenge that requires advancements in both hardware and software components. By leveraging hardware accelerators, optimizing memory and bandwidth utilization, and employing distributed training strategies, practitioners can enhance the scalability of deep learning applications. Despite the challenges associated with communication overhead, resource utilization, and model complexity, ongoing research and innovation continue to drive the development of scalable deep learning systems. As the field progresses, the ability to effectively scale deep learning models will unlock new opportunities and applications, further solidifying the transformative impact of deep learning across industries.

Conclusion

The exploration of scalable machine learning infrastructure in this chapter underscores the intricate interplay between technological advancements and methodologies necessary for managing large-scale ML workloads. As models grow in complexity and data volumes expand, robust infrastructure becomes essential. Distributed training architectures were examined, highlighting the significance of data and model parallelism in optimizing computational efficiency. By distributing workloads across multiple nodes, these architectures reduce training times and enhance scalability. The chapter also addressed model serving and inference strategies, emphasizing the importance of high throughput and low latency in production environments. These capabilities are crucial for delivering real-time predictions, ensuring seamless transitions from research to operational settings.

The role of AutoML and hyperparameter optimization was explored, revealing their impact on streamlining model development. AutoML democratizes access to machine learning by automating model selection and tuning, allowing practitioners to focus on strategic problem-solving. Additionally, MLOps practices were introduced, applying DevOps principles to the ML lifecycle to ensure continuous integration, deployment, and monitoring, thus enhancing reliability and compliance. Emerging paradigms such as edge AI and federated learning, alongside the scaling of deep learning systems, were discussed. These approaches address challenges related to data privacy, real-time processing, and model complexity, paving the way for scalable and efficient ML solutions across diverse industries. As machine learning evolves, integrating these elements will be crucial for unlocking AI's full potential.

The next chapter will look into real-time AI systems and stream processing, exploring architectures and strategies for low-latency, high throughput processing. This will include discussions on online learning, adaptive models, and integrating real-time features into ML workflows, setting the stage for responsive AI applications in dynamic environments.

Join our Discord space

Join our Discord workspace for latest updates, offers, tech happenings around the world, new releases, and sessions with the authors:

CHAPTER 9

Real-time AI Systems and Stream Processing

Introduction

The advent of real-time **artificial intelligence** (**AI**) systems has marked a significant milestone in the evolution of data-driven technologies, enabling organizations to process and analyze data instantaneously. As industries increasingly rely on data to drive decision-making, the ability to extract timely insights from continuous data streams has become a critical competitive advantage. This chapter looks into the intricate world of real-time AI systems and stream processing, exploring their architecture, methodologies, and applications across various domains.

The foundation of real-time AI systems lies in their capacity to handle high-velocity data streams, a capability that traditional batch processing systems lack. These systems are designed to ingest, process, and output data with minimal latency, ensuring that insights are delivered promptly and actions can be taken in real-time. The integration of advanced stream processing frameworks, such as Apache Kafka, Apache Flink, and Apache Spark Streaming, provides the necessary infrastructure to achieve this level of performance, enabling the seamless flow of data through complex processing pipelines. A key aspect of real-time AI systems is their architectural design, which must support scalability, fault tolerance, and low-latency processing. This chapter examines the architectural components and design principles that underpin successful real-time AI deployments, highlighting the role of distributed computing frameworks and microservices architectures.

Real-time feature engineering and latency management are critical components of these systems, ensuring that features are both timely and relevant while minimizing processing delays. The chapter explores various techniques employed to achieve these objectives, such as sliding windows, online learning, and in-memory processing.

In summary, this chapter provides a comprehensive overview of real-time AI systems and stream processing, offering insights into their design, implementation, and application. As the demand for real-time AI continues to grow, understanding these systems' intricacies will be essential for researchers and practitioners aiming to harness the full potential of continuous data streams.

Structure

The chapter covers the following topics:

- Architectures for real-time AI systems
- Stream processing frameworks with AI capabilities
- Online learning and adaptive models for streaming
- Real-time feature engineering techniques
- Latency management in AI-driven stream processing
- Scalability challenges in real-time AI
- Complex event processing for AI applications
- Use cases and best practices for AI deployment

Objectives

The primary objective of this chapter is to provide a thorough exploration of real-time AI systems and stream processing, emphasizing their transformative impact on data-driven decision-making across various industries. This chapter aims to elucidate the fundamental principles and architectures that underpin real-time AI systems, offering a detailed examination of the technologies and methodologies that enable the processing of high-velocity data streams with minimal latency.

A key focus of this chapter is to dissect the architectural components and design strategies that facilitate the scalability, fault tolerance, and efficiency of real-time AI systems. By delving into distributed computing frameworks and microservices architectures, the chapter seeks to highlight how these technologies contribute to the seamless distribution of processing workloads, ensuring that systems remain responsive even as data volumes increase.

Another objective is to explore the methodologies employed in real-time feature engineering and latency management. The chapter aims to provide insights into techniques such as sliding windows, online learning, and in-memory processing, which are crucial for maintaining the accuracy and relevance of AI models in dynamic environments. These methodologies are dissected to understand their role in minimizing latency and enhancing the timeliness of insights.

Furthermore, the chapter seeks to address the scalability challenges inherent in real-time AI systems, examining the solutions that have been developed to overcome these obstacles. By investigating cloud-based solutions and containerization technologies, the chapter aims to demonstrate how organizations can achieve the necessary elasticity and scalability to accommodate fluctuating workloads.

Architectures for real-time AI systems

The advent of real-time AI systems marks a pivotal shift in the landscape of data processing and analytics. These systems are designed to handle data streams that continuously evolve, necessitating architectures that can process, analyze, and respond to data in near real-time. The architecture of real-time AI systems must be robust, scalable, and capable of integrating seamlessly with various data sources and processing frameworks. This section explores the foundational elements of real-time AI architecture, emphasizing their design principles, components, and the challenges they address.

Design principles of real-time AI architectures

At the core of designing real-time AI architectures is the principle of low-latency processing. Real-time systems are characterized by their ability to ingest, process, and output data with minimal delay. To achieve this, architectures must be optimized for speed, often leveraging in-memory data processing and parallel computing techniques. Scalability is another critical design principle, as real-time systems must handle varying data loads efficiently. This requires architecture that can dynamically allocate resources and scale horizontally across distributed environments.

Fault tolerance and reliability are also paramount. Real-time AI systems must maintain operational continuity despite hardware failures or network disruptions. This is typically achieved through redundant components and failover mechanisms that ensure data integrity and system availability. Furthermore, architecture must support seamless integration with existing data infrastructure, enabling interoperability across diverse platforms and technologies.

Core components of real-time AI architectures

Real-time AI architectures are composed of several interconnected components, each serving a specific function in the data processing pipeline. The data ingestion layer is responsible for capturing data from various sources, such as IoT devices, social media feeds, and transactional systems. This layer often employs stream processing frameworks like Apache Kafka or Apache Flink, which provide robust capabilities for handling high throughput data streams.

Following data ingestion, the processing layer performs real-time analytics and decision-making. This layer utilizes distributed computing frameworks, such as Apache Spark or Apache Storm, to execute complex algorithms and machine learning models at scale. The choice of framework depends on the specific requirements of the application, including latency constraints and computational complexity.

The storage layer is crucial for maintaining state and persisting data for future analysis. Real-time systems often employ a combination of in-memory databases and distributed storage solutions, such as Apache Cassandra or Amazon DynamoDB, to balance speed and durability. This layer must support efficient data retrieval and update operations to facilitate real-time analytics.

Finally, the output and visualization layer presents processed data to end-users or downstream systems. This layer may involve dashboards, alerting systems, or automated actions triggered by AI insights. The architecture must ensure that output is delivered promptly and accurately, enabling users to make informed decisions based on real-time data. *Figure 9.1* demonstrates the core components of a real-time AI system:

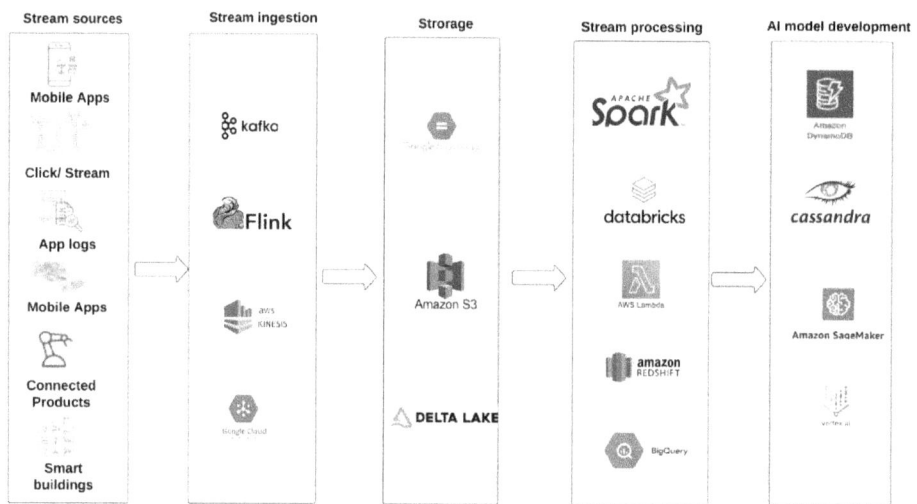

Figure 9.1: *Core components of a real-time AI system*

Challenges in real-time AI architectures

Designing and implementing real-time AI architecture presents several challenges. One of the primary challenges is managing data velocity and volume. Real-time systems must handle continuous data streams that can vary significantly in size and speed. This requires architectures that can efficiently process large volumes of data without compromising performance.

Latency management is another critical challenge. Real-time AI systems must minimize processing delays to deliver timely insights. This involves optimizing data flow across the architecture, reducing bottlenecks, and employing techniques such as data partitioning and parallel processing.

Data quality and consistency are also vital considerations. Real-time systems must ensure that data is accurate and reliable, as errors can propagate quickly and affect decision-making. This necessitates robust data validation and cleansing mechanisms integrated into the architecture.

Security and compliance are additional challenges, particularly in domains where sensitive data is processed. Real-time AI architectures must incorporate security measures, such as encryption and access controls, to protect data integrity and privacy. Compliance with regulatory requirements, such as GDPR or CCPA, must also be considered in architecture design.

Architecture for real-time AI systems represents a critical advancement in the field of data processing and analytics. By adhering to design principles of low-latency processing, scalability, and fault tolerance, these architectures enable organizations to harness the power of real-time data for enhanced decision-making. The integration of core components, including data ingestion, processing, storage, and output, forms the backbone of these systems, facilitating seamless data flow and analytics. Despite the challenges associated with data velocity, latency management, and security, real-time AI architecture offers transformative potential across various industries, paving the way for more responsive and intelligent applications. As technology continues to evolve, the development and refinement of real-time AI architectures will remain a focal point for researchers and practitioners alike.

Stream processing frameworks with AI capabilities

Stream processing frameworks are at the heart of real-time AI systems, enabling the continuous analysis and processing of data streams. These frameworks provide the necessary infrastructure to handle high throughput, low-latency data, making them indispensable for applications that require immediate insights and actions. In this section, we look into the architecture and functionalities of leading stream processing frameworks, examining their capabilities in supporting AI workloads. We explore how these frameworks integrate with AI models, facilitating the deployment of intelligent applications that respond to real-time data.

Architecture of stream processing frameworks

Stream processing frameworks are designed to process data in motion, as opposed to traditional batch processing systems that handle static datasets. At their core, these frameworks consist of several key components: data ingestion, processing, and output. The data ingestion component is responsible for capturing and queuing incoming data streams from various sources, such as sensors, logs, or message brokers. This component ensures that data is ingested in a timely manner, ready for processing.

The processing component is where the core logic of the framework resides. It typically consists of a distributed, fault-tolerant architecture that can scale horizontally to accommodate varying data loads. This component executes a series of transformations and computations on the data, such as filtering, aggregation, and enrichment. The processing logic is often defined using a high-level programming model that abstracts the complexities of distributed computing, allowing developers to focus on the business logic.

The output component is responsible for delivering processed data to downstream systems or end-users. This component can interface with a variety of data sinks, including databases, data warehouses, or visualization tools. The architecture of stream processing frameworks is designed to ensure that data flows seamlessly from ingestion to output, with minimal latency and maximum reliability.

Integration with AI models

One of the most significant advancements in stream processing frameworks is their ability to integrate with AI models, enabling the deployment of intelligent applications that leverage real-time data. This integration is achieved through several mechanisms, including model serving, online learning, and adaptive processing.

Model serving involves deploying pre-trained AI models within the stream processing framework, allowing them to make predictions or classifications on incoming data streams. This approach is particularly useful for applications that require immediate decision-making, such as fraud detection or recommendation systems. Stream processing frameworks provide APIs and libraries that facilitate the integration of AI models, ensuring that they can be invoked efficiently within the processing pipeline. Online learning is another capability that enhances the AI potential of stream processing frameworks. Unlike traditional batch learning, which requires static datasets, online learning allows models to be updated incrementally as new data arrives. This enables AI systems to adapt to changing data patterns and maintain high accuracy over time. Stream processing frameworks support online learning by providing mechanisms for model updates and versioning, ensuring that AI models remain relevant and effective.

Adaptive processing is a capability that allows stream processing frameworks to adjust their behavior based on the context or state of the data stream. This is particularly useful for AI applications that require dynamic decision-making, such as adaptive traffic management or personalized content delivery. Stream processing frameworks enable adaptive processing by providing access to contextual information and state management APIs, allowing AI models to tailor their predictions based on the current environment.

Leading stream processing frameworks

Several stream processing frameworks have emerged as leaders in the field, each offering unique features and capabilities tailored for AI workloads. Apache Kafka, Apache Flink, and Apache Spark Streaming are among the most prominent frameworks, widely adopted across various industries for their robustness and scalability.

Apache Kafka is a distributed streaming platform that excels in data ingestion and message brokering. It is designed to handle high throughput data streams with low latency, making it ideal for real-time applications. Kafka's architecture is based on a publish-subscribe model, where data producers publish messages to topics, and consumers subscribe to these topics to receive data. Kafka's integration with AI models is facilitated through its stream processing library, Kafka Streams, which provides a lightweight and scalable processing layer for real-time analytics. Apache Flink is a powerful stream processing framework known for its stateful processing capabilities and event-time semantics. Flink's architecture is designed to handle complex event processing and real-time analytics, making it suitable for applications that require sophisticated data transformations. Flink's integration with AI models is achieved through its machine learning library, Flink ML, which supports a range of algorithms for real-time prediction and classification. Flink's ability to manage state efficiently allows AI models to maintain context and adapt to changing data patterns seamlessly. Apache Spark Streaming is an extension of the Apache Spark platform, designed for processing live data streams. Spark Streaming's architecture is built on a micro-batch processing model, where data streams are divided into small batches for processing. This approach allows Spark Streaming to leverage Spark's powerful batch processing capabilities while maintaining low latency. Spark Streaming's integration with AI models is facilitated through its MLlib library, which provides a comprehensive set of machine learning algorithms for real-time analytics. Spark Streaming's compatibility with the broader Spark ecosystem enables seamless integration with other data processing and storage solutions.

Table 9.1 compares the capabilities of these stream processing frameworks on multiple dimensions:

Dimension	Apache Kafka	Apache Flink	Spark Streaming
Architecture and processing model	Primarily recognized as a distributed streaming platform excelling in data ingestion and message brokering. Built on a publish-subscribe model, enabling continuous processing through Kafka Streams. Suitable for low-latency data processing and applications requiring immediate insights.	Designed as a dedicated stream processing framework with stateful processing and event-time semantics. Its architecture supports both stream and batch processing, offering flexibility in handling various data workloads. Flink's continuous data flow processing model enables real-time analytics with precise event-time processing capabilities.	Extension of Apache Spark adopts a micro-batch processing model. Divides streams into small batches, leveraging Spark's powerful batch capabilities while maintaining low latency. Integrated with the broader Spark ecosystem.

Dimension	Apache Kafka	Apache Flink	Spark Streaming
Scalability and fault tolerance	Highly scalable, capable of handling millions of messages/second with low latency through distributed architecture and horizontal scaling. Fault tolerance via data replication.	Supports dynamic scaling of stateful applications across distributed environments. Handles large-scale data processing with low latency. Fault tolerance via a checkpointing mechanism.	Scales across large clusters via Spark's distributed processing. Handles high throughput streams with horizontal scaling. Fault tolerance through a lineage-based recovery mechanism, periodically saving state to durable storage.
Integration with AI models	Integrates via Kafka Streams, supporting deployment of pre-trained models for real-time prediction and classification. Lightweight processing enables immediate insights.	Robust AI integration via Flink ML library. Supports online learning and adaptive processing through state management, ideal for dynamic model updates.	Leverages Spark's MLlib for real-time analytics. Supports wide range of ML algorithms and advanced machine learning workflows. Tight integration with the Spark ecosystem.

Table 9.1: *Comparison of streaming frameworks*

Stream processing frameworks play a crucial role in enabling real-time AI systems, providing the infrastructure necessary to process and analyze continuous data streams. Their architecture, characterized by components for data ingestion, processing, and output, ensures efficient data flow with minimal latency. The integration of AI models within these frameworks enhances their capabilities, allowing for intelligent decision-making and adaptive processing. Leading frameworks such as Apache Kafka, Apache Flink, and Apache Spark Streaming offer robust solutions for deploying AI workloads in real-time environments, each with unique features tailored to specific use cases. As the demand for real-time AI applications continues to grow, stream processing frameworks will remain a vital component of modern data architecture, driving innovation and enabling new possibilities across various industries.

Online learning and adaptive models for streaming

The dynamic nature of streaming data presents unique challenges and opportunities for AI systems. Traditional batch learning methods are often inadequate for real-time applications due to their reliance on static datasets. In contrast, online learning and adaptive models offer a robust framework for handling continuous data streams, enabling AI systems to learn and adapt in real-time. This section explores the principles, methodologies, and applications of online learning and adaptive models in the context of streaming data, emphasizing their significance in modern AI architectures.

Principles of online learning

Online learning is a machine learning paradigm where models are trained incrementally as new data becomes available. Unlike batch learning, which processes data in fixed-size chunks, online learning continuously updates the model with each new data point. This approach is particularly advantageous in environments where data arrives sequentially and must be processed in real-time. The primary goal of online learning is to maintain model accuracy and relevance by continuously adapting to evolving data patterns.

One of the core principles of online learning is the minimization of memory and computational resources. Online algorithms are designed to operate efficiently with limited resources, making them suitable for deployment in resource-constrained environments such as edge devices or IoT networks. Additionally, online learning emphasizes the importance of quick adaptation to changes in data distribution. This is achieved through mechanisms such as concept drift detection, which identifies shifts in the underlying data patterns and triggers model updates accordingly.

Methodologies for online learning

Several methodologies have been developed to facilitate online learning, each with its own strengths and limitations. One of the most widely used approaches is **Stochastic Gradient Descent (SGD)**, which updates model parameters incrementally based on each new data point. SGD is particularly effective in online learning due to its simplicity and scalability, allowing models to be trained efficiently on large-scale streaming data.

Another popular methodology is the use of ensemble learning techniques, where multiple models are trained simultaneously, and their predictions are combined to improve accuracy. In the context of online learning, ensemble methods such as online bagging and boosting have been adapted to handle streaming data. These methods leverage the diversity of models to enhance robustness against concept drift and improve generalization.

Adaptive filtering is another methodology employed in online learning, particularly in signal processing applications. Adaptive filters adjust their parameters in real-time based on incoming data, making them suitable for tasks such as noise reduction or signal enhancement. The **least mean squares (LMS)** algorithm is a classic example of an adaptive filter used in online learning scenarios.

Adaptive models in streaming data

Adaptive models extend the capabilities of online learning by incorporating mechanisms that allow them to adjust their structure and parameters dynamically. These models are particularly useful in environments where data characteristics change over time, necessitating continuous adaptation. Adaptive models can be categorized into several types, including parameter-adaptive models, structure-adaptive models, and context-adaptive models.

Parameter-adaptive models focus on adjusting the parameters of the model in response to changes in data distribution. Techniques such as adaptive learning rates or regularization parameters are employed to ensure that the model remains responsive to new data while avoiding overfitting. These models are well-suited for applications where data patterns exhibit gradual changes over time.

Structure-adaptive models, on the other hand, allow for changes in the model architecture itself. This includes adding or removing neurons in neural networks or adjusting the topology of decision trees. Structure-adaptive models are particularly effective in scenarios where data complexity varies significantly, requiring the model to adjust its capacity dynamically.

Context-adaptive models incorporate external contextual information to enhance their predictive capabilities. This includes factors such as time of day, location, or user preferences, which can influence the model's predictions. By integrating contextual information, these models can provide more accurate and personalized predictions, making them valuable in applications such as recommendation systems or personalized marketing.

Applications of online learning and adaptive models

The application of online learning and adaptive models spans a wide range of domains, from finance and healthcare to autonomous systems and cybersecurity. In the financial sector, online learning is used for real-time trading and fraud detection, where models must respond quickly to market changes and identify anomalies in transaction patterns. Adaptive models enable financial institutions to maintain high levels of accuracy and reliability, even in volatile market conditions.

In healthcare, online learning and adaptive models are employed for personalized medicine and real-time patient monitoring. These models can continuously update their predictions based on new patient data, providing clinicians with timely insights and recommendations. The ability to adapt to individual patient characteristics and treatment responses makes these models particularly valuable in precision medicine.

Autonomous systems, such as self-driving cars and drones, rely heavily on online learning and adaptive models to navigate dynamic environments. These models process sensor data in real-time, allowing the system to adapt to changing road conditions, obstacles, and traffic patterns. The continuous learning capability ensures that autonomous systems can improve their performance over time, enhancing safety and reliability.

In cybersecurity, online learning is used for intrusion detection and malware classification, where models must identify and respond to threats in real-time. Adaptive models enable security systems to adjust their detection strategies based on evolving threat landscapes, ensuring robust protection against cyberattacks.

Online learning and adaptive models represent a significant advancement in the field of AI, offering a powerful framework for processing streaming data in real-time. By continuously updating and adapting to new information, these models maintain high levels of accuracy and relevance, making them indispensable in dynamic environments. The methodologies and applications explored in this section highlight the versatility and potential of online learning and adaptive models across various domains. As the demand for real-time AI systems continues to grow, the development and refinement of these models will remain a focal point for researchers and practitioners, driving innovation and enabling new possibilities in the era of streaming data.

Real-time feature engineering techniques

Feature engineering is a critical step in the development of machine learning models, as it involves transforming raw data into meaningful features that can enhance model performance. In the context of real-time AI systems, feature engineering must be conducted on-the-fly, processing data streams as they arrive to extract relevant features efficiently. This section looks into the methodologies and challenges of real-time feature engineering, exploring techniques that enable the extraction and transformation of features in real-time environments.

Importance of real-time feature engineering

Real-time feature engineering is essential for applications that require immediate insights and decision-making. In such scenarios, the ability to process and transform data into actionable features directly impacts the effectiveness of the AI system. The primary objective of real-time feature engineering is to ensure that features are both timely and relevant, capturing the dynamic nature of streaming data. This requires a balance between computational efficiency and the richness of the features extracted, as overly complex transformations can introduce latency and hinder real-time processing.

Moreover, real-time feature engineering plays a vital role in adapting models to changing data patterns. By continuously updating features based on new data, models can maintain their accuracy and relevance over time. This adaptability is particularly crucial in environments characterized by non-stationary data distributions, where traditional feature engineering methods may fall short.

Techniques for real-time feature engineering

Several techniques have been developed to facilitate real-time feature engineering, each tailored to specific data characteristics and application requirements. One of the foundational techniques is the use of sliding windows and time-based aggregations. Sliding windows allow data streams to be partitioned into manageable segments, enabling the computation of aggregate statistics such as moving averages, sums, or counts. These aggregates serve as features that capture temporal trends and patterns, providing valuable context for real-time decision-making.

Another technique involves the use of feature extraction algorithms that operate directly on streaming data. These algorithms, such as online **principal component analysis (PCA)** or incremental clustering, are designed to update feature representations incrementally as new data arrives. By maintaining a compact and evolving representation of the data, these algorithms enable the extraction of features that reflect the current state of the data stream.

Real-time feature engineering also employs techniques for handling categorical data, such as one-hot encoding or embedding representations. In streaming environments, categorical features may evolve over time, necessitating dynamic encoding strategies that can accommodate new categories as they emerge. Embedding representations, in particular, offers a powerful approach for capturing semantic relationships between categories, allowing for more nuanced feature representations.

Feature selection is another critical aspect of real-time feature engineering. As data streams can generate a vast number of potential features, selecting the most relevant ones is essential to avoid overfitting and reduce computational overhead. Techniques such as online feature selection or adaptive feature pruning are employed to identify and retain the most informative features, ensuring that the model remains efficient and interpretable.

Challenges in real-time feature engineering

Real-time feature engineering presents several challenges that must be addressed to ensure the effectiveness of AI systems. One of the primary challenges is managing the trade-off between feature complexity and computational efficiency. Complex feature transformations can provide richer representations but may introduce latency, undermining the real-time capabilities of the system. Balancing this trade-off requires careful consideration of the computational resources available and the latency constraints of the application.

Another challenge is dealing with concept drift, where the statistical properties of the data stream change over time. Concept drift can render previously engineered features obsolete, necessitating continuous monitoring and adaptation of the feature set. Techniques such as drift detection and adaptive feature engineering are employed to identify and respond to changes in data distribution, ensuring that features remain relevant and informative.

Data quality is also a significant concern in real-time feature engineering. Streaming data is often noisy and incomplete, requiring robust preprocessing techniques to ensure the reliability of the features extracted. This includes handling missing values, outlier detection, and data normalization, all of which must be performed in real-time to maintain the integrity of the feature set.

Applications for real-time feature engineering

Real-time feature engineering is applied across a wide range of domains, each with its unique requirements and challenges. In finance, real-time feature engineering is used for algorithmic trading and fraud detection, where timely and accurate features are critical for making informed decisions. By continuously updating features based on market data and transaction patterns, financial institutions can enhance their predictive capabilities and mitigate risks.

In healthcare, real-time feature engineering is employed for patient monitoring and early warning systems. By extracting features from continuous streams of physiological data, healthcare providers can detect anomalies and intervene promptly, improving patient outcomes. The ability to adapt feature representations based on individual patient characteristics further enhances the personalization of healthcare interventions.

In the realm of autonomous systems, real-time feature engineering is crucial for navigation and control. Autonomous vehicles, for example, rely on real-time features derived from sensor data to make split-second decisions in dynamic environments. The continuous adaptation of features ensures that the vehicle can respond effectively to changing road conditions, obstacles, and traffic patterns.

Real-time feature engineering is a cornerstone of modern AI systems, enabling the extraction and transformation of features from streaming data in real-time. By employing techniques such as sliding windows, online algorithms, and adaptive feature selection, AI systems can maintain their accuracy and relevance in dynamic environments. The challenges of computational efficiency, concept drift, and data quality highlight the complexity of real-time feature engineering, necessitating ongoing research and innovation. As real-time applications continue to expand across various domains, the development of robust and efficient feature engineering techniques will remain a critical focus for researchers and practitioners, driving the advancement of intelligent systems capable of processing and responding to continuous data streams.

Latency management in AI-driven stream processing

In the realm of AI-driven stream processing, latency management is a critical concern that directly impacts the performance and effectiveness of real-time applications. Latency, defined as the time delay between data ingestion and the generation of actionable insights, must be minimized to ensure timely and accurate decision-making. This section explores the principles, strategies, and challenges associated with latency management in AI-driven stream processing, emphasizing its significance in the design and implementation of real-time systems.

Principles of latency management

The primary principle of latency management is the optimization of data flow through the processing pipeline. This involves reducing the time taken for data to traverse from ingestion to output, ensuring that insights are delivered promptly. Achieving low latency requires a holistic approach that considers the architecture, algorithms, and infrastructure supporting the stream processing system. The goal is to create a seamless data flow that minimizes bottlenecks and maximizes throughput, enabling real-time responsiveness.

Another key principle is the prioritization of critical tasks within the processing pipeline. In many real-time applications, certain tasks or computations are more time-sensitive than others. By identifying and prioritizing these tasks, systems can allocate resources more effectively, ensuring that latency-sensitive operations are completed swiftly. This requires a deep understanding of the application domain and the specific requirements of the AI models employed.

Strategies for latency reduction

Several strategies have been developed to reduce latency in AI-driven stream processing, each addressing different aspects of the processing pipeline. One of the most effective strategies is the use of in-memory data processing. By storing and processing data in memory rather than on disk, systems can significantly reduce I/O latency, accelerating data access and computation. In-memory processing frameworks, such as Apache Ignite or Redis, are commonly employed to facilitate this approach, providing high-speed data retrieval and manipulation capabilities.

Parallel processing is another strategy that can dramatically reduce latency. By distributing data processing tasks across multiple nodes or processors, systems can perform computations concurrently, reducing the overall processing time. This approach leverages the power of distributed computing frameworks, such as Apache Spark or Apache Flink, which are designed to handle large-scale data processing with low latency. Parallel processing is particularly effective for tasks that can be decomposed into independent subtasks, allowing for efficient resource utilization.

Data partitioning is also a crucial strategy for latency reduction. By dividing data streams into smaller, manageable partitions, systems can process each partition independently, reducing contention and improving throughput. This approach is often combined with load balancing techniques to ensure that processing resources are evenly distributed across partitions, preventing bottlenecks and maintaining consistent performance.

Challenges in latency management

Despite the availability of various strategies, latency management in AI-driven stream processing presents several challenges that must be addressed to achieve optimal performance. One of the primary challenges is the inherent trade-off between latency and accuracy. In many cases, reducing latency may involve simplifying computations or using approximate algorithms, which can impact the accuracy of the results. Balancing this trade-off requires careful consideration of the application requirements and the acceptable levels of accuracy and latency.

Another challenge is the variability of data streams, which can fluctuate in volume and velocity over time. This variability can lead to unpredictable latency spikes, particularly in systems with limited scalability or resource constraints. To address this challenge, systems must be designed with elasticity in mind, allowing them to scale dynamically in response to changing data loads. This involves the use of cloud-based infrastructure and containerization technologies, such as Kubernetes, which provide the flexibility and scalability needed to handle variable workloads.

Network latency is an additional challenge that can impact the performance of distributed stream processing systems. Data must often be transmitted across multiple nodes or data centers, introducing delays that can accumulate and affect overall latency. To mitigate network latency, systems can employ techniques such as data locality optimization, which aims to process data as close to its source as possible, reducing the need for data transmission. Additionally, the use of high-speed networking technologies and protocols can help minimize transmission delays, ensuring efficient data flow across the network.

Applications of latency management

Effective latency management is crucial in a wide range of real-time applications, where timely insights and actions are essential. In financial trading, for example, latency management is paramount, as even microsecond delays can result in significant financial losses. By optimizing data flow and employing high-speed processing techniques, trading systems can execute transactions swiftly, capitalizing on market opportunities and mitigating risks.

In healthcare, latency management plays a vital role in patient monitoring and emergency response systems. Real-time processing of physiological data enables healthcare providers to detect anomalies and intervene promptly, improving patient outcomes. The ability to deliver timely alerts and recommendations is contingent upon minimizing latency throughout the processing pipeline.

Autonomous vehicles also rely heavily on effective latency management to ensure safe and reliable operation. These systems must process sensor data in real-time to make split-second decisions, such as obstacle avoidance and path planning. By employing low-latency processing techniques, autonomous vehicles can navigate complex environments with precision and agility, enhancing safety and efficiency.

Latency management is a critical component of AI-driven stream processing, directly influencing the performance and effectiveness of real-time applications. By adhering to principles of optimized data flow and task prioritization, and employing strategies such as in-memory processing, parallel processing, and data partitioning, systems can achieve low latency and deliver timely insights. However, challenges such as the trade-off between latency and accuracy, data stream variability, and network latency must be carefully managed to ensure optimal performance. As real-time applications continue to expand across various domains, the development of robust latency management techniques will remain a focal point for researchers and practitioners, driving the advancement of intelligent systems capable of processing and responding to continuous data streams with minimal delay.

Scalability challenges in real-time AI

The increasing demand for real-time AI systems has brought scalability to the forefront of challenges faced by researchers and practitioners. As data volumes grow and applications become more complex, ensuring that AI systems can scale to meet these demands is both a technical and architectural challenge. This section explores the scalability challenges inherent in real-time AI systems and examines the solutions that have been developed to address these issues. The discussion is framed within the context of data processing, model training, and infrastructure management, providing a comprehensive overview of the strategies employed to achieve scalability.

Understanding the challenges

Scalability in real-time AI systems is primarily challenged by the exponential growth in data volumes and the need for rapid processing. The continuous influx of data from diverse sources, such as IoT devices, social media feeds, and transactional systems, requires architectures that can handle high throughput data streams without compromising performance. This necessitates the development of systems that can scale horizontally, distributing workloads across multiple nodes to maintain efficiency and responsiveness. However, achieving such scalability is complicated by the need to preserve data consistency and integrity across distributed environments.

Another significant scalability challenge is the training and deployment of AI models in real-time settings. Traditional model training approaches, which often involve batch processing of large datasets, are ill-suited for real-time applications where models must be updated continuously. The need for incremental learning and model adaptation introduces additional complexity, as systems must balance the computational demands of training with the latency constraints of real-time processing. This challenge is further exacerbated by the heterogeneity of data sources and the variability of data streams, which require models to be both flexible and robust.

Infrastructure management is also a critical aspect of scalability in real-time AI systems. The dynamic nature of real-time applications necessitates infrastructure that can scale elastically in response to changing workloads. This involves managing resources efficiently to prevent bottlenecks and ensure that the system can accommodate peak loads without degradation in performance. The integration of cloud-based solutions and containerization technologies has provided some relief, but the complexity of orchestrating distributed resources remains a formidable challenge.

Solutions for scalability in real-time AI

To address the scalability challenges in real-time AI systems, several solutions have been developed, each targeting different aspects of the problem. One of the most effective solutions is the adoption of distributed computing frameworks, such as Apache Kafka, Apache Flink, and Apache Spark. These frameworks provide the infrastructure necessary to process large-scale data streams in parallel, distributing workloads across multiple nodes to achieve high throughput and low latency. By leveraging the capabilities of these frameworks, real-time AI systems can scale horizontally, accommodating increasing data volumes and complexity.

In addition to distributed computing, the use of microservices architecture has emerged as a powerful solution for scalability. Microservices decompose applications into smaller, independent services that can be developed, deployed, and scaled independently. This modular approach allows real-time AI systems to scale specific components as needed, optimizing resource utilization and enhancing system flexibility. The integration of microservices with containerization technologies, such as Docker and Kubernetes, further facilitates the orchestration and management of distributed resources, enabling seamless scaling and deployment.

For model training and adaptation, online learning and incremental training techniques provide a scalable solution. These approaches allow models to be updated continuously as new data arrives, eliminating the need for batch retraining and reducing the computational overhead associated with traditional training methods. By employing algorithms that support online learning, such as stochastic gradient descent and adaptive filtering, real-time AI systems can maintain model accuracy and relevance in dynamic environments.

Cloud computing has also played a pivotal role in addressing scalability challenges. The elasticity and scalability offered by cloud platforms, such as **Amazon Web Services** (**AWS**), Microsoft Azure, and **Google Cloud Platform** (**GCP**), enable real-time AI systems to scale resources dynamically in response to changing workloads. Cloud-based solutions provide the infrastructure necessary to handle peak loads, ensuring that systems remain responsive and efficient. Additionally, the integration of serverless computing models allows developers to focus on application logic without the burden of managing the underlying infrastructure, further enhancing scalability.

Complex event processing for AI applications

In the rapidly evolving landscape of real-time AI systems, **complex event processing** (**CEP**) has emerged as a pivotal technology, enabling the detection and analysis of patterns and relationships within streams of data. CEP provides the capability to process and analyze multiple event streams in real-time, extracting actionable insights that drive decision-making in AI applications. This section looks into the principles, methodologies, and applications of CEP within the context of AI, highlighting its significance and potential to enhance the capabilities of intelligent systems.

Principles of complex event processing

CEP is grounded in the principle of identifying meaningful patterns and correlations within streams of events. Unlike traditional data processing systems that focus on individual data points, CEP operates on the premise that valuable insights often arise from the relationships and interactions between events. This paradigm shift allows CEP to detect complex patterns, such as sequences, aggregations, and temporal relationships, that are not readily apparent in isolated data points.

At the core of CEP is the event-driven architecture, which enables the continuous processing of data as it flows through the system. This architecture is characterized by the use of event streams, which are sequences of data points that represent occurrences or changes of state in the system. CEP systems are designed to ingest these streams and apply a set of predefined rules or queries to identify patterns of interest. The real-time nature of CEP ensures that insights are generated promptly, allowing AI applications to respond to changing conditions with agility and precision.

Methodologies for complex event processing

The methodologies employed in CEP are diverse, reflecting the complexity and variability of the patterns being detected. One of the foundational methodologies is the use of event pattern matching, which involves defining rules or templates that describe the structure of the patterns of interest. These patterns can be simple, such as detecting a specific sequence of events, or complex, involving multiple conditions and constraints. The pattern matching process is typically implemented using query languages, such as the **event processing language** (**EPL**), which provide a high-level abstraction for defining and executing event patterns.

Temporal reasoning is another critical methodology in CEP, enabling the analysis of time-dependent patterns and relationships. Temporal reasoning involves the use of time windows, which define the temporal scope within which events are considered for pattern detection. By applying time-based constraints, CEP systems can detect patterns that occur within specific time intervals, such as bursts of activity or trends over time. This capability is particularly valuable in applications where timing and sequence are crucial, such as fraud detection or network monitoring.

Aggregation and correlation are also central methodologies in CEP, allowing the system to combine and relate events from different streams. Aggregation involves computing summary statistics, such as counts or averages, over a set of events, providing a high-level view of the data. Correlation, on the other hand, focuses on identifying relationships between events, such as causality or co-occurrence. These methodologies enable CEP systems to derive insights from complex interactions and dependencies, enhancing the depth and richness of the analysis.

Applications of complex event processing in AI

The application of CEP in AI spans a wide range of domains, each leveraging the technology to enhance decision-making and responsiveness. In the financial sector, CEP is used for real-time trading and risk management, where the ability to detect patterns and anomalies in market data is critical. By processing streams of financial transactions and market indicators, CEP systems can identify trading opportunities and risks, enabling traders to make informed decisions in volatile markets.

In the realm of cybersecurity, CEP plays a vital role in intrusion detection and threat analysis. By analyzing streams of network traffic and security logs, CEP systems can detect suspicious patterns and behaviors indicative of cyberattacks. The real-time capabilities of CEP allow security teams to respond swiftly to emerging threats, mitigating potential damage and ensuring the integrity of the network.

Healthcare is another domain where CEP has significant applications, particularly in patient monitoring and alerting systems. By processing streams of physiological data from medical devices, CEP systems can detect critical events, such as changes in vital signs or the onset of medical conditions. This enables healthcare providers to intervene promptly, improving patient outcomes and reducing the risk of adverse events.

In the context of smart cities, CEP is employed to enhance urban management and sustainability. By analyzing streams of data from sensors and IoT devices, CEP systems can monitor and optimize various aspects of city operations, such as traffic flow, energy consumption, and environmental conditions. The ability to detect patterns and trends in real-time allows city planners to make data-driven decisions, improving the quality of life for residents and promoting sustainable development.

CEP represents a transformative approach to real-time data analysis, enabling AI applications to detect and respond to patterns and relationships within streams of events. By leveraging methodologies such as event pattern matching, temporal reasoning, and aggregation, CEP systems provide the tools necessary to extract actionable insights from complex data interactions. The diverse applications of CEP in domains such as finance, cybersecurity, healthcare, and smart cities underscore its potential to enhance decision-making and responsiveness in real-time environments. As the demand for intelligent systems capable of processing continuous data streams continues to grow, the development and refinement of CEP technologies will remain a focal point for researchers and practitioners, driving innovation and enabling new possibilities in the era of real-time AI.

Use cases and best practices for AI deployment

The deployment of real-time AI systems represents a significant advancement in the capability of organizations to process and respond to data instantaneously. This capability is increasingly critical across various industries, from finance and healthcare to transportation and telecommunications. This section explores prominent use cases for real-time AI deployment and outlines best practices that can guide the successful implementation of these systems, ensuring they deliver timely and accurate insights while maintaining operational efficiency and robustness.

Use cases of real-time AI

Real-time AI systems are transforming the financial industry by enabling rapid analysis and decision-making. In algorithmic trading, real-time AI models process market data streams to identify trading opportunities and execute transactions within milliseconds. This capability allows traders to capitalize on fleeting market inefficiencies, enhancing profitability. Additionally, real-time AI is pivotal in fraud detection, where systems continuously monitor transaction streams to identify suspicious patterns indicative of fraudulent activity. By analyzing these patterns in real-time, financial institutions can intervene promptly, mitigating potential losses and safeguarding customer trust.

In healthcare, real-time AI systems play a crucial role in patient monitoring and emergency response. By processing continuous streams of physiological data from wearable devices and medical sensors, these systems can detect anomalies and alert healthcare providers to potential health crises. This capability is particularly valuable in intensive care units, where timely intervention can significantly impact patient outcomes. Furthermore, real-time AI is used in personalized medicine, where models analyze patient data to tailor treatment plans dynamically, improving the efficacy of medical interventions.

The transportation sector also benefits from real-time AI through applications in autonomous vehicles and traffic management. Autonomous vehicles rely on real-time AI to process sensor data and make split-second decisions, such as obstacle avoidance and route planning. This capability enhances the safety and efficiency of autonomous driving systems. In urban environments, real-time AI is used to optimize traffic flow by analyzing data from traffic cameras and sensors, enabling dynamic traffic signal adjustments and reducing congestion.

Telecommunications companies leverage real-time AI for network optimization and customer experience enhancement. By analyzing network traffic in real-time, AI systems can identify and mitigate issues such as congestion or outages, ensuring seamless connectivity for users. Additionally, real-time AI is employed in customer service applications, where chatbots and virtual assistants provide instant support and resolution to customer inquiries, improving satisfaction and loyalty.

Best practices for real-time AI deployment

Deploying real-time AI systems requires careful planning and execution to ensure they operate effectively and efficiently. One of the best practices is to establish a robust data infrastructure that supports high throughput data ingestion and processing. This involves selecting appropriate data storage and processing frameworks that can handle the volume and velocity of real-time data streams. Technologies such as Apache Kafka for data ingestion and Apache Flink or Spark Streaming for processing are commonly used to achieve this capability.

Another best practice is to implement scalable and resilient system architectures. Real-time AI systems must be designed to scale horizontally, accommodating increasing data loads without degradation in performance. This requires the use of distributed computing frameworks and cloud-based solutions that provide elasticity and scalability. Additionally, systems should be designed with fault tolerance in mind, incorporating redundancy and failover mechanisms to ensure continuous operation in the face of hardware or software failures.

Ensuring data quality and integrity is also critical in real-time AI deployments. Data streams are often noisy and incomplete, necessitating robust preprocessing techniques to clean and validate data before it is fed into AI models. This includes handling missing values, filtering outliers, and normalizing data to ensure consistency. Implementing real-time data validation and monitoring tools can help maintain data quality and prevent erroneous insights.

Security and compliance are paramount considerations in real-time AI deployments, particularly in industries handling sensitive data. Best practices include implementing encryption and access controls to protect data privacy and integrity. Compliance with regulatory requirements, such as GDPR or HIPAA, must be ensured through comprehensive data governance frameworks that define policies and procedures for data handling and protection.

Finally, continuous monitoring and optimization of real-time AI systems are essential to maintain their performance and relevance. This involves setting up monitoring tools to track system metrics, such as latency, throughput, and error rates, and using these insights to identify areas for improvement. Regular model retraining and tuning are also necessary to adapt to changing data patterns and maintain model accuracy. Incorporating feedback loops and automated retraining pipelines can streamline this process, ensuring that AI models remain effective over time.

The deployment of real-time AI systems offers transformative potential across various industries, enabling organizations to process and respond to data with unprecedented speed and accuracy. The use cases explored in this section highlight the diverse applications of real-time AI, from financial trading and fraud detection to patient monitoring and autonomous driving. To realize the full potential of real-time AI, organizations must adhere to best practices that ensure robust data infrastructure, scalable architectures, data quality, security, and continuous optimization. As the demand for real-time AI continues to grow, these best practices will serve as a foundation for successful deployments, driving innovation and enabling new possibilities in the era of real-time data processing.

Conclusion

The exploration of real-time AI systems and stream processing in this chapter has illuminated the profound impact these technologies have across diverse sectors. By enabling the continuous processing and analysis of data streams, real-time AI systems are transforming how organizations derive insights and make decisions. The integration of sophisticated stream processing frameworks, such as Apache Kafka, Apache Flink, and

Apache Spark Streaming, is crucial in providing the infrastructure needed for handling high throughput, low-latency data, thereby facilitating timely and actionable intelligence.

Central to the discussion is the architecture of real-time AI systems, which must be meticulously designed to support low-latency processing while ensuring scalability and resilience. The adoption of distributed computing frameworks and microservices architectures emerges as a robust solution to these challenges, allowing systems to scale horizontally and efficiently manage distributed resources. Furthermore, the use of cloud-based solutions enhances scalability by offering the elasticity required to adapt to fluctuating workloads.

The chapter also looks into the methodologies and applications of stream processing frameworks, emphasizing their role in supporting AI models. By enabling real-time data ingestion, processing, and output, these frameworks facilitate the deployment of intelligent applications capable of agile and precise responses to dynamic conditions. The integration of AI models within these pipelines enhances decision-making processes, enabling systems to be adaptive and context-aware, with the ability to learn and evolve continuously.

Real-time feature engineering and latency management are highlighted as critical components of real-time AI systems, ensuring that features are both timely and relevant while minimizing processing delays. Techniques such as sliding windows, online learning, and in-memory processing are employed to achieve these goals, striking a balance between computational efficiency and the richness of the features extracted. Effective latency management is essential for maintaining the responsiveness of real-time applications, particularly in domains where timely insights are crucial.

The chapter concludes by addressing the scalability challenges and solutions in real-time AI, underscoring the importance of robust data infrastructure and scalable architectures. Successful deployment of real-time AI systems necessitates adherence to best practices that ensure data quality, security, and continuous optimization. As the demand for real-time AI continues to expand, these best practices will form the foundation for successful deployments, driving innovation and enabling new possibilities in the era of real-time data processing.

Looking ahead, the next chapter will look into the integration of real-time AI systems with edge computing. It will explore how edge computing complements real-time AI by bringing computation closer to the data source, thereby reducing latency and enhancing data privacy. The chapter will examine the synergies between these technologies and how they can be leveraged to develop more efficient and responsive AI applications. This exploration will provide insights into the future trajectory of AI development, highlighting the potential for edge-integrated AI systems to revolutionize industries by delivering intelligent insights at unprecedented speeds.

CHAPTER 10
Data Visualization and Explainable AI

Introduction

Artificial intelligence (**AI**) is transforming industries from the medical and finance sectors to the automotive and entertainment sectors. AI systems are poring over gigantic datasets, seeking patterns and predictions, sometimes with breathtaking accuracy. For all their growing prowess, much of AI is a mysterious black box, churning out outputs that are difficult to explain or understand. When AI is making decisions that have an impact on human lives, such as loan approvals, medical diagnoses, or hiring decisions, it is crucial to understand how and why such decisions are being made. Without transparency, trust in AI is fragile.

Here, we talk about high-end visualization techniques that make AI explainable. We will explore how to visually represent high-dimensional data, model predictions, and uncertainty, and how interactive dashboards can provide real-time insights into AI systems. Additionally, we will examine the role of AI-driven storytelling, which combines data analysis with compelling narratives to make insights more accessible and engaging. Finally, we will emphasize the necessity of accessibility and inclusivity so that AI visualization tools reach varied audiences and are designed in an equitable manner.

Finally, AI does not have to be a machine that operates beyond human understanding. With the integration of data visualization and explainability techniques, we can certainly have AI systems that are intelligent and yet interpretable, ethical, and contribute to society meaningfully.

Structure

The chapter covers the following topics:

- Advanced data visualization techniques for AI insights
- XAI techniques and tools
- Visualizing model predictions and uncertainties
- Interactive dashboards for AI systems
- Time-series and high-dimensional data visualization in AI
- Network and graph visualization for AI applications
- Augmented analytics and AI-driven data storytelling
- Accessibility and inclusivity in AI visualizations

Objectives

This chapter looks into the pivotal role of data visualization and explainable AI in enhancing the interpretability and usability of AI systems. As AI technologies continue to evolve and permeate various sectors, the ability to effectively visualize and comprehend complex data and model outputs has become increasingly crucial. This chapter systematically explores the methodologies and applications of visualization techniques that cater to different data types and structures, alongside strategies for making AI systems more interpretable and accessible.

The discussion begins with an examination of time series and high-dimensional data visualization. These data types are prevalent in numerous AI applications, and their complexity necessitates advanced visualization techniques that can reveal underlying patterns and relationships. Through interactive and intuitive visualizations, users can engage with these data forms to extract actionable insights, thereby supporting more informed decision-making processes.

Following this, the chapter addresses network and graph visualization, which are essential for representing relational data structures. Graphs are particularly valuable in domains such as social network analysis and knowledge graph exploration, where understanding the interconnections and interactions within datasets is crucial. The visualization techniques discussed in this section enable practitioners to navigate and interpret complex networks, facilitating the discovery of meaningful insights.

The chapter then transitions to augmented analytics and AI-driven data storytelling, highlighting their transformative impact on data interpretation and communication. By leveraging AI technologies such as machine learning and natural language generation, augmented analytics automates the analysis process, while data storytelling crafts compelling narratives that make complex insights accessible to diverse audiences. These approaches democratize data access and empower users to engage with data in a more meaningful way, enhancing the overall impact of AI-driven insights.

Finally, the chapter emphasizes the importance of accessibility and inclusivity in AI visualizations. Ensuring that visualizations are designed to accommodate diverse user needs is essential for promoting equitable access to AI insights. This section explores the principles and practices of accessible design, underscoring the need to adhere to established guidelines and consider cultural, linguistic, and contextual differences in visualization design.

Advanced data visualization techniques for AI insights

AI changes how we work, make decisions, and interact with technology. It powers everything from medical diagnoses and self-driving cars to anti-fraud and recommendations. However, the more sophisticated AI becomes, the less we understand it. When AI systems decide about your credit score, job interview, or even your health, how do we know why they did so?

That is where data visualization comes in. AI burrows through large amounts of data in ways indistinguishable to us, but with the proper graphics, we can break it down into something valuable. Visualization lets us peer into patterns, find biases, and expose AI model decision-making so that we can make it more understandable and trustworthy.

In this section, we will explore why visualization is crucial for AI, how it helps make sense of high-dimensional data, and how it can explain complex AI decisions. We will also look at how interactive dashboards and visualization tools bring AI insights to life, making them easier to use and act upon.

Importance of data visualization in AI

AI is changing businesses, making forecasts, taking decisions, and identifying patterns that would take decades for people to identify. The irony is that AI likes to act as a black box and gives outputs, but we are not sure of the how or the why that it reached any decision. It is a treasure chest filled with valuable stuff, but without the mechanism to open it.

That is where visualization enters the picture. Visualization serves as a key, unlocking the insights of AI and rendering them transparent, understandable, and actionable for humans. By transforming raw data, mathematical calculations, and complex models into simple charts, graphs, and interactive dashboards, visualization makes AI more accessible, easier to analyze, and simpler to refine.

Here is why it is important:

- **Transparency matters**: AI is already making decisions that affect actual people, whether it is issuing a mortgage, detecting a disease, or choosing which recruitment candidates appear on the shortlist. If we do not understand why AI makes these decisions, how can we ever rely on them? Visualization helps to uncover the reasoning of AI and thereby guarantees fairness, accountability, and transparency.

- **Debugging and improving AI models**: AI is not flawless. It can develop biases, make miscalculations, or overlook important factors. Visualization helps researchers and developers pinpoint errors, refine models, and improve accuracy, ensuring that AI systems function as intended.

- **Building trust**: Humans do not trust what they do not know. If AI choices are black boxes that generate results out of an unseen process, distrust will grow. Successful visualization helps to make the AI decision-making process clearer, fostering belief in its reliability. Whether a doctor reviewing an AI-generated diagnosis or a business leader relying on AI analytics, trust is created from knowledge.

- **Making AI insights actionable**: AI is capable of spotting trends and generating insights that could transform industries. However, if those insights are buried in complex algorithms and endless numbers, they will not be useful. Visualization translates AI's raw output into meaningful, interactive stories that drive better decisions.

Without visualization, AI is a mystery, powerful but inaccessible. The more we can visualize how AI thinks, the more we can rely on it, refine it, and ensure that it works for all people equally and well.

Reading high-dimensional data

AI is great at number-crunching and finding patterns in massive datasets. However, what if a model is dealing with hundreds or thousands of variables at once? How do we even read it? Imagine trying to find patterns in a million-piece puzzle without seeing what the finished picture is supposed to look like. That is what working with high-dimensional data feels like without the right tools.

This is where visualization steps in as a game changer. Visualization helps us pierce through complexity, draw focus to vital relationships, and make AI-generated insights more meaningful.

Dimensionality reduction

Think about a 1,000-page book; you do not necessarily need to memorize every word to be familiar with the book. Dimensionality reduction does the same for an AI: it compresses large datasets but keeps the most important information. The following are the two popular dimensionality reduction techniques:

- **PCA**: The technique gets rid of the noise and finds the principal trends in data, just like cutting down a large book into a concise summary.

- **t-SNE and UMAP**: **t-Distributed Stochastic Neighbor Embedding (t-SNE)** and **Uniform Manifold Approximation and Projection (UMAP)** apply very complex data and transform it into easy-to-visualize 2D or 3D graphs so that patterns, clusters, and trends stand out at once. It is comparable to taking an intricate research paper and turning it into an easy-to-grasp infographic.

- **Correspondence analysis (CA)**: Often used for categorical data, CA visualizes relationships between rows and columns in a contingency table, akin to summarizing the interactions between characters and chapters in a novel.

- **Latent Dirichlet Allocation (LDA)**: A probabilistic technique primarily used in text analysis, LDA uncovers hidden thematic structures in large corpora, like identifying the underlying topics that thread through a long anthology.

Heatmaps

Let us be realistic; staring at raw numbers can be exhausting, but colors make patterns pop. Heatmaps translate data into a color-coded picture, and it is easy to spot trends and relationships in an instant. Two such variations of heatmaps are as follows:

- **Correlation heatmaps**: These show how different factors influence each other. For example, they can allow AI researchers to quickly see which variables are most important in a model, such as whether education level has a significant effect on income predictions.

- **Activation heatmaps**: Used in deep learning, they indicate what an AI model is examining. Imagine an AI scanning X-Rays for disease; on an X-Ray, an activation heatmap would highlight the exact areas the AI examined to diagnose a disease.

By turning numbers into colors, heatmaps explain AI decision-making more clearly and simply.

Correlation matrices

A correlation matrix is like a map of data relationships, showing how highly correlated features are with one another, how little those that do not contribute much, and perhaps even redundant.

For example:

- A marketing team would use a correlation matrix to see whether more social media activity translates to more product sales or whether opinions are more important.

- A medical researcher might explore whether certain lifestyle tendencies correlate with heart disease.

By mapping out latent connections, correlation matrices render AI models more efficient, precise, and insightful.

Visualization AI decision-making process

AI is incredible; it can predict outcomes, sort information, and make decisions in ways that almost feel like magic. Here is the thing: if we do not understand why it makes certain choices, how can we really trust it?

Visualization enables us to peer into AI's brain, to observe how it is deciding. Such transparency is necessary—not just for data scientists but for all those using AI for important decisions, from medicine to finance to everyday life.

Decision boundaries

Take the example of sorting emails into spam and not spam. You would likely search for keywords such as lottery or free money. AI-aided visualizations show them in the following way:

- Decision boundary visualizations show how AI is splitting up various categories. They let us observe whether the AI is making intelligent distinctions or just guessing.

- These visualizations can also reveal biases and blind spots. Is the AI unfairly flagging certain emails based on subtle, irrelevant patterns?

It is helpful to observe these boundaries to adapt and tweak AI models so they make more knowledgeable, fairer decisions.

Feature importance and saliency maps

AI considers numerous factors while making a decision. Feature importance can be gauged in the following ways:

- **Feature importance scores (SHAP, LIME)**: Imagine an AI system that decides if you qualify for a loan. Is it looking at your credit score, income, or something unexpected like your ZIP code? **SHapley Additive exPlanations** (**SHAP**) and **Local Interpretable Model-Agnostic Explanations** (**LIME**) techniques identify which factors had the highest impact.

- **Saliency maps**: When AI is examining images, how can we be sure it is looking at the right thing? If an AI finds a dog in an image, is it looking at the face of the dog or the background? Saliency maps show which parts of an image the AI was looking at.

By observing what the AI is thinking, we can rely on it to make decisions for the right reasons, not because of irrelevant patterns or hidden biases.

Making AI insights interactive and actionable

A spreadsheet filled with lots of numbers or an opaque AI model you cannot interact with is useless.

For AI to really help human beings, it must be easy to use and understand. Interactive visualizations are, therefore, essential as they make AI insights visible, tactile, and interactive.

Interactive dashboards

Instead of thick, technical reports, imagine interactive dashboards where you can:

- Adjust filters and instantly see how AI predictions change.

- Watch AI performance in real time.

- Explore trends with just a few clicks.

- Power BI, Tableau, Streamlit, and Dash make AI insights accessible, even if you are not a data scientist.

- TensorBoard lets AI engineers track deep learning models, helping them spot issues early.

With the right tools, AI stops being a mystery and becomes a tool anyone can use to make informed decisions.

Visualization at model development and deployment

Visualization is not only for the end results. It is helpful at each phase:

- **During training**: Allows developers to identify issues early.

- **During deployment**: Allows companies to monitor AI in real time.

- **For decision-makers**: Ensures insights are clear, actionable, and useful.

By making AI more interactive, we close the gap between complicated technology and actual decisions.

AI is changing the world, but its real potential can be achieved only when it is understood and trusted.

Visualization is the key to that trust. It enables us to:

- See what AI is doing.

- Understand why it makes certain decisions.

- Ensure fairness, accuracy, and transparency.

AI does not need to be a type of black box enigma. The more we can see, touch, and learn about AI, the more we can harness it to build a smarter, fairer, and more ethical tomorrow.

XAI techniques and tools

AI is making big decisions, whether it is accepting loans, diagnosing disease, or screening job candidates. Here is the problem: How do we know whether AI is making the right decision?

If someone decides, we can explain why. AI, on the other hand, tends to be a black box, delivering output without an explanation of why. That is where XAI begins.

XAI helps us look inside the mind of AI, making AI more transparent, credible, and fair. Let us break down why explainability is important, how we do it, and what tools we use.

Why explainability matters

Imagine you apply for a mortgage loan and are rejected. If you request a reason why, the bank responds, *The AI algorithm made the decision*. Such a response would not be helpful.

Imagine a physician employing AI to diagnose a patient. If the AI reports, *This patient is at high risk of heart disease*, but cannot tell you why, how can the physician rely on the outcome?

That is why explainability is important. Without it, AI choices can seem arbitrary, unjust, or even discriminatory.

The importance of **explainable AI (XAI)** is explained as follows:

- **Trust and confidence**: If humans do not comprehend AI's choices, they will not trust them.

- **Fairness and bias detection**: AI can, at times, discriminate against one group and favor another. Explainability helps us detect and remove biases.

- **Accountability**: Who is responsible when AI makes a mistake? Explainability helps organizations hold themselves accountable.

- **Regulatory compliance**: Laws like the GDPR (in Europe) and AI Act require AI decisions to be transparent.

Finally, AI needs to work for humankind, not against it. Explainability provides transparency to AI decisions, fairness, and openness to human examination.

Making AI explainable

There exist some AI models that are inherently easy to interpret and some that require extra effort to explain. Let us cover both.

Intrinsic interpretability

Some AI models are inherently transparent. These models use basic logic, so we do not have any problem seeing how they reach a conclusion. The following are a few examples:

- **Decision trees**: Very much like a flowchart, it shows step by step how the AI makes a decision.

- **Linear regression**: Can easily see how every parameter (e.g., income, age, education) affects predictions.

- **Rule-based models**: Uses plain if-then rules to reach conclusions, so one can simply read them.

These models are great at transparency but struggle with complex issues. That is when more powerful (but less interpretable) models come into play.

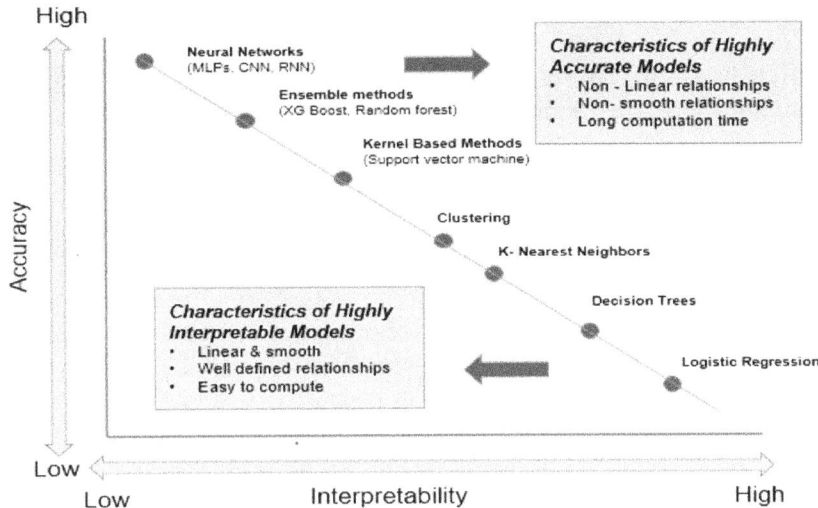

Figure 10.1: *Trade-off between accuracy and interpretability in ML models*

This shows the compromise between machine learning model interpretability and accuracy. Highly accurate models like neural networks and ensemble techniques are powerful, but are black boxes, and their decision-making process becomes difficult to justify. Less complicated models like logistic regression and decision trees are simple to interpret but may not provide optimal accuracy.

Post-hoc interpretability

Deep learning and advanced machine learning models are very accurate, but they do not explain their choices. The following are some post-hoc methods to interpret them:

- **Feature importance analysis**: Tells us what factors played the largest role in AI's choice.

- **Surrogate models**: Uses a simpler model (like a decision tree) to mimic and explain the behavior of a complex AI model.

- **Local explanations (LIME, SHAP)**: Explains individual decisions by showing how small changes in input data affect the AI's predictions.

These methods bridge the gap between AI's power and its understandability.

Seeing AI's thought process using visualization methods

Most people do not understand AI models in lines of code. Visualization is the key reason why; it makes AI's logic real and interactive so that we can understand it.

Major visualization methods are listed as follows:

- **Feature importance charts**: Shows us which features (e.g., salary, employment history) played the largest role in AI's decision.

- **Decision boundary plots**: Allows us to see how AI separates different groups (e.g., spam vs. regular emails).

- **Saliency maps**: Shines a light on the part of the image AI was considering when it made a prediction.

- **Partial dependence plots (PDPs)**: Shows how AI's predictions would change if we alter one variable at a time.

- **Counterfactual explanations**: These show what differences would have led to a different decision (e.g., *If your credit score was 20 points better, you would have been accepted*).

These tools render the choices made by AI transparent, making it easier for businesses, researchers, and normal users to know why AI is making a particular decision.

Tools for implementing XAI

AI engineers put XAI into practice with the right tools. Some of the tools are as follows:

- **InterpretML**:
  - A framework for transforming AI models to make them explainable.
  - Intrinsic models and post-hoc explanations are both supported.
  - Enables developers to build fair and accountable AI systems.

- **SHAP and LIME**:
  - **SHapley Additive exPlanations (SHAP)**: Mathematically breaks down AI decisions, showing exactly how much each attribute contributed.
  - **Local Interpretable Model-Agnostic Explanations (LIME)**: This creates a simpler model that can account for a single AI prediction.

- **TensorBoard**:
  - Deep learning model visualization tool.
  - Enables AI engineers to track training progress, model accuracy, and bias detection.
  - Useful for debugging neural networks and optimizing model performance.

These are some of the most widely used tools in the AI space. Together with these tools, AI becomes less of a black box and more something that we can see, question, and enhance.

AI is changing our world, but its true value lies in being understood and trusted.

With the right techniques, visualizations, and tools, we can:

- See why AI makes certain choices.
- Identify and remove biases.
- Make AI fair, transparent, and accountable.

AI should never be a mere acceptance on our part without questioning. Instead, it should be a system we understand, trust, and continuously improve. By embracing explainable AI, we make sure AI really serves the people who rely on it, not just the engineers who design it.

Visualizing model predictions and uncertainties

Predictions are great, but predictions alone are not enough; we also want to be aware of how sure we are about them. Are we certain about what the model is predicting, or is there a lot of uncertainty?

That is where we need visualization. With a graphical representation of prediction and uncertainty, we can set confidence in AI models, flag errors, and make better decisions based on the output of the model.

Need to visualize predictions

Think about an autonomous car observing pedestrians. If the AI provides you with a 95% prediction that a person will be in the crosswalk, you feel comforted. If 60%, perhaps not?

Now, think about a medical AI predicting whether a tumor is cancerous. If AI predicts cancer but only with low confidence, a second opinion is needed.

This is why visualizing predictions is so important. It helps:

- **Improve trust and transparency**: Seeing predictions visually makes it easier to interpret AI's decisions.
- **Detect bias and errors**: Patterns in predictions can reveal biases or inconsistencies in the model.
- **Support decision-making**: Quickly act on high-confidence predictions, but human validation might be necessary for uncertain ones.

Numbers in a display do not speak the whole truth, but an effectively designed visualization does.

Visualization techniques for predictions

Not every prediction is equal. Some models label data as categories (e.g., spam or not spam), while others estimate continuous values (e.g., house prices). Here are the optimal visualization techniques for various kinds of predictions:

- **Confusion matrices and ROC curves**:
  - o **Confusion matrix**: A table to see where the model was right and where it was wrong.
  - o **Receiver operating characteristic (ROC) curve**: Illustrates the trade-off between true positive rate and false positive rate, which allows us to assess how good the model is.
  - o **Use case**: Spam detection, medical diagnosis, and fraud detection.
- **Scatter plots and regression lines**:
  - o **Scatter plots**: Plot predicted against actual values, showing how well the model fits the data.
  - o **Regression lines**: A regression line representing the model's forecasts, easy to spot outliers and errors.
  - o **Use case**: Forecasting stock prices, demand prediction, and house prices.
- **Heatmaps and probability distributions**:
  - o **Heatmaps**: Illustrate patterns in high-dimensional data, highlighting trends not readily evident in raw data.
  - o **Probability distributions**: Show how probable various outcomes are and assist us in making sense of uncertainty.
  - o **Use case**: Predicting the weather, sentiment analysis, and recommendation systems.

Through these visualizations, we can make more sense of AI's predictions and enhance its accuracy.

Visualizing uncertainties in predictions

Predictions are not always 100% certain, so how do we know when to trust AI and when to be wary?

That is where uncertainty visualization enters the scene. AI models not only give answers but also quantify how certain they are about their answers.

Types of uncertainty in AI predictions are:

- **Aleatoric uncertainty (data noise)**: Arises due to randomness in the data itself (e.g., volatile stock market trends).

- **Epistemic uncertainty (model uncertainty)**: Arises due to a lack of knowledge (e.g., AI has not had enough similar instances).

Both types of uncertainty are quantifiable and can be visualized to improve the trustworthiness of AI.

Some techniques for visualizing uncertainty are as follows:

- **Confidence intervals and prediction intervals**:
    - o **Confidence intervals**: Show how certain we are regarding the average prediction of the model.
    - o **Prediction intervals**: Show a band in which future data points will fall.
    - o **Use case**: Medical diagnoses, financial forecasting

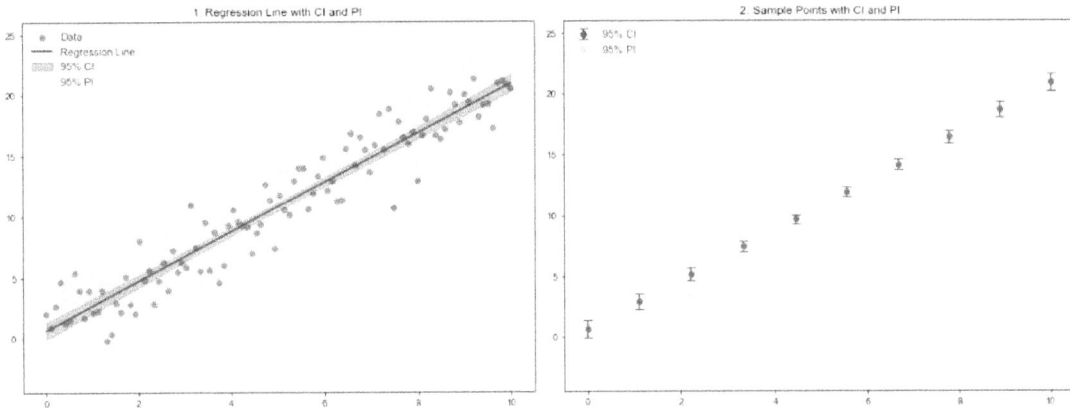

Figure 10.2: Plots for confidence and prediction interval

- **Bayesian methods and Monte Carlo simulations**:
    - o **Bayesian models**: Provide probability distributions instead of a single point, enabling us to understand uncertainty.
    - o **Monte Carlo simulations**: Run multiple simulations to simulate multiple possible outcomes and their probabilities.
    - o **Use case**: Risk assessment, climate simulation, robotics.

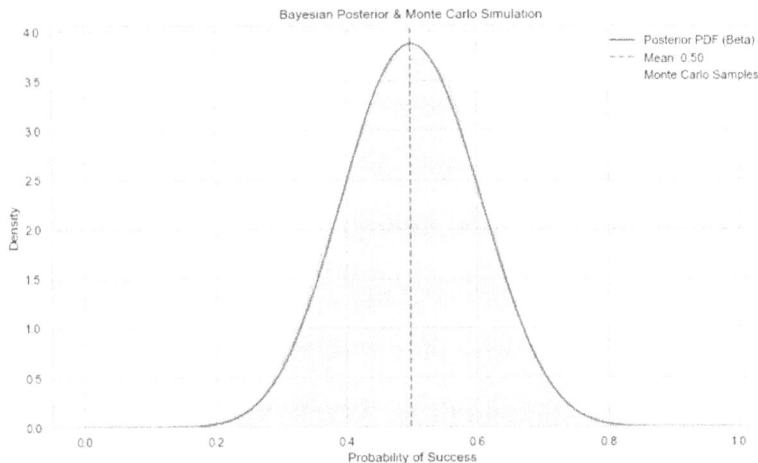

Figure 10.3: Plots for Bayesian methods and Monte Carlo simulation

- **Error bars and uncertainty bands**:
  - o **Error bars**: Put visual markers on points, showing the level of uncertainty with each point.
  - o **Uncertainty bands**: A filled-in region around a regression line, indicating the uncertainty range of possible outcomes.
  - o **Use case**: Predicting sales of products, demand forecasting.

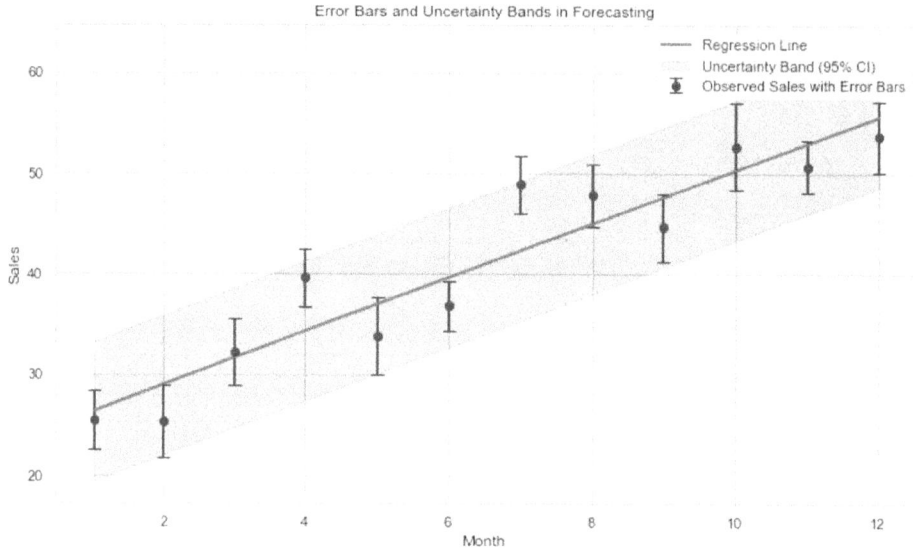

Figure 10.4: *Plots for error bars and uncertainty bands*

By experiencing uncertainty, we do not just get to see what AI is forecasting but how confident it is in its forecasts.

AI predictions are powerful, but they are only useful if others can understand and rely on them.

By using the right visualization techniques, we can:

- Make AI choices transparent.
- Catch errors and biases before they become issues.
- Help people and companies make good decisions.

In the real world, uncertainty matters, whether in medical diagnosis, investment guidance, or self-driving cars. By seeing predictions and uncertainties, we not only ensure that AI makes correct decisions but also ethical decisions.

Interactive dashboards for AI systems

AI is transforming industry by enabling customers to forecast actions, allowing physicians to diagnose diseases sooner, and informing investors to make wiser financial choices. Here is the catch: if individuals are unable to comprehend AI insights, they will not trust or utilize them. This is where interactive dashboards come in.

Instead of scanning overblown reports, a meaning-imparting AI dashboard would have users observe forecasts coalesce in an image, find patterns, and be able to adjust inputs to find out how conclusions were reached.

AI is not an algorithm issue; it is a problem of humans harnessing AI to make better decisions. Interactive dashboards can bridge the gap there.

Role of interactive dashboards in AI

AI is strong, but if it is not accompanied by the proper tools, its knowledge stays imprisoned within spreadsheets, raw data, or difficult reports. A nicely designed AI dashboard could convert deep predictions into uncomplicated, actionable knowledge that anyone can exploit.

Why dashboards matter:

- **They make AI insights accessible**: No coding or data science expertise is needed.
- **They enable people to make improved decisions**: Visual trends and real-time updates eliminate guessing.
- **Foster trust and openness**: No longer an enigmatic black box, AI can be understood and engaged with.

Here are some real-world examples:

- **Self-driving cars**: A dashboard could show what the AI sees, what it is going to do, and how confident it is in its actions.
- **Bank loan approvals**: A dashboard can show credit scores, risk indicators, and why a customer was approved or denied.
- **Monitoring of healthcare risk**: AI determines which patients are at risk for complications. A dashboard flags priority cases, trends, and recommended actions for doctors.

Instead of making AI distant and daunting, dashboards bring it closer to the people who need it most.

Design principles for effective dashboard

A dashboard must be a useful guide. Proper design is the difference between an adored dashboard and one that is avoided. The following are the aspects of design for a dashboard that help with its acceptability amongst users:

- **Usability and user centric**:
  - o **Reveal only what is important**: Do not clog it up. Only provide the most critical insights that influence decisions.

o **Make it easy to navigate**: Users must discover what they want in seconds, not minutes.

o **Appropriate for various users**: An executive needs an executive summary; an analyst would want more advanced figures.

- **Clarity and simplicity**:

  o **Charts, bars, and color**: A well-positioned bar chart is easier to understand than a page of figures.

  o **Interactive features**: Enable individuals to drill down through the data, adjust inputs, and explore what-ifs.

  o **Inbuilt explanations**: Concise explanations allow users to comprehend outcomes.

- **Real-time data integration**:

  o **Live updates**: The dashboard should refresh in real-time as fresh data comes in.

  o **Drill-down feature**: Users can click through on insights to drill down further.

  o **Forecasting analytics**: AI-powered dashboards should forecast trends instead of reporting on happenings after they have occurred.

Implementing interactive dashboards

Interactive dashboards have emerged as a crucial tool in the realm of AI, offering dynamic interfaces that enable users to engage with complex datasets and model outputs effectively. These dashboards provide a platform for real-time data exploration, allowing users to manipulate variables, filter data, and visualize changes instantaneously. The integration of interactive elements facilitates a deeper understanding of AI-driven insights by providing users with the flexibility to look into specific areas of interest. Moreover, interactive dashboards enhance decision-making processes by presenting data in a visually intuitive format, supporting the identification of trends, anomalies, and correlations. This capability is particularly essential in domains requiring rapid responses to evolving data, such as finance, healthcare, and logistics. By empowering users to interact with AI systems in a more meaningful and accessible manner, interactive dashboards play a vital role in bridging the gap between complex AI models and practical, actionable insights.

Choosing the right tools

There are some tools for building dashboards, but the right tool depends on who it will be for and which AI model it is associated with. The following are some popular dashboarding tools:

- **Power BI and Tableau**: Best for business teams and executives who need high-level, sharp reports.

- **Streamlit and Dash (Python libraries)**: Best for data scientists needing dynamic, AI-generated dashboards.

- **Google Data Studio**: Cloud-based, easy pick for speedy data discovery.

- **TensorBoard:** Best for graphing deep learning models and AI training monitoring.

Embedding AI forecasts into dashboards

A good dashboard is not just a report; it needs to be connected to AI models in real-time so that users can experiment with live predictions. The following ways enable embedding an AI forecast in dashboards:

- **API connections**: Predictions need to feed directly into the dashboard from AI models.

- **Scenario testing**: Users need to be able to adjust inputs and see how predictions respond.

- **Automated alerts**: In case AI discovers something important (like a risk of fraud or a patient emergency), the dashboard needs to notify it immediately.

Data protection and control

Since AI generally deals with sensitive data, security is as important as functionality. The following are the three important aspects of data protection and control:

- **Role-based access control**: Different users need different degrees of access to AI insights.

- **Compliance with privacy legislation**: If AI handles personal data (finance, healthcare, HR), it must adhere to regulations like GDPR and HIPAA.

- **Audit logs**: Record who accessed or changed data for accountability.

Interactive dashboards revolutionizing AI

The following are the benefits of interactive dashboards in a typical AI-driven enterprise:

- **Intelligent, speedy decision-making**:
  o AI dashboards help business leaders, doctors, and analysts make informed decisions in real-time.
  o They allow users to test different scenarios instead of relying on a one-size-fits-all prediction.
  o AI recommendations can be immediately put into action instead of getting buried in a report.
  o **Example**: A supply chain manager can adjust delivery routes in a dashboard and instantly see AI's predictions for cost savings and efficiency.

- **More transparency, less black box AI**:
  - o   Dashboards explain how AI makes decisions, building trust and accountability.
  - o   They make it easier to spot biases or unexpected patterns in AI predictions.
  - o   Dashboards can be utilized by organizations to showcase compliance with ethical AI standards.
  - o   **Example**: An HR dashboard illustrates to hiring teams why AI ranked candidates in a particular order, in order to preserve fairness.

- **Enhanced human-AI collaboration**:
  - o   AI dashboards bring teams together as different departments are able to view insights.
  - o   Instead of AI as a technical tool, dashboards make it a collaborative decision-making ally.
  - o   Customization allows users to focus on what matters to them, not generic one-size-fits-all reports.
  - o   **Example**: Doctors, nurses, and administrators can use a patient risk dashboard to coordinate care more effectively.

Interactive dashboards push AI from a conceptual, technical notion and turn it into an ordinary tool that can be employed by anyone in the following ways:

- From raw data to clear, visual insights.
- From invisible AI processes to transparent, explainable decisions.
- From passive reports to interactive, hands-on decision-making.

Dashboards will be even more adaptive and AI-driven in the future, providing personalized recommendations, forecasting trends before they happen, and integrating into day-to-day work.

Time-series and high-dimensional data visualization in AI

The visualization of time series and high-dimensional data has become increasingly crucial in the context of AI, where the ability to interpret complex data structures is paramount. As AI systems evolve to handle more intricate datasets, the need for advanced visualization techniques that can effectively represent temporal patterns and multidimensional relationships is more pressing than ever. This section looks into the methodologies and tools employed in visualizing time series and high-dimensional data, providing insights into their application within AI systems.

Time-series data visualization

Time-series data visualization is a critical component of data analysis, particularly in fields that require the monitoring and forecasting of trends over time, such as finance, healthcare, and environmental studies. This visualization technique involves plotting data points sequentially over intervals, allowing for the identification of temporal patterns, trends, and anomalies. Line charts are commonly utilized due to their effectiveness in depicting continuous data over time. Advanced methods, such as heatmaps and interactive dashboards, enhance the exploration of complex datasets by enabling dynamic manipulation and comparative analysis. These visualizations facilitate the comprehension of temporal dynamics, supporting data-driven decision-making processes.

Characteristics and challenges

Time-series data, characterized by observations recorded at successive time intervals, is prevalent in various domains such as finance, healthcare, and IoT. The primary challenge in visualizing time-series data lies in capturing temporal patterns and trends while accommodating the potential for high variability and noise. Effective visualization must also enable the detection of anomalies and the identification of seasonal or cyclical patterns.

Techniques for time-series visualization

Several techniques have been developed to address the visualization of time-series data. Line charts remain the most common approach due to their simplicity and effectiveness in illustrating trends over time. However, for more complex datasets, advanced techniques such as heatmaps, which use color gradients to represent values across time, can be employed to highlight patterns that may not be immediately apparent in line charts.

Another technique, the use of interactive dashboards, allows users to manipulate the time axis, zoom into specific periods, and overlay multiple time-series data for comparative analysis. These dashboards often integrate with AI systems to provide real-time analytics, enabling dynamic exploration of temporal data.

Applications in AI

In AI, time-series visualization plays a critical role in model evaluation and feature engineering. By visualizing temporal data, practitioners can better understand the underlying patterns that influence model predictions, facilitating the development of more accurate and robust AI models. Additionally, time-series visualization aids in the monitoring of AI systems in real-time applications, such as predictive maintenance and anomaly detection, where timely insights are crucial.

High-dimensional data visualization

High-dimensional data visualization presents a unique challenge in the realm of data analysis due to the complexity inherent in datasets with numerous variables. Traditional visualization methods are often inadequate for capturing the intricate relationships within such data. These techniques enable the visualization of clusters and patterns, providing insights into variable interactions. Advanced tools like scatter plots and parallel coordinates plots further aid in exploring the multidimensional feature space, enhancing analytical comprehension and supporting robust data-driven conclusions.

Understanding high-dimensional data

High-dimensional data refers to datasets with many features or variables. In AI, such data is common in fields like genomics, image processing, and natural language processing. The complexity of high-dimensional data poses significant challenges for visualization, as traditional two-dimensional plots are inadequate for capturing the intricate relationships between variables.

Dimensionality reduction techniques

To visualize high-dimensional data, dimensionality reduction techniques are often employed to project the data into lower-dimensional spaces while preserving its essential structure. Techniques such as PCA and **t-distributed Stochastic Neighbor Embedding (t-SNE)** are widely used in this context. PCA reduces dimensionality by transforming the data into a set of orthogonal components, while t-SNE focuses on maintaining the local structure of the data, making it particularly effective for visualizing clusters in high-dimensional space.

Visualization tools and methods

Several visualization tools have been developed to facilitate the exploration of high-dimensional data. Scatter plots, enhanced by dimensionality reduction techniques, are commonly used to visualize the relationships between variables in a two or three-dimensional space. Parallel coordinates plots provide an alternative approach by representing each dimension as a vertical axis, allowing users to trace data points across multiple dimensions simultaneously. Interactive visualization platforms, such as Plotly and Tableau, offer robust capabilities for exploring high-dimensional data. These platforms enable users to dynamically adjust parameters, filter data, and apply various dimensionality reduction techniques, providing a comprehensive view of the data's structure.

Implications for AI

High-dimensional data visualization is integral to the development and refinement of AI models. By visualizing the feature space, practitioners can gain insights into the distribution and relationships of variables, aiding in feature selection and engineering. Moreover, visualization techniques help in diagnosing model performance, identifying potential overfitting, and understanding the decision boundaries of complex models such as deep neural networks.

The visualization of time series and high-dimensional data is a critical component of modern AI systems. By employing advanced visualization techniques and tools, practitioners can gain deeper insights into complex datasets, enhancing their ability to develop, evaluate, and deploy AI models effectively. As AI continues to advance, the integration of sophisticated visualization methodologies will remain essential in unlocking the full potential of data-driven insights.

Network and graph visualization for AI applications

In the field of AI, network and graph visualization have emerged as a powerful tool for interpreting complex relational data structures. Graphs, which consist of nodes and edges, are inherently suited to represent relationships and interactions in various domains, such as social networks, biological systems, and knowledge graphs. The visualization of these structures not only aids in the comprehension of intricate data but also enhances the interpretability and trustworthiness of AI models that leverage such data. This section explores the methodologies and applications of network and graph visualization within AI, highlighting their significance in unraveling complex interdependencies.

Graph structures and their representation

Graphs are versatile data structures that can model a wide array of phenomena, from social interactions to molecular structures. In AI, graphs are frequently employed to represent knowledge bases, where nodes symbolize entities and edges denote relationships. The challenge in visualizing graphs lies in their potential complexity, as large graphs can become unwieldy and difficult to interpret. Effective graph visualization requires techniques that can manage this complexity while preserving the essential structure and relationships inherent in the data.

Visualization techniques

Several techniques have been developed to facilitate the visualization of graphs. Force-directed layouts, for instance, are popular for their ability to intuitively position nodes based on repulsive and attractive forces, creating aesthetically pleasing representations that reveal clusters and connections. These layouts are particularly effective for medium-sized graphs, where the spatial arrangement can highlight community structures and key nodes.

Hierarchical layouts offer an alternative approach, organizing nodes into levels based on their relationships, which is useful for visualizing directed acyclic graphs such as organizational charts or dependency graphs. This method provides clarity by emphasizing the flow and directionality of relationships, making it easier to trace paths and dependencies.

For large-scale graphs, techniques such as graph clustering and simplification are essential. Clustering algorithms group nodes into communities, reducing the overall complexity and making it feasible to visualize large networks by focusing on inter-cluster relationships. Simplification techniques, such as edge bundling, further enhance readability by aggregating similar edges, reducing visual clutter.

Applications in AI

Network and graph visualization play a pivotal role in AI by facilitating the interpretation of complex relational data structures. In social network analysis, visualizations help uncover influential nodes and community structures, enabling insights into information dissemination and social dynamics. Knowledge graphs, which represent entities and their interconnections, benefit from visualization techniques that elucidate relationships, supporting tasks such as semantic search and natural language processing. Furthermore, **graph neural networks (GNNs)** leverage graph structures to enhance learning processes, and visualizing these graphs aids in understanding model behavior and decision-making pathways. These applications underscore the importance of graph visualization in advancing AI's capabilities across diverse domains.

Social network analysis

In social network analysis, graph visualization plays a crucial role in understanding the dynamics of social interactions. By visualizing social graphs, AI systems can identify influential nodes, detect communities, and analyze the spread of information or behaviors. This capability is invaluable in applications ranging from marketing and recommendation systems to the study of misinformation and sentiment analysis.

Knowledge graphs

Knowledge graphs, which represent structured information in a graph format, are increasingly used in AI for tasks such as natural language processing and semantic search. The visualization of knowledge graphs enables researchers and practitioners to explore the interconnectedness of concepts, facilitating the discovery of new insights and relationships. This is particularly beneficial in domains like biomedical research, where understanding the complex interactions between genes, proteins, and diseases can lead to breakthroughs in treatment and diagnosis.

Graph neural networks

The advent of GNNs has further underscored the importance of graph visualization in AI. GNNs leverage the structure of graphs to perform tasks such as node classification and link prediction, making them powerful tools for relational learning. Visualizing the input graphs and the learned embeddings can provide insights into the model's decision-making process, enhancing interpretability and aiding in model refinement.

Challenges and future directions

Despite the advancements in graph visualization, several challenges remain. The scalability of visualization techniques is a persistent issue, particularly as datasets continue to grow in size and complexity. Developing methods that can efficiently process and visualize large-scale graphs without sacrificing detail or clarity is an ongoing area of research.

Another challenge lies in the dynamic nature of graphs, where relationships and nodes may change over time. Visualizing these temporal dynamics requires innovative approaches that can capture changes and trends without overwhelming the viewer. Interactive visualization tools that allow users to explore different time slices or simulate the evolution of the graph are promising solutions to this challenge.

Looking forward, the integration of AI and graph visualization holds significant potential. AI-driven visualization techniques, which leverage machine learning to automatically adjust layouts or highlight significant patterns, could revolutionize the way graphs are interpreted. Additionally, the incorporation of **augmented reality** (**AR**) and **virtual reality** (**VR**) technologies could provide immersive visualization experiences, enabling users to explore complex graphs in three-dimensional space.

Network and graph visualization is a vital component of AI applications, offering insights into relational data that are crucial for understanding complex systems. Through advanced visualization techniques, practitioners can uncover hidden patterns, enhance model interpretability, and drive informed decision-making. As AI continues to evolve, the synergy between graph visualization and AI promises to unlock new frontiers in data analysis and interpretation, paving the way for more transparent and effective AI systems.

Augmented analytics and AI-driven data storytelling

In the modern data-driven landscape, the ability to transform complex datasets into actionable insights is paramount. Augmented analytics and AI-driven data storytelling have emerged as transformative approaches in this context, leveraging advanced technologies to enhance data interpretation and communication. These methodologies empower users to derive meaningful narratives from data, facilitating informed decision-making and fostering a deeper understanding of complex phenomena. This section explores the principles and applications of augmented analytics and AI-driven data storytelling, emphasizing their significance in the realm of AI.

Augmented analytics for enhancing data interpretation

Augmented analytics refers to the use of machine learning, natural language processing, and other AI technologies to automate and enhance data analysis processes. By integrating these advanced capabilities, augmented analytics platforms can sift through vast datasets, identify patterns, and generate insights with minimal human intervention. This automation not only accelerates the analytical process but also reduces the potential for human error, ensuring more accurate and reliable outcomes.

One of the key features of augmented analytics is its ability to democratize data access and analysis. Traditional data analysis often requires specialized skills and knowledge, creating barriers for non-expert users. Augmented analytics platforms, however, are designed to be user-friendly, enabling individuals across an organization to engage with data and extract insights without the need for extensive technical expertise. This democratization is achieved through intuitive interfaces, natural language queries, and automated insight generation, allowing users to interact with data in a more accessible manner.

The integration of AI into analytics processes also enhances the depth and quality of insights. Machine learning algorithms can uncover hidden patterns and correlations that may not be immediately apparent through traditional analysis methods. For instance, predictive analytics can forecast future trends based on historical data, while anomaly detection algorithms can identify outliers that warrant further investigation. These capabilities enable organizations to anticipate changes, optimize operations, and make data-driven decisions with greater confidence.

AI-driven data storytelling for compelling narratives

While augmented analytics focuses on the analysis and interpretation of data, AI-driven data storytelling emphasizes the communication of insights in a compelling and understandable manner. Data storytelling combines the power of narrative with data visualization, transforming raw data into stories that resonate with audiences. This approach not only enhances comprehension but also engages stakeholders, facilitating more effective communication and decision-making.

AI-driven data storytelling leverages natural language generation and advanced visualization techniques to create narratives that are both informative and engaging. Natural language generation algorithms can automatically generate textual descriptions and explanations of data insights, making complex information more accessible to non-technical audiences. These narratives are often complemented by dynamic visualizations that illustrate key points and trends, providing a holistic view of the data.

The effectiveness of data storytelling lies in its ability to contextualize data within a broader narrative framework. By framing data insights within a story, organizations can convey the relevance and implications of their findings, helping stakeholders understand the significance of the data and its impact on strategic objectives. This narrative approach also facilitates the identification of key takeaways and action points, ensuring that insights are not only understood but also acted upon.

Applications and implications

Augmented analytics and AI-driven data storytelling have a wide range of applications across various domains. In business, these methodologies are used to enhance decision-making processes, optimize operations, and drive innovation. For example, marketing teams can leverage augmented analytics to identify customer segments and personalize campaigns, while finance departments can use data storytelling to communicate financial performance and projections to stakeholders.

In healthcare, augmented analytics can assist in diagnosing diseases and predicting patient outcomes, while data storytelling can be used to communicate treatment plans and progress to patients and their families. Similarly, in the public sector, these approaches can enhance policy analysis and communication, enabling governments to make informed decisions and engage with citizens more effectively.

The implications of augmented analytics and AI-driven data storytelling extend beyond individual applications. By enhancing data literacy and fostering a culture of data-driven decision-making, these methodologies contribute to the overall effectiveness and competitiveness of organizations. They also promote transparency and accountability, as stakeholders are better equipped to understand and scrutinize data-driven decisions.

Challenges and future directions

Despite their potential, augmented analytics and AI-driven data storytelling face several challenges. One of the primary concerns is data privacy and security, as the automation and integration of data processes increase the risk of unauthorized access and misuse. Ensuring compliance with data protection regulations and implementing robust security measures are essential to mitigate these risks.

Another challenge is the potential for algorithmic bias, which can arise from the data used to train machine learning models. Bias in data can lead to skewed insights and reinforce existing inequalities, undermining the credibility and fairness of data-driven decisions. Addressing this issue requires careful data curation and the development of algorithms that are transparent and accountable.

Looking forward, the future of augmented analytics and AI-driven data storytelling is promising. Advances in AI and machine learning will continue to enhance the capabilities of these methodologies, enabling more sophisticated and nuanced insights. The integration of emerging technologies such as augmented reality and virtual reality could further revolutionize data storytelling, providing immersive and interactive experiences that enhance engagement and understanding.

Augmented analytics and AI-driven data storytelling represent a paradigm shift in the way organizations engage with data. By automating analysis and crafting compelling narratives, these methodologies empower users to derive meaningful insights and communicate them effectively. As AI continues to evolve, the synergy between augmented analytics and data storytelling will play an increasingly vital role in shaping the future of data-driven decision-making and innovation.

Accessibility and inclusivity in AI visualizations

In the rapidly advancing field of AI, the visualization of data and model outputs plays a critical role in enhancing comprehension and facilitating informed decision-making. However, as AI systems become increasingly integrated into various aspects of society, ensuring that visualizations are accessible and inclusive for all users, regardless of their abilities or backgrounds, has become paramount. This section examines the principles and practices of accessibility and inclusivity in AI visualizations, highlighting their importance in fostering equitable access to AI-driven insights.

Importance of accessibility in AI visualizations

Accessibility in AI visualizations refers to the design and implementation of visual content that can be effectively perceived and understood by individuals with diverse abilities, including those with visual, auditory, cognitive, or motor impairments. Ensuring accessibility is not only a legal and ethical obligation but also a crucial factor in maximizing the reach and impact of AI systems.

Visualizations that are accessible enable individuals with disabilities to engage with data on an equal footing with their peers, promoting inclusivity and diversity in data-driven decision-making. This is particularly important in contexts where AI insights influence critical areas such as healthcare, education, and public policy. By designing visualizations that accommodate a wide range of user needs, organizations can ensure that their AI systems serve the entire population, not just a select group.

To achieve accessibility, AI visualizations must adhere to established guidelines and standards, such as the **Web Content Accessibility Guidelines** (**WCAG**), which provide recommendations for making web content more accessible. These guidelines emphasize the importance of providing alternative text for images, ensuring sufficient color contrast, and enabling keyboard navigation, among other considerations.

Techniques for enhancing accessibility

Several techniques can be employed to enhance the accessibility of AI visualizations. One fundamental approach is the use of alternative text descriptions, which provide concise explanations of visual content for individuals who use screen readers. These descriptions should convey the essential information and insights depicted in the visualization, allowing users to understand the data without relying solely on visual cues.

Color contrast is another critical consideration in accessible design. Visualizations should use color palettes that provide sufficient contrast between text and background elements, ensuring readability for individuals with visual impairments, such as color blindness. Tools and resources are available to assist designers in selecting accessible color schemes that meet contrast ratio requirements.

Interactive elements within visualizations should also be designed with accessibility in mind. This includes ensuring that all interactive features, such as buttons and sliders, are operable via keyboard and compatible with assistive technologies. Providing clear labels and instructions for interactive components can further enhance usability for individuals with cognitive or motor impairments.

Inclusivity in AI visualizations

Inclusivity in AI visualizations extends beyond accessibility to encompass the representation and consideration of diverse user perspectives and experiences. Inclusive visualizations are designed to resonate with a broad audience, considering cultural, linguistic, and contextual differences that may influence how data is perceived and interpreted.

One aspect of inclusivity is the use of culturally sensitive and representative imagery and symbols. Visualizations should avoid relying on culturally specific icons or metaphors that may not be universally understood. Instead, designers should strive to use neutral and universally recognizable symbols that convey information clearly across different cultural contexts.

Language is another important factor in inclusive design. Visualizations should be available in multiple languages to accommodate users from diverse linguistic backgrounds. Providing language options and ensuring that text is clear and concise can help bridge language barriers and enhance comprehension.

Inclusivity also involves considering the diverse contexts in which visualizations may be used. For example, visualizations intended for use in educational settings should be designed to support diverse learning styles and preferences. This may include offering multiple modes of engagement, such as auditory descriptions or interactive simulations, to cater to different learning needs.

Challenges and future directions

Despite the growing recognition of the importance of accessibility and inclusivity in AI visualizations, several challenges remain. One of the primary challenges is the need for increased awareness and education among designers and developers regarding accessibility best practices. Many individuals involved in the creation of visualizations may lack the knowledge or resources to implement accessible and inclusive designs effectively.

Another challenge is the dynamic and complex nature of AI-generated visualizations, which can make it difficult to apply traditional accessibility techniques. As AI systems generate increasingly sophisticated and interactive visual content, new approaches and technologies will be required to ensure accessibility and inclusivity.

Looking forward, the integration of AI technologies themselves holds promise for enhancing accessibility and inclusivity in visualizations. AI-driven tools can assist in the automated generation of alternative text, the evaluation of color contrast, and the translation of content into multiple languages. By leveraging AI to address accessibility challenges, organizations can create more inclusive visualizations that cater to a diverse audience.

Accessibility and inclusivity are essential components of effective AI visualizations, ensuring that all individuals, regardless of their abilities or backgrounds, can engage with and benefit from AI-driven insights. By adhering to accessibility guidelines and embracing inclusive design principles, organizations can create visualizations that are not only legally and ethically compliant but also impactful and meaningful for a wide range of users. As AI continues to evolve, the commitment to accessibility and inclusivity will be crucial in realizing the full potential of AI systems and fostering a more equitable and inclusive society.

Conclusion

This chapter has explored the critical role of data visualization and explainable AI in enhancing the interpretability and usability of AI systems. Through the examination of time series and high-dimensional data visualization, we have highlighted the importance of intuitive and interactive methods for uncovering patterns and relationships within complex datasets. These visualization techniques are essential for enabling users to derive meaningful insights, thereby supporting informed decision-making processes across various domains. The discussion on network and graph visualization emphasized their utility in representing relational data structures, facilitating the exploration of interconnected systems. These visualizations are invaluable in domains such as social network analysis and knowledge graph exploration, where understanding relationships and interactions is crucial for deriving insights.

Furthermore, the chapter looked into augmented analytics and AI-driven data storytelling as transformative approaches that leverage advanced technologies to enhance data interpretation and communication. By automating analysis and crafting compelling narratives, these methodologies empower users to engage with data in a more accessible and meaningful way. In the subsequent chapter, we will explore the future trends and emerging technologies in AI data architecture. This exploration will include advances such as quantum computing and decentralized AI, providing insights into the future trajectory of AI data architecture and its implications for various industries and applications.

In the next chapter, we will be exploring the emerging trends in AI data architecture. We will primarily explore AI's transformative impact on data management, highlighting innovative methodologies and future data architecture. It will examine AI's role in enhancing efficiency, scalability, and decision-making across sectors. The chapter will elucidate AI-powered solutions like **natural language processing (NLP)** interfaces and self-optimizing systems, addressing data complexities and democratizing access. It will also investigate emerging trends in data synthesis and simulation to overcome data scarcity and privacy concerns, emphasizing robust model validation for reliable AI systems.

CHAPTER 11

Emerging Trends in AI Data Architecture

Introduction

The landscape of data management is undergoing a profound transformation, driven by the rapid advancements in **artificial intelligence** (**AI**) technologies. As organizations grapple with the challenges posed by the exponential growth in data volume, velocity, and complexity, there is an increasing need for innovative approaches to data architecture that can harness the power of AI to enhance efficiency, scalability, and decision-making capabilities. This chapter looks into the future trends and emerging technologies shaping AI data architecture, offering insights into how these developments are redefining the way data is processed, analyzed, and utilized.

AI technologies are at the forefront of this transformation, providing the tools necessary to manage and derive insights from vast and complex datasets. From natural language processing interfaces that democratize data access to self-optimizing systems that autonomously enhance performance, AI is revolutionizing traditional data management practices. These advancements are not only addressing current challenges but also opening new avenues for innovation and efficiency across various industries.

The exploration of future trends in AI data architecture encompasses a diverse array of methodologies and technologies, each contributing to the evolution of data systems. The integration of AI-driven solutions such as data synthesis and simulation, along with cutting-edge developments like digital twins and high-fidelity simulations, highlights the potential for AI to reshape data architectures fundamentally. As these technologies continue to mature, they promise to offer unprecedented capabilities for optimizing data processes and enhancing decision-making.

This chapter aims to provide a comprehensive overview of these emerging trends and technologies, examining their implications for data architecture and their potential to drive innovation in data management practices. By understanding and embracing these advancements, organizations can position themselves at the forefront of the digital age, ensuring that their data systems are robust, efficient, and capable of meeting the demands of an increasingly complex and dynamic world.

Structure

The chapter covers the following topics:

- Quantum computing for AI
- Neuromorphic computing architectures
- AI-driven data architecture optimization
- Decentralized AI and blockchain
- Green AI and sustainable data architectures
- Natural language interfaces for data management
- Data synthesis and simulation
- AI-powered self-optimizing data systems

Objectives

The primary objective of this chapter is to explore the transformative potential of artificial intelligence in redefining data management practices. This chapter seeks to provide a comprehensive analysis of the innovative methodologies and technologies shaping the future of data architecture, focusing on how AI is driving efficiency, scalability, and enhanced decision-making capabilities across diverse sectors. By examining these advancements, the chapter aims to equip readers with a nuanced understanding of the opportunities and challenges associated with integrating AI into data systems.

A key objective is to elucidate the role of AI-powered solutions, such as natural language processing interfaces and self-optimizing systems, in addressing the complexities associated with modern data environments. This involves an in-depth exploration of how these technologies democratize data access, optimize performance, and reduce operational costs. The chapter endeavors to highlight the practical applications of these solutions, demonstrating their impact on industries such as telecommunications, finance, and healthcare, where data-driven decision-making is critical to success.

Furthermore, the chapter aims to investigate the emerging trends in data synthesis and simulation, emphasizing their significance in overcoming data scarcity and privacy concerns. By showcasing the methodologies that enable the generation of synthetic data and the simulation of complex systems, the chapter seeks to underscore the importance of robust model validation and testing in ensuring the reliability of AI systems.

Quantum computing for AI

Quantum computing represents a paradigm shift in computational capabilities, leveraging the principles of quantum mechanics to process information in ways that classical computers cannot. At its core, quantum computing utilizes quantum bits, or qubits, which, unlike classical bits, can exist in multiple states simultaneously due to the phenomenon known as superposition. This ability allows quantum computers to perform complex calculations at exponentially faster rates compared to their classical counterparts. Furthermore, quantum entanglement, another key principle, enables qubits that are entangled to be interdependent, allowing for highly efficient parallel processing. This transformative technology holds significant promise for artificial intelligence, particularly in areas requiring vast computational power and sophisticated data processing.

Quantum computing and AI synergy

The intersection of quantum computing and artificial intelligence offers unprecedented opportunities to enhance AI capabilities. Quantum algorithms, such as Shor's and Grover's algorithms, have already demonstrated potential in solving problems deemed intractable for classical computers. In AI, these quantum algorithms can be adapted to optimize machine learning models, improve data search and retrieval processes, and enhance pattern recognition. **Quantum machine learning** (QML) is an emerging field that seeks to harness quantum computing to accelerate AI tasks, such as training deep neural networks and performing complex simulations. The synergy between quantum computing and AI promises to unlock new levels of efficiency and accuracy in data processing and model training.

Quantum algorithms for AI

Quantum algorithms are designed to exploit the unique properties of quantum mechanics to solve specific problems more efficiently than classical algorithms. In the context of AI, quantum algorithms can significantly accelerate tasks such as optimization, sampling, and classification. For instance, the **quantum approximate optimization algorithm** (QAOA) is particularly suited for solving combinatorial optimization problems, which are prevalent in AI applications. Similarly, quantum-enhanced sampling algorithms can improve the efficiency of probabilistic models by generating more accurate samples from complex distributions. These advancements in quantum algorithms are poised to revolutionize AI by enabling faster and more precise data analysis and decision-making processes.

Quantum machine learning

Quantum machine learning (**QML**) represents a convergence of quantum computing and AI, aiming to leverage quantum algorithms to enhance machine learning processes. QML explores the use of quantum computers to accelerate the training of machine learning models, optimize hyperparameters, and improve feature selection. **Quantum neural networks** (**QNNs**), a subset of QML, seek to replicate the structure and function of classical neural networks using quantum circuits. These quantum circuits can potentially process information more efficiently by exploiting quantum parallelism. QML also investigates quantum kernel methods, which can transform data into higher-dimensional spaces, enabling more effective pattern recognition and classification.

Challenges and opportunities

While the potential of quantum computing for AI is immense, several challenges must be overcome to realize its full benefits. One of the primary challenges is the development of stable and scalable quantum hardware. Quantum computers are highly sensitive to external disturbances, leading to errors and decoherence. Therefore, significant advancements in error correction and quantum coherence are necessary to build reliable quantum systems. Additionally, the integration of quantum computing into existing AI frameworks requires the development of new algorithms and software tools. Despite these challenges, the opportunities presented by quantum computing for AI are vast. Quantum computing can enhance AI's ability to process large-scale datasets, optimize complex models, and perform real-time data analysis, paving the way for more sophisticated and intelligent AI systems.

Applications and implications

The application of quantum computing in AI has far-reaching implications across various industries. In finance, quantum computing can optimize trading strategies and risk management by processing large volumes of data more efficiently. In healthcare, quantum-enhanced AI can accelerate drug discovery and personalized medicine by analyzing complex biological data. In logistics, quantum algorithms can optimize supply chain operations and route planning. Furthermore, the integration of quantum computing into AI systems can lead to the development of more intelligent autonomous systems, capable of making real-time decisions in dynamic environments. As quantum computing technology matures, its impact on AI will likely extend to numerous domains, transforming how data is processed and analyzed.

Quantum computing for AI represents a frontier in computational innovation, offering the potential to transform data architecture and AI capabilities. By harnessing the principles of quantum mechanics, quantum computing can accelerate AI processes, enhance data analysis, and improve decision-making. While challenges remain in developing stable and scalable quantum systems, the opportunities presented by quantum computing are immense. As research and development in quantum computing continue to advance, its integration with AI is poised to revolutionize data architecture, enabling more efficient and intelligent AI systems across various industries. The future of AI data architecture will likely be shaped by the continued exploration and application of quantum computing technologies.

Neuromorphic computing architectures

Neuromorphic computing is an innovative approach to computation that seeks to emulate the architecture and functionality of the human brain. Unlike traditional computing architectures, which rely on sequential processing, neuromorphic systems are designed to mimic the parallel processing capabilities of biological neural networks. This paradigm shift is achieved through the use of specialized hardware known as **neuromorphic chips**, which incorporate artificial neurons and synapses to process information in a manner akin to the brain's neural activity. Neuromorphic computing holds significant promise for advancing artificial intelligence by offering new ways to process data, recognize patterns, and adapt to changing environments.

Principles of neuromorphic computing

The principles underlying neuromorphic computing are rooted in the study of neuroscience and the structure of biological neural networks. Neuromorphic systems are characterized by their ability to perform event-driven computation, allowing them to process information asynchronously and in parallel. This is facilitated by the use of **spiking neural networks (SNNs)**, which emulate the way neurons communicate through electrical impulses or spikes. Unlike conventional artificial neural networks, SNNs leverage temporal dynamics and spike timing to encode and transmit information, enabling more efficient and biologically plausible computation. Neuromorphic architectures also prioritize energy efficiency, utilizing low-power hardware to perform complex computations with minimal energy consumption, a feature crucial for the development of sustainable AI systems.

Neuromorphic hardware and design

Neuromorphic hardware represents a departure from traditional silicon-based processors, incorporating novel materials and designs to replicate neural functions. Neuromorphic chips, such as IBM's TrueNorth and Intel's Loihi, are engineered to simulate the behavior of neurons and synapses, enabling them to perform cognitive tasks with high efficiency. These chips consist of arrays of artificial neurons interconnected by synapses, capable of processing information in parallel and adapting to new patterns through learning mechanisms. The design of neuromorphic hardware is informed by insights from neuroscience, with the aim of achieving brain-like computation in terms of speed, adaptability, and energy efficiency. The development of neuromorphic hardware is a critical step toward realizing the potential of neuromorphic computing for AI applications.

Advantages of neuromorphic computing

Neuromorphic computing offers several advantages over traditional computing architectures, particularly in the context of AI. One of the primary benefits is its ability to perform real-time processing and pattern recognition, making it well-suited for applications requiring rapid decision-making and adaptation. Neuromorphic systems excel at handling unstructured and noisy data, leveraging their brain-inspired architecture to identify patterns and correlations in complex datasets. Additionally, neuromorphic computing is inherently energy-efficient, capable of performing computations with significantly lower power consumption compared to conventional processors. This energy efficiency is crucial for the development of sustainable AI systems and is particularly beneficial for applications in mobile and edge computing, where power constraints are a critical consideration.

Applications in artificial intelligence

The application of neuromorphic computing in artificial intelligence spans a wide range of domains, offering new possibilities for enhancing AI capabilities. In robotics, neuromorphic systems can facilitate real-time sensory processing and decision-making, enabling robots to interact with their environment in a more adaptive and intelligent manner. In computer vision, neuromorphic architectures can improve image recognition and object detection by processing visual information in a manner similar to the human visual system. Neuromorphic computing also holds promise for advancing natural language processing, with the potential to enhance speech recognition and language understanding through brain-inspired models. Furthermore, neuromorphic systems can contribute to the development of autonomous vehicles, providing the computational power needed for real-time navigation and obstacle avoidance.

Challenges and future directions

Despite the promising potential of neuromorphic computing, several challenges must be addressed to fully realize its benefits for AI. One of the primary challenges is the development of scalable neuromorphic hardware that can accommodate large-scale neural networks and complex computations. Additionally, the integration of neuromorphic systems into existing AI frameworks requires the development of new algorithms and software tools that can leverage the unique capabilities of neuromorphic architectures. The complexity of designing and programming neuromorphic systems presents a significant hurdle, necessitating advancements in both hardware design and algorithm development. However, ongoing research and development in neuromorphic computing are paving the way for overcoming these challenges, with the potential to transform AI data architecture in the coming years.

Neuromorphic computing architecture represents a groundbreaking approach to computation, offering new possibilities for advancing artificial intelligence through brain-inspired design. By emulating the parallel processing capabilities and energy efficiency of biological neural networks, neuromorphic systems hold significant promise for enhancing AI's ability to process data, recognize patterns, and adapt to dynamic environments. While challenges remain in the development and integration of neuromorphic hardware and algorithms, the potential benefits of neuromorphic computing for AI are immense. As research in this field continues to advance, neuromorphic computing is poised to play a pivotal role in shaping the future of AI data architecture, enabling more intelligent and sustainable AI systems across various domains.

AI-driven data architecture optimization

In the rapidly evolving landscape of data management and artificial intelligence, the optimization of data architectures has become a critical concern for organizations seeking to harness the full potential of AI technologies. AI-driven data architecture optimization refers to the use of artificial intelligence techniques to enhance the design, efficiency, and scalability of data systems. This approach leverages machine learning algorithms, predictive analytics, and automated decision-making processes to optimize data storage, retrieval, and processing, thereby improving overall system performance and reducing operational costs. This section explores the various dimensions of AI-driven data architecture optimization, highlighting its significance, methodologies, and implications for the future of data management.

Role of AI in data architecture

Artificial intelligence plays a pivotal role in transforming traditional data architectures into dynamic and adaptive systems capable of meeting the demands of modern applications. By integrating AI into data architecture, organizations can achieve greater flexibility and responsiveness in managing large volumes of data. AI techniques facilitate the automation of routine tasks, such as data cleansing, integration, and transformation, thereby reducing the burden on human operators and minimizing the risk of errors. Moreover, AI-driven optimization enables real-time monitoring and analysis of data flows, allowing organizations to identify bottlenecks and inefficiencies in data processing pipelines. This proactive approach to data management enhances system reliability and ensures that data architectures can scale effectively to accommodate growing data volumes.

Methodologies for AI-driven optimization

The methodologies employed in AI-driven data architecture optimization are diverse and multifaceted, encompassing a wide range of AI techniques and tools. Machine learning algorithms, particularly those based on reinforcement learning and deep learning, are commonly used to model and predict data access patterns, enabling the dynamic allocation of resources and optimization of data storage strategies. Predictive analytics plays a crucial role in forecasting future data requirements and guiding the design of scalable data architectures. Additionally, AI-driven optimization often involves the use of automated decision-making systems that can adjust data processing workflows in response to changing conditions, such as variations in data volume or user demand. These methodologies are supported by advanced data analytics platforms and cloud-based services, which provide the computational power and flexibility needed to implement AI-driven optimization at scale.

Benefits of AI-driven optimization

The benefits of AI-driven data architecture optimization are manifold, offering significant advantages in terms of performance, cost-efficiency, and adaptability. One of the primary benefits is the ability to enhance system performance by optimizing data processing workflows and reducing latency. AI-driven optimization enables organizations to achieve faster data retrieval and processing times, thereby improving the overall responsiveness of applications and services. Cost-efficiency is another critical benefit, as AI techniques can identify and eliminate redundant data storage and processing activities, leading to substantial savings in infrastructure and operational costs. Furthermore, AI-driven optimization enhances the adaptability of data architectures, allowing organizations to quickly respond to changes in data volume, user demand, and technological advancements. This adaptability is crucial for maintaining a competitive edge in a rapidly changing business environment.

Challenges and considerations

Despite its potential benefits, AI-driven data architecture optimization presents several challenges and considerations that must be addressed to ensure successful implementation. One of the primary challenges is the complexity of integrating AI techniques into existing data architectures, which often requires significant changes to infrastructure and workflows. Organizations must also consider the ethical implications of AI-driven optimization, particularly in terms of data privacy and security. The use of AI algorithms to analyze and optimize data architectures raises concerns about the potential misuse of sensitive information and the need for robust data governance frameworks. Additionally, the reliance on AI-driven systems necessitates a high level of transparency and interpretability, ensuring that decision-making processes are understandable and accountable. Addressing these challenges requires a comprehensive approach that combines technical expertise with ethical and regulatory considerations.

Future directions and implications

The future of AI-driven data architecture optimization is likely to be shaped by ongoing advancements in AI technologies and the increasing demand for efficient and scalable data management solutions. As AI techniques continue to evolve, organizations will have access to more sophisticated tools and methodologies for optimizing data architectures, enabling them to achieve even greater levels of performance and efficiency. The integration of AI-driven optimization with emerging technologies, such as edge computing and the **Internet of Things** (**IoT**), will further enhance the capabilities of data architectures, allowing organizations to process and analyze data at the network edge in real time. This development has significant implications for industries such as healthcare, finance, and manufacturing, where real-time data processing is critical for operational success. As AI-driven optimization becomes more prevalent, organizations will need to adapt their data management strategies to leverage the full potential of AI technologies, ensuring that their data architectures remain competitive and capable of meeting future challenges.

AI-driven data architecture optimization represents a transformative approach to data management, offering significant benefits in terms of performance, cost-efficiency, and adaptability. By leveraging AI techniques, organizations can enhance the design and operation of their data architectures, enabling them to respond effectively to changing data requirements and technological advancements. While challenges remain in terms of integration, ethics, and transparency, the potential of AI-driven optimization to revolutionize data management is undeniable. As the field continues to evolve, organizations that embrace AI-driven optimization will be well-positioned to capitalize on the opportunities presented by the digital age, ensuring that their data architectures remain robust, efficient, and future-ready.

Decentralized AI and blockchain

The convergence of decentralized AI and blockchain technology represents a transformative shift in the way data architectures are designed and managed. This integration is poised to address some of the most pressing challenges in AI, such as data privacy, security, and transparency, by leveraging the inherent characteristics of blockchain: decentralization, immutability, and trustlessness. In this section, we explore the synergies between decentralized AI and blockchain, examining their potential to redefine data architectures and enhance AI systems' robustness and reliability.

Concept of decentralized AI

Decentralized AI refers to the distribution of AI processes across multiple nodes or agents, rather than relying on a centralized server or authority. This approach mirrors the decentralized nature of blockchain technology, where data is stored and verified across a distributed network. Decentralized AI systems are designed to operate autonomously, with each node capable of performing computations and making decisions based on local data and interactions with other nodes. This architecture offers several advantages, including enhanced resilience to single points of failure, improved scalability, and the ability to operate in environments with limited connectivity.

Blockchain as an enabler for decentralized AI

Blockchain technology provides a robust framework for implementing decentralized AI systems by offering a secure and transparent platform for data exchange and collaboration.

The decentralized ledger of a blockchain ensures that all transactions and data exchanges are recorded immutably, providing a verifiable and tamper-proof history of interactions. This transparency is particularly valuable in AI applications, where the provenance and integrity of data are critical for building trustworthy models. Furthermore, the use of smart contracts—self-executing contracts with the terms of the agreement directly written into code—enables automated and conditional interactions between AI agents, facilitating complex workflows and decision-making processes.

Data privacy and security

One of the most significant benefits of integrating blockchain with decentralized AI is the enhancement of data privacy and security. Traditional AI systems often rely on centralized data repositories, which can be vulnerable to breaches and unauthorized access. In contrast, a blockchain-based decentralized AI system can implement advanced cryptographic techniques, such as zero-knowledge proofs and homomorphic encryption, to ensure that data remains private while still being used for AI computations. These techniques allow AI models to be trained and deployed without exposing sensitive data, addressing privacy concerns and compliance requirements in sectors such as healthcare and finance.

Trust and transparency in AI systems

Trust and transparency are critical components of any AI system, particularly in applications that impact decision-making and human interactions. Blockchain technology enhances trust in decentralized AI systems by providing an immutable and transparent record of all data exchanges and model updates. This transparency allows stakeholders to verify the integrity of AI models and ensure that they have not been tampered with or biased. Additionally, blockchain can facilitate the creation of decentralized marketplaces for AI models and data, where participants can exchange resources and services with confidence, knowing that all transactions are recorded and auditable.

Challenges and limitations

Despite the promising potential of decentralized AI and blockchain, several challenges and limitations must be addressed to fully realize their benefits. One of the primary challenges is the scalability of blockchain networks, which can be constrained by the need for consensus among nodes and the computational overhead of maintaining a distributed ledger. These scalability issues can impact the performance and responsiveness of decentralized AI systems, particularly in real-time applications. Furthermore, the integration of AI and blockchain requires the development of new algorithms and protocols that can efficiently leverage the strengths of both technologies while mitigating their weaknesses. There is also a need for standardized frameworks and interoperability solutions to ensure that decentralized AI systems can operate seamlessly across different blockchain platforms.

Future directions

The future of decentralized AI and blockchain is likely to be shaped by ongoing advancements in both fields, as well as the increasing demand for secure and transparent AI solutions. Research efforts are focused on developing more scalable and efficient blockchain architectures, such as sharding and layer-two solutions, which can support the computational demands of decentralized AI systems. Additionally, the exploration of hybrid models that combine centralized and decentralized elements may offer a pragmatic approach to balancing performance and security. As these technologies continue to evolve, they are expected to play a pivotal role in enabling new applications and business models, from **decentralized finance (DeFi)** to autonomous supply chains and smart cities.

Decentralized AI and blockchain represent a powerful combination that has the potential to revolutionize data architectures and enhance the capabilities of AI systems. By leveraging the decentralized, secure, and transparent nature of blockchain, AI systems can achieve greater levels of privacy, trust, and efficiency. While challenges remain in terms of scalability and integration, the ongoing development of these technologies promises to unlock new opportunities and applications across various industries. As organizations continue to explore and adopt decentralized AI and blockchain, they will be better positioned to address the complex challenges of the digital age and build more resilient and trustworthy AI systems.

Green AI and sustainable data architectures

As AI continues to permeate various sectors, the environmental impact of AI technologies has become a growing concern. The computational demands of AI, particularly in data-intensive tasks such as training large models, contribute significantly to energy consumption and carbon emissions. This has led to the emergence of Green AI, an initiative aimed at developing AI technologies with minimal environmental impact. Green AI emphasizes the importance of sustainability in AI development, advocating for practices that reduce energy usage and promote environmental responsibility. In tandem with Green AI, sustainable data architectures are being designed to optimize data storage, processing, and management in ways that align with ecological goals. This section explores the principles and practices of Green AI and sustainable data architectures, highlighting their significance, methodologies, and implications for the future of AI.

Environmental impact of AI

The environmental impact of AI is largely driven by the energy-intensive processes required for data management and model training. The exponential growth of data and the increasing complexity of AI models necessitate substantial computational resources, often resulting in high energy consumption. Data centers, which house the infrastructure needed for AI processing, are significant contributors to global energy usage and carbon emissions. The training of large-scale AI models, such as deep neural networks, can consume vast amounts of electricity, exacerbating the environmental footprint of AI technologies. This impact is particularly concerning in the context of climate change, where reducing energy consumption and carbon emissions is critical for achieving sustainability goals.

Principles of Green AI

Green AI is founded on the principle of balancing AI advancement with environmental stewardship. This involves the development of AI technologies that prioritize energy efficiency and sustainability without compromising performance. Green AI advocates for transparency in reporting the environmental impact of AI systems, encouraging researchers and developers to consider energy consumption and carbon emissions as key metrics in AI evaluation. This transparency fosters accountability and promotes the adoption of environmentally responsible practices in AI development. Additionally, Green AI emphasizes the importance of interdisciplinary collaboration, bringing together experts from AI, environmental science, and engineering to develop innovative solutions that address the ecological challenges associated with AI.

Sustainable data storage solutions

Sustainable data storage solutions are central to the goal of reducing the environmental impact of AI systems. As data volumes continue to grow exponentially, driven by the proliferation of digital devices and the increasing complexity of AI models, the demand for efficient and sustainable storage solutions becomes paramount. This section explores the strategies and technologies employed to optimize data storage, focusing on energy efficiency and environmental sustainability.

Data deduplication is a critical technique in sustainable data storage, aimed at minimizing redundancy and optimizing storage capacity. This process involves identifying and eliminating duplicate copies of data, ensuring that only unique instances are stored. By reducing the overall data footprint, deduplication decreases the need for extensive storage infrastructure and the associated energy consumption. The implementation of deduplication algorithms can significantly enhance storage efficiency, contributing to both cost savings and environmental benefits.

Compression techniques further complement sustainable data storage efforts by reducing the size of data files, thereby optimizing storage space and minimizing resource usage. Data compression algorithms, such as lossless and lossy compression, enable the efficient encoding of information, allowing for reduced storage requirements without compromising data integrity. The application of compression techniques is particularly beneficial in handling large datasets and multimedia files, where storage demands are substantial. By leveraging compression, organizations can achieve more sustainable data management practices, aligning with the broader goals of Green AI.

The adoption of tiered storage architectures represents another strategy for sustainable data storage, optimizing resource allocation based on data access patterns and importance.

Tiered storage systems classify data into different levels, each with varying performance and cost characteristics. Frequently accessed data is stored on high-performance, energy-efficient storage media, while less critical data is relegated to lower-cost, energy-saving storage solutions. This hierarchical approach ensures that storage resources are utilized effectively, reducing energy consumption and enhancing overall efficiency. The implementation of tiered storage aligns with the principles of sustainable data management, promoting resource optimization and environmental responsibility.

The role of renewable energy in powering data storage infrastructure is increasingly recognized as a vital component of sustainable data architectures. By transitioning to renewable energy sources, such as solar and wind power, organizations can significantly reduce their reliance on fossil fuels and decrease carbon emissions. The integration of renewable energy into data storage operations is facilitated by advancements in energy storage and distribution technologies, ensuring a stable and reliable energy supply even during periods of low generation. This shift not only supports sustainability goals but also offers potential cost savings in energy procurement, contributing to the economic viability of sustainable data storage solutions.

Moreover, the design and operation of energy-efficient data centers are integral to the realization of sustainable data storage solutions. Data centers, which house the infrastructure for data storage and processing, are significant contributors to global energy consumption. Implementing advanced cooling systems, efficient power distribution, and dynamic load balancing can substantially reduce energy usage and enhance overall efficiency. These practices, when combined with renewable energy adoption, create a comprehensive approach to sustainable data management, ensuring that data storage solutions are both ecologically and economically sustainable.

In conclusion, sustainable data storage solutions are essential for achieving the goals of Green AI and minimizing the environmental impact of AI technologies. By employing strategies such as data deduplication, compression, tiered storage, and renewable energy integration, organizations can optimize data storage practices, reducing energy consumption and promoting sustainability. As data volumes continue to grow, the importance of sustainable storage solutions will only increase, necessitating ongoing research and innovation in this field. The future of AI data architecture will likely be shaped by these sustainability initiatives, fostering the development of data systems that are both efficient and environmentally responsible.

Energy-efficient AI models

The pursuit of energy-efficient AI models is a cornerstone of Green AI, driven by the need to balance computational power with environmental sustainability. As AI models, particularly deep learning networks, grow in complexity, they demand substantial computational resources, leading to increased energy consumption and carbon emissions. Addressing this challenge requires innovative techniques that optimize the efficiency of AI models without compromising their performance.

One prominent approach to achieving energy efficiency is model pruning. This technique involves the systematic removal of redundant or non-essential parameters from AI models, effectively reducing their size and complexity. By eliminating these unnecessary components, pruned models require fewer computational resources for training and inference, thereby lowering energy consumption. Pruning can be applied at various stages of model development, from initial design to post-training refinement, offering flexibility in optimizing model efficiency.

Quantization is another critical technique employed to enhance the energy efficiency of AI models. It involves reducing the precision of model parameters, typically from floating-point to fixed-point representations. This reduction in precision translates to decreased memory and computational requirements, enabling more efficient processing and storage. Quantization is particularly beneficial for deploying AI models on resource-constrained devices, such as mobile phones and edge computing platforms, where energy efficiency is paramount.

In addition to pruning and quantization, model distillation plays a vital role in developing energy-efficient AI systems. Distillation involves transferring knowledge from a large, complex model (often referred to as the **teacher**) to a smaller, more efficient model (the **student**). The student model, trained to replicate the behavior of the teacher, achieves comparable performance with significantly reduced resource demands. This technique is instrumental in creating lightweight AI models that maintain high accuracy while minimizing energy consumption.

The development of energy-efficient AI models also benefits from advancements in hardware design. Specialized hardware accelerators, such as GPUs and TPUs, are optimized for AI workloads, delivering enhanced performance per watt compared to traditional CPUs. These accelerators, when combined with energy-efficient model architectures, contribute to the broader goals of Green AI by reducing the environmental impact of AI processes.

Role of renewable energy

The integration of renewable energy sources into AI infrastructure is a critical strategy for promoting sustainability and reducing the carbon footprint of AI technologies. As data centers and AI systems continue to expand, their reliance on traditional energy sources, primarily fossil fuels, contributes significantly to global carbon emissions. Transitioning to renewable energy sources, such as solar, wind, and hydroelectric power, offers a viable solution to mitigate these environmental impacts.

Renewable energy sources provide several advantages for powering AI infrastructure. They offer a sustainable and inexhaustible supply of energy, reducing dependency on finite fossil fuels and contributing to energy security. Additionally, renewable energy technologies have seen significant advancements in efficiency and cost-effectiveness, making them increasingly accessible for large-scale deployment. By harnessing renewable energy, organizations can power their data centers and AI systems with clean energy, significantly reducing their carbon emissions and contributing to global sustainability efforts.

The adoption of renewable energy in AI infrastructure is facilitated by innovations in energy storage and distribution technologies. Energy storage solutions, such as advanced battery systems and grid-scale storage, enable the efficient capture and utilization of renewable energy, even during periods of low generation. These storage technologies ensure a stable and reliable energy supply, addressing the intermittent nature of renewable sources and supporting continuous AI operations.

Moreover, the strategic placement of data centers in regions with abundant renewable energy resources can further enhance sustainability efforts. By locating data centers near sources of solar, wind, or hydroelectric power, organizations can optimize energy procurement and reduce transmission losses. This geographical alignment with renewable energy resources not only supports sustainability goals but also offers potential cost savings in energy procurement.

The transition to renewable energy is complemented by the implementation of energy-efficient practices within data centers. Techniques such as advanced cooling systems, efficient power distribution, and dynamic load balancing contribute to reducing energy consumption and enhancing overall efficiency. These practices, when combined with renewable energy adoption, create a comprehensive approach to sustainable data management and AI operations.

The pursuit of energy-efficient AI models and the integration of renewable energy sources are pivotal components of Green AI. These strategies address the dual challenges of performance optimization and environmental responsibility, ensuring that AI technologies contribute positively to global sustainability efforts. As organizations continue to embrace these practices, they will be better positioned to leverage the transformative potential of AI while minimizing its ecological impact. The future of AI data architecture will likely be shaped by these sustainability initiatives, fostering the development of AI systems that are both powerful and environmentally conscious.

Future directions

The future of Green AI and sustainable data architectures is likely to be shaped by ongoing advancements in AI technologies and the increasing demand for environmentally responsible practices. Research efforts are focused on developing more efficient AI models and data architectures that minimize energy consumption and environmental impact. The exploration of alternative computing paradigms, such as neuromorphic and quantum computing, offers promising avenues for achieving energy-efficient AI systems. As these technologies continue to evolve, they are expected to play a pivotal role in enabling sustainable AI practices and reducing the ecological footprint of AI technologies. Additionally, the integration of AI with emerging technologies, such as the **Internet of Things (IoT)** and edge computing, will further enhance the capabilities of sustainable data architectures, allowing organizations to process and analyze data in energy-efficient ways.

Green AI and sustainable data architectures represent a transformative approach to AI development, emphasizing the importance of environmental responsibility and sustainability. By prioritizing energy efficiency and reducing the environmental impact of AI processes, these initiatives offer significant opportunities to align AI advancement with ecological goals. While challenges remain in terms of performance optimization and infrastructure transition, the potential benefits of Green AI are immense. As organizations continue to explore and adopt sustainable practices, they will be better positioned to address the ecological challenges of the digital age and build AI systems that are both powerful and environmentally responsible. The future of AI data architecture will likely be shaped by the continued pursuit of sustainability, ensuring that AI technologies contribute positively to the global effort to combat climate change and promote environmental stewardship.

Natural language interfaces for data management

The advent of **natural language processing** (**NLP**) technologies has revolutionized the way humans interact with computers, enabling more intuitive and accessible interfaces for various applications. In the realm of data management, **natural language interfaces** (**NLIs**) have emerged as powerful tools that facilitate seamless communication between users and data systems. By leveraging NLP, NLIs allow users to query, manipulate, and analyze data using human language, thereby democratizing data access and enhancing user experience. This section explores the principles, applications, and implications of natural language interfaces for data management, highlighting their transformative potential in modern data architectures.

Role of NLP

NLP serves as the foundational technology that enables the creation and functionality of **natural language interfaces** (**NLIs**) within data management systems. As a subfield of artificial intelligence, NLP focuses on the interaction between computers and human language, encompassing a wide array of techniques designed to understand, interpret, and generate human language in a way that is both meaningful and actionable. This capability is crucial for bridging the gap between complex data systems and the intuitive, conversational interactions preferred by human users.

Understanding and interpretation

At the core of NLP is the ability to understand and interpret human language, which is inherently complex and nuanced. Human language is characterized by ambiguity, variability, and context dependence, posing significant challenges for computational models. NLP techniques address these challenges by employing sophisticated algorithms that parse and analyze linguistic structures, such as syntax and semantics, to derive meaning from text. This process involves the disambiguation of words and phrases, the recognition of named entities, and the extraction of relationships between linguistic elements. Through these capabilities, NLP enables computers to comprehend human language inputs, transforming them into structured data that can be processed by data management systems.

Generation and interaction

Beyond understanding, NLP also encompasses the generation of human language, enabling computers to produce responses and outputs that are coherent and contextually appropriate. This aspect of NLP is critical for facilitating interactive dialogues between users and data systems, allowing for dynamic exchanges of information. Techniques such as **natural language generation** (**NLG**) are employed to construct responses that are not only grammatically correct but also tailored to the user's query and context. This capability enhances the user experience by providing outputs that are easily interpretable and relevant, fostering more effective communication between users and data systems.

Machine learning and deep learning

The advancements in NLP have been significantly propelled by the integration of machine learning and deep learning techniques, which have revolutionized the way language models are developed and trained. Machine learning algorithms, particularly those based on neural networks, have demonstrated remarkable success in capturing the intricate patterns and dependencies inherent in human language. The advent of deep learning, with its capacity to model complex, non-linear relationships, has further enhanced NLP capabilities, enabling the development of models that can process vast amounts of linguistic data with high accuracy and efficiency. These models, such as transformers and recurrent neural networks, have set new benchmarks in NLP performance, driving the evolution of more sophisticated natural language interfaces.

Applications in data management

In the context of data management, NLP plays a pivotal role in enabling natural language interfaces to perform a variety of tasks, from query formulation and data retrieval to analytics and report generation. By translating human language queries into structured data commands, NLP empowers users to interact with data systems using conversational language, thereby democratizing data access. This capability is particularly valuable in environments where traditional query languages and interfaces may pose barriers to non-technical users. Moreover, NLP enhances the adaptability and responsiveness of data management systems, allowing them to cater to a diverse range of user needs and preferences. The role of natural language processing in enabling natural language interfaces for data management is both foundational and transformative. By facilitating the understanding, interpretation, and generation of human language, NLP bridges the gap between complex data systems and intuitive user interactions. As NLP technologies continue to advance, they will play an increasingly critical role in shaping the future of data management, ensuring that data systems are accessible, efficient, and capable of meeting the evolving demands of users in the digital age.

Natural language interfaces have wide-ranging applications in data management, offering new opportunities for enhancing data accessibility and usability. One of the primary applications is in query formulation and data retrieval, where NLIs enable users to express complex queries in natural language, bypassing the need for specialized query languages such as SQL. This capability is particularly beneficial for non-technical users, who may lack the expertise required to construct traditional data queries. By simplifying the query process, NLIs democratize data access, allowing users from diverse backgrounds to engage with data systems effectively.

In addition to query formulation, natural language interfaces facilitate report generation and analytics, enabling users to request and receive data insights in conversational language. This functionality supports decision-making processes by providing users with timely and relevant information, presented in an easily digestible format. The integration of NLIs with AI-driven analytics platforms further enhances their capabilities, allowing users to extract insights and make informed decisions based on natural language interactions. These applications contribute to more efficient and responsive data management practices, aligning with the goals of modern data architectures.

Designing user-centric interfaces

The design of user-centric interfaces is a critical component in the development of NLIs for data management systems. This approach emphasizes the creation of interfaces that prioritize the needs, preferences, and behaviors of users, ensuring that interactions with data systems are intuitive, efficient, and satisfying. The design process is informed by principles of **human-computer interaction** (**HCI**) and **user experience** (**UX**) design, which collectively aim to enhance the usability and accessibility of technological solutions.

Understanding user needs and contexts

A fundamental aspect of designing user-centric interfaces is a thorough understanding of the diverse needs and contexts of potential users. This involves conducting comprehensive user research to gather insights into the specific tasks users aim to accomplish, the challenges they face, and the environments in which they operate. Techniques such as interviews, surveys, and observational studies are employed to capture a holistic view of user requirements and expectations. By gaining a deep understanding of user contexts, designers can tailor interfaces to support a wide range of use cases, from simple data queries to complex analytical tasks, thereby ensuring that the interface is relevant and valuable to all users.

Prioritizing usability and accessibility

Usability and accessibility are paramount in the design of user-centric interfaces. Usability refers to the ease with which users can learn and effectively use an interface to achieve their goals. To enhance usability, designers focus on creating clear and consistent navigation structures, intuitive workflows, and responsive interactions. The interface should facilitate seamless user journeys, minimizing cognitive load and reducing the likelihood of errors. Accessibility, on the other hand, ensures that interfaces are usable by individuals with varying abilities and disabilities. This involves adhering to accessibility standards and guidelines, such as the **Web Content Accessibility Guidelines** (**WCAG**), to provide features like screen reader compatibility, keyboard navigation, and adjustable text sizes. By prioritizing usability and accessibility, designers create inclusive interfaces that cater to a broad spectrum of users.

Iterative design and user feedback

The process of designing user-centric interfaces is inherently iterative, involving continuous refinement based on user feedback and testing. Prototyping is a key method used to explore and evaluate design concepts, allowing designers to create low-fidelity models of the interface that can be tested with users. User testing sessions provide valuable insights into how users interact with the interface, revealing areas of friction and opportunities for improvement. Feedback gathered from these sessions informs iterative design cycles, where modifications are made to address identified issues and enhance overall user experience. This iterative approach ensures that the final interface is well-aligned with user needs and expectations, resulting in a more effective and engaging interaction.

Enhancing user engagement and satisfaction

Ultimately, the goal of designing user-centric interfaces is to enhance user engagement and satisfaction. Engagement is fostered through the creation of interfaces that are not only functional but also aesthetically pleasing and emotionally resonant. Visual design elements, such as color schemes, typography, and iconography, are carefully crafted to create an appealing and cohesive interface that resonates with users. Satisfaction is achieved when users feel empowered and confident in their ability to interact with the data system, experiencing minimal frustration and achieving their objectives efficiently. By focusing on user engagement and satisfaction, designers contribute to the development of interfaces that not only meet functional requirements but also deliver a positive and memorable user experience. The design of user-centric interfaces for natural language interfaces in data management systems is a multifaceted process that requires a deep understanding of user needs, a commitment to usability and accessibility, and an iterative approach to design refinement. By prioritizing these elements, designers can create interfaces that facilitate intuitive and effective interactions, ultimately enhancing the overall user experience and promoting the widespread adoption of natural language interfaces in data management.

Challenges and considerations

Despite their promising potential, the implementation of natural language interfaces in data management presents several challenges and considerations. One of the primary challenges is ensuring the accuracy and reliability of NLP models, which are critical for interpreting and processing natural language inputs. NLP models must be trained on diverse and representative datasets to achieve high levels of accuracy and generalization, necessitating ongoing research and development. Additionally, the integration of NLIs into existing data systems requires the development of new algorithms and protocols that can effectively translate natural language queries into actionable data tasks.

The ethical implications of natural language interfaces also warrant careful consideration, particularly in terms of data privacy and security. The use of NLIs raises concerns about the potential misuse of sensitive information, necessitating robust data governance frameworks to ensure the responsible handling of user data. Furthermore, the reliance on NLP models necessitates a high level of transparency and interpretability, ensuring that decision-making processes are understandable and accountable. Addressing these challenges requires a comprehensive approach that combines technical expertise with ethical and regulatory considerations.

Future directions and implications

The future of natural language interfaces for data management is likely to be shaped by ongoing advancements in NLP technologies and the increasing demand for intuitive and accessible data systems. As NLP techniques continue to evolve, organizations will have access to more sophisticated tools and methodologies for developing NLIs, enabling them to achieve even greater levels of usability and efficiency. The integration of NLIs with emerging technologies, such as voice recognition and augmented reality, offers promising avenues for enhancing user interaction and engagement. These developments have significant implications for industries such as healthcare, finance, and education, where natural language interfaces can facilitate more responsive and personalized data management practices. Natural language interfaces represent a transformative approach to data management, offering significant benefits in terms of accessibility, usability, and efficiency. By leveraging NLP technologies, NLIs enable users to interact with data systems using human language, democratizing data access and enhancing user experience. While challenges remain in terms of accuracy, integration, and ethics, the potential of natural language interfaces to revolutionize data management is undeniable. As organizations continue to explore and adopt NLIs, they will be better positioned to leverage the opportunities presented by the digital age, ensuring that their data architectures remain competitive and capable of meeting future challenges.

Data synthesis and simulation

In the rapidly evolving landscape of AI and data science, the ability to generate and manipulate data effectively is paramount. Data synthesis and simulation have emerged as critical methodologies that enable researchers and practitioners to create artificial datasets and model complex systems, addressing challenges such as data scarcity, privacy concerns, and the need for robust model validation. This section looks into the principles, methodologies, and applications of data synthesis and simulation, highlighting their significance in advancing AI technologies and enhancing data-driven decision-making.

Importance of data synthesis

Data synthesis refers to the process of generating artificial data that mimics the characteristics and patterns of real-world datasets. This capability is crucial in scenarios where access to real data is limited, either due to privacy restrictions, proprietary constraints, or the inherent scarcity of certain types of data. Synthetic data provides a viable alternative, enabling the training and testing of AI models without compromising sensitive information. Moreover, data synthesis allows for the creation of diverse and representative datasets, which are essential for developing robust and generalizable AI models. By simulating various scenarios and conditions, synthetic data can enhance model performance and reduce biases, contributing to more accurate and reliable AI systems.

Techniques for data synthesis

Data synthesis is a pivotal process in AI and data science, enabling the creation of artificial datasets that replicate the characteristics and patterns of real-world data. This capability is essential for addressing challenges such as data scarcity, privacy concerns, and the need for diverse training data in AI model development. Several sophisticated techniques have been developed to facilitate data synthesis, each offering unique advantages and applications.

Generative adversarial networks

GANs represent a groundbreaking approach to data synthesis, characterized by their ability to generate high-quality synthetic data through adversarial training. Introduced by *Ian Goodfellow* and colleagues in 2014, GANs consist of two neural networks: a generator and a discriminator. The generator's role is to produce synthetic data samples, while the discriminator's function is to evaluate the authenticity of these samples compared to real data. The two networks are trained simultaneously in a competitive process, where the generator strives to create realistic data that can deceive the discriminator, and the discriminator aims to distinguish between real and synthetic data. This adversarial dynamic drives the generator to improve iteratively, resulting in synthetic datasets that closely resemble the original data distribution. GANs have been successfully applied in various domains, including image synthesis, text generation, and anomaly detection, demonstrating their versatility and efficacy in data synthesis.

Variational autoencoders

Variational autoencoders (VAEs) offer a probabilistic approach to data synthesis, leveraging latent variable models to generate new data samples. VAEs consist of an encoder and a decoder, which work together to transform input data into a latent space and subsequently reconstruct it. The encoder maps input data to a latent representation, characterized by a distribution over latent variables. From this latent space, new data samples can be drawn by decoding latent variables, allowing for the generation of continuous and structured data. VAEs are particularly effective in applications where data synthesis requires the preservation of underlying structures and relationships, such as in image synthesis and generative modeling. The probabilistic nature of VAEs ensures that synthetic data retains the variability and complexity of real-world data, contributing to more robust and generalizable AI models.

Rule-based and statistical methods

In addition to neural network-based approaches, rule-based and statistical methods are employed for data synthesis, offering flexibility and control over the data generation process. Rule-based methods involve the use of predefined rules and logic to generate synthetic data, ensuring that specific patterns and structures are maintained. These methods are particularly useful in domains where data generation requires adherence to strict guidelines or regulations, such as in financial modeling and healthcare data synthesis. Statistical methods, such as Monte Carlo simulations and agent-based modeling, employ probabilistic techniques to model the distributions and interactions of variables within a system. Monte Carlo simulations utilize random sampling to explore a wide range of possible outcomes, providing insights into the variability and uncertainty inherent in complex systems. Agent-based modeling simulates the interactions of autonomous agents within a defined environment, offering valuable insights into emergent phenomena and system-level dynamics.

The techniques for data synthesis are diverse and multifaceted, encompassing neural network-based approaches, probabilistic models, and rule-based and statistical methods. Each technique offers distinct advantages, enabling the generation of synthetic data that is realistic, diverse, and representative of real-world datasets. By leveraging these techniques, researchers and practitioners can address critical challenges in AI model development, enhancing data availability, privacy, and robustness. As data synthesis techniques continue to evolve, they will play an increasingly vital role in shaping the future of AI and data science, ensuring that synthetic data contributes positively to the advancement of AI technologies and data-driven decision-making.

Simulation for model validation

Simulation is a fundamental methodology in the validation and testing of AI models, providing a controlled environment in which model performance can be rigorously assessed under a variety of conditions. The use of simulation techniques enables researchers to replicate real-world scenarios, thereby facilitating a comprehensive evaluation of model accuracy, robustness, and scalability. This process is critical in ensuring that AI models are reliable and effective prior to deployment in real-world applications.

In the realm of AI model validation, simulation serves as a tool for exploring the dynamics and interactions within complex systems. Agent-based modeling is one such simulation technique that is particularly useful for studying systems characterized by autonomous agents operating within a defined environment. This approach allows researchers to simulate the behavior and interactions of individual agents, providing insights into emergent phenomena and system-level dynamics. By modeling the decision-making processes and interactions of agents, researchers can assess the impact of various factors on system behavior, thereby informing the development of more effective AI models. Agent-based modeling is employed in diverse fields, including social networks, ecological systems, and market dynamics, where understanding the intricacies of agent interactions is paramount.

Monte Carlo simulations represent another widely utilized technique in model validation, particularly in scenarios where uncertainty and variability are inherent. This statistical method employs random sampling to model the probability distributions of uncertain variables, enabling the exploration of a wide range of possible outcomes. By simulating numerous iterations, Monte Carlo simulations provide a comprehensive understanding of model behavior and performance, supporting robust and informed decision-making. This technique is particularly valuable in risk analysis, financial modeling, and decision-making processes, where accurately capturing the variability of inputs is essential for predicting outcomes and assessing risks.

The advancement of simulation technologies has significantly enhanced the capabilities of model validation processes. High-fidelity simulations, which aim to accurately replicate the physical and functional characteristics of real-world systems, offer unprecedented opportunities for detailed and realistic representations of complex systems. These simulations leverage advanced computational models and high-performance computing resources to achieve precision and accuracy in replicating system behavior. High-fidelity simulations are increasingly being used in engineering, healthcare, and autonomous systems, where understanding the nuances of system behavior is crucial for ensuring reliability and effectiveness. By providing a comprehensive understanding of system dynamics, high-fidelity simulations facilitate the testing and validation of AI models, ensuring their robustness and efficacy in real-world applications.

Digital twins, which are virtual replicas of physical assets or processes, represent a cutting-edge advancement in simulation technologies. These virtual models enable real-time monitoring and analysis, providing valuable insights into system performance and potential improvements. By integrating AI and machine learning algorithms, digital twins can simulate various scenarios and predict future outcomes, supporting proactive decision-making and optimization. The use of digital twins in model validation offers significant advantages, allowing researchers to test AI models in a dynamic and interactive environment that closely mirrors real-world conditions. Simulation for model validation is a critical component of the AI development process, offering valuable insights into model performance and reliability. Through techniques such as agent-based modeling, Monte Carlo simulations, high-fidelity simulations, and digital twins, researchers can rigorously assess AI models, ensuring their robustness and effectiveness prior to deployment. As simulation technologies continue to evolve, they will play an increasingly vital role in shaping the future of AI model validation, contributing to the development of AI systems that are both reliable and capable of meeting the demands of complex and dynamic environments.

Advancements in simulation technologies

The field of simulation technologies has experienced significant advancements over recent years, fundamentally transforming the way AI models are validated and tested. These innovations have enabled more precise and detailed representations of complex systems, facilitating comprehensive evaluations of AI model performance under various conditions. As simulation technologies continue to evolve, they offer unprecedented opportunities for enhancing the reliability and effectiveness of AI systems across diverse applications.

High-fidelity simulations

High-fidelity simulations have emerged as a pivotal advancement in the realm of simulation technologies, offering detailed and realistic representations of real-world systems. These simulations leverage sophisticated computational models and high-performance computing resources to replicate the physical and functional characteristics of complex systems with precision. The ability to model intricate interactions and dynamics within a system allows researchers to gain a deeper understanding of system behavior, informing the development of more robust AI models. High-fidelity simulations are increasingly employed in fields such as engineering, healthcare, and autonomous systems, where accurately capturing the nuances of system behavior is crucial for ensuring reliability and effectiveness. By providing a comprehensive understanding of system dynamics, high-fidelity simulations facilitate rigorous testing and validation processes, ensuring that AI models are equipped to handle real-world challenges.

Digital twins

Digital twins represent a cutting-edge advancement in simulation technologies, offering dynamic and interactive virtual replicas of physical assets or processes. These virtual models enable real-time monitoring and analysis, providing valuable insights into system performance and potential improvements. By integrating AI and machine learning algorithms, digital twins can simulate various scenarios and predict future outcomes, supporting proactive decision-making and optimization. The use of digital twins in model validation offers significant advantages, allowing researchers to test AI models in environments that closely mirror real-world conditions. This capability is particularly valuable in industries such as manufacturing, energy, and transportation, where understanding the intricacies of system behavior is essential for optimizing operations and enhancing efficiency. The dynamic nature of digital twins allows for continuous updates and refinements, ensuring that simulations remain relevant and accurate as system conditions evolve.

Computational advancements

The advancements in simulation technologies have been significantly propelled by developments in computational power and resources. **High-performance computing (HPC)** systems provide the necessary infrastructure for conducting complex simulations, enabling the processing of large datasets and intricate models with speed and efficiency. The integration of parallel computing techniques further enhances the capabilities of simulation technologies, allowing for the simultaneous execution of multiple simulation tasks and the exploration of diverse scenarios. These computational advancements have facilitated the scalability of simulation processes, enabling researchers to conduct detailed analyses of large-scale systems and environments. The ability to harness computational power effectively is critical for advancing simulation technologies and ensuring that they remain capable of addressing the demands of increasingly complex and dynamic systems.

Implications for AI model validation

The advancements in simulation technologies have profound implications for AI model validation, offering new possibilities for enhancing the reliability and effectiveness of AI systems. By providing detailed and realistic representations of complex systems, high-fidelity simulations, and digital twins enable researchers to conduct comprehensive evaluations of model performance, identifying potential limitations and areas for improvement. These technologies facilitate the testing of AI models in diverse scenarios, ensuring that they are equipped to handle real-world challenges and uncertainties. The integration of advanced computational techniques further enhances the scalability and efficiency of simulation processes, supporting robust and informed decision-making. As simulation technologies continue to evolve, they will play an increasingly vital role in shaping the future of AI model validation, contributing to the development of AI systems that are both reliable and capable of meeting the demands of complex and dynamic environments.

The advancements in simulation technologies represent a transformative development in the field of AI model validation, offering significant benefits in terms of precision, realism, and scalability. Through innovations such as high-fidelity simulations and digital twins, researchers can gain valuable insights into system behavior and dynamics, informing the development of robust and effective AI models. As computational power continues to advance, the capabilities of simulation technologies will expand, enabling more comprehensive and detailed analyses of complex systems. These advancements are essential for ensuring that AI models are equipped to handle real-world challenges, contributing to the reliability and effectiveness of AI systems across diverse applications.

Applications in AI and data science

Data synthesis and simulation have wide-ranging applications in AI and data science, offering new possibilities for enhancing model development, testing, and deployment.

In the field of healthcare, synthetic data is used to train AI models for medical imaging, diagnostics, and personalized medicine, addressing privacy concerns and enabling the exploration of rare conditions. In autonomous systems, simulation environments provide a safe and controlled setting for testing self-driving cars, drones, and robotics, ensuring their safety and reliability before real-world deployment.

In finance, data synthesis and simulation are employed for risk assessment, fraud detection, and algorithmic trading, enabling the modeling of complex market dynamics and the evaluation of investment strategies. In manufacturing and supply chain management, digital twins and high-fidelity simulations support predictive maintenance, process optimization, and resource allocation, driving efficiency and reducing operational costs.

Data synthesis and simulation represent transformative methodologies in the realm of AI and data science, offering significant benefits in terms of data availability, model validation, and system optimization. By enabling the generation of realistic synthetic data and the simulation of complex systems, these techniques address critical challenges such as data scarcity, privacy, and model robustness. As research and development in data synthesis and simulation continue to advance, they will play an increasingly vital role in shaping the future of AI data architecture, ensuring that AI technologies are robust, reliable, and capable of meeting the demands of a rapidly changing world.

AI-powered self-optimizing data systems

The rapid evolution of AI and machine learning technologies has ushered in a new era of data management, characterized by self-optimizing data systems. These systems leverage AI to autonomously monitor, analyze, and optimize data processes, enhancing efficiency, scalability, and reliability. This paper explores the principles, architecture, and implications of AI-powered self-optimizing data systems, highlighting their transformative potential in modern data environments.

In the contemporary landscape of data management, the volume, velocity, and variety of data have increased exponentially, presenting significant challenges for traditional data systems. To address these challenges, AI-powered self-optimizing data systems have emerged as a promising solution. These systems utilize AI algorithms to continuously monitor data operations, identify inefficiencies, and implement optimization strategies autonomously. By integrating AI into data management processes, self-optimizing systems enhance performance, reduce operational costs, and improve data quality, aligning with the goals of modern data architectures.

Principles of self-optimization

The concept of self-optimization in data systems revolves around the ability to adapt and improve autonomously in response to changing conditions and requirements. This is achieved through the integration of AI algorithms that analyze data operations in real-time, identifying patterns, anomalies, and opportunities for optimization. Key principles underpinning self-optimization include adaptability, scalability, and autonomy. Adaptability ensures that the system can respond to dynamic data environments, adjusting processes to maintain optimal performance. Scalability allows the system to handle increasing data volumes and complexities without compromising efficiency. Autonomy enables the system to operate independently, minimizing the need for human intervention and streamlining data management processes.

Architecture of AI-powered self-optimizing systems

The architecture of AI-powered self-optimizing data systems is a sophisticated construct designed to enable autonomous monitoring, analysis, and optimization of data processes. This architecture integrates advanced AI and machine learning algorithms with robust data management frameworks, ensuring that the system can adapt to dynamic environments and improve performance continuously. This section looks into the key components and functionalities that define the architecture of self-optimizing systems, exploring how these elements work together to achieve autonomy and efficiency.

AI and machine learning models

At the heart of self-optimizing systems are AI and machine learning models that process real-time data streams to extract actionable insights. These models are trained on extensive datasets to recognize patterns, identify anomalies, and predict future trends. The training process involves the use of supervised, unsupervised, and reinforcement learning techniques, depending on the specific requirements and objectives of the system. Supervised learning models are employed to make predictions based on labeled data, while unsupervised learning models are used to identify patterns and structures in unlabeled data. Reinforcement learning models, on the other hand, enable the system to learn optimal strategies through trial and error, adapting to changing conditions and improving over time.

The integration of these models into the system architecture allows for continuous monitoring and analysis of data operations. By processing data in real-time, the models can detect inefficiencies, bottlenecks, and opportunities for optimization, informing the system's decision-making processes. This capability is critical for ensuring that the system remains responsive and adaptable, maintaining optimal performance in dynamic data environments.

Data ingestion and processing layers

The architecture of self-optimizing systems includes data ingestion and processing layers that facilitate the seamless flow of data throughout the system. The data ingestion layer is responsible for collecting data from various sources, including databases, sensors, and external systems. This layer ensures that data is captured in a timely and efficient manner, supporting real-time analysis and decision-making. The processing layer, meanwhile, is tasked with transforming raw data into a format suitable for analysis by AI models. This involves data cleaning, normalization, and integration, ensuring that the data is accurate, consistent, and comprehensive.

These layers are designed to handle diverse data types and formats, enabling the system to process structured, semi-structured, and unstructured data efficiently. The flexibility of the data ingestion and processing layers is crucial for ensuring that the system can accommodate a wide range of data sources and applications, supporting scalability and adaptability.

Feedback loops and learning mechanisms

A defining feature of self-optimizing systems is the incorporation of feedback loops and learning mechanisms that enable the system to refine its optimization strategies over time. Feedback loops involve the continuous monitoring of system performance and the evaluation of optimization actions. By analyzing the outcomes of these actions, the system can assess its effectiveness and make necessary adjustments to improve future performance.

Learning mechanisms, such as reinforcement learning, play a critical role in this process, allowing the system to learn from its experiences and develop more effective strategies. These mechanisms enable the system to adapt to changing conditions and requirements, ensuring that it can maintain optimal performance in dynamic environments. The integration of feedback loops and learning mechanisms is essential for achieving autonomy, minimizing the need for human intervention, and enhancing the system's ability to self-optimize.

Integration with existing data systems

The architecture of AI-powered self-optimizing systems is designed to integrate seamlessly with existing data systems and infrastructures. This integration is facilitated through the use of standardized protocols and interfaces, ensuring compatibility and interoperability with legacy systems. By leveraging existing data infrastructures, self-optimizing systems can enhance their capabilities and extend their reach, supporting a broader range of applications and use cases.

The integration process involves the alignment of data models, schemas, and workflows, ensuring that the self-optimizing system can access and utilize relevant data effectively. This alignment is critical for ensuring that the system can operate efficiently within existing data environments, minimizing disruptions and maximizing the benefits of self-optimization.

The architecture of AI-powered self-optimizing data systems is a complex and multifaceted construct that integrates advanced AI and machine learning models with robust data management frameworks. By incorporating real-time data processing, feedback loops, and learning mechanisms, these systems achieve autonomy and adaptability, enabling continuous optimization of data processes. The architecture's ability to integrate with existing data systems further enhances its capabilities, supporting a wide range of applications and use cases. As research and development in AI technologies continue to advance, the architecture of self-optimizing systems will play an increasingly vital role in shaping the future of data management, ensuring that data systems are efficient, scalable, and capable of meeting the demands of a rapidly changing world.

Applications and use cases

AI-powered self-optimizing data systems are increasingly being recognized for their transformative potential across various industries. These systems leverage artificial intelligence to autonomously monitor, analyze, and optimize data processes, leading to enhanced efficiency, reduced operational costs, and improved data quality. This section explores the diverse applications and use cases of self-optimizing data systems, highlighting their impact in sectors such as telecommunications, finance, and healthcare.

Telecommunications

In the telecommunications industry, AI-powered self-optimizing data systems play a crucial role in optimizing network performance and ensuring seamless connectivity. The exponential growth in data traffic, driven by the proliferation of digital devices and services, necessitates efficient resource management to maintain service quality. Self-optimizing systems address this need by analyzing network traffic patterns in real-time and predicting demand fluctuations. By dynamically allocating resources, such as bandwidth and processing power, these systems enhance network efficiency and reduce latency. The ability to autonomously adjust network configurations based on real-time data insights ensures that telecommunications providers can deliver high-quality services while minimizing operational costs.

Finance

The financial sector benefits significantly from the deployment of self-optimizing data systems, particularly in the areas of fraud detection and risk management. Financial institutions face the ongoing challenge of safeguarding against fraudulent activities and managing risks associated with transactions and investments. Self-optimizing systems offer a proactive solution by continuously monitoring financial transactions and analyzing patterns to identify suspicious activities. Through the application of machine learning algorithms, these systems can detect anomalies and implement preventive measures in real-time, enhancing security and reducing the financial impact of fraud. Additionally, self-optimizing systems contribute to risk management by analyzing market data and predicting trends, enabling financial institutions to make informed decisions and optimize investment strategies.

Healthcare

In the healthcare industry, AI-powered self-optimizing data systems are instrumental in improving patient care and resource management. The complexity and variability of healthcare data present challenges in delivering personalized and effective treatment plans. Self-optimizing systems address these challenges by analyzing patient data to identify optimal treatment pathways, ensuring that healthcare providers can deliver tailored care that meets individual patient needs. Furthermore, these systems enhance resource allocation within healthcare facilities, optimizing the management of patient loads and reducing wait times. By autonomously adjusting resource distribution based on real-time data insights, self-optimizing systems contribute to more efficient healthcare operations and improved patient outcomes.

AI-powered self-optimizing data systems have demonstrated their value across a range of industries, offering significant benefits in terms of efficiency, cost savings, and data quality. In telecommunications, finance, and healthcare, these systems enhance operational performance by autonomously optimizing data processes based on real-time insights. The ability to dynamically adjust configurations and resource allocations ensures that organizations can respond effectively to changing conditions and demands. As the adoption of self-optimizing systems continues to grow, their impact will likely expand, driving innovation and efficiency in data management practices across diverse sectors. The ongoing advancements in AI technologies will further enhance the capabilities of self-optimizing systems, solidifying their role as a critical component of modern data architectures.

Challenges and considerations

Despite their promising potential, the implementation of AI-powered self-optimizing data systems presents several challenges and considerations. One of the primary challenges is ensuring the accuracy and reliability of AI models, which are critical for effective optimization. These models must be trained on diverse and representative datasets to achieve high levels of accuracy and generalization, necessitating ongoing research and development.

Data privacy and security are also significant considerations in the deployment of self-optimizing systems. The continuous monitoring and analysis of data raise concerns about the potential misuse of sensitive information, necessitating robust data governance frameworks to ensure responsible data handling. Additionally, the reliance on AI algorithms requires a high level of transparency and interpretability, ensuring that decision-making processes are understandable and accountable.

Future directions and implications

The future of AI-powered self-optimizing data systems is likely to be shaped by ongoing advancements in AI technologies and the increasing demand for efficient and scalable data management solutions. As AI algorithms become more sophisticated, self-optimizing systems will be able to handle more complex data environments, enhancing their capabilities and applications. The integration of emerging technologies, such as edge computing and the IoT, will further enhance the potential of self-optimizing systems, enabling real-time optimization in distributed and decentralized environments.

The implications of AI-powered self-optimizing data systems are profound, offering new opportunities for enhancing efficiency, reducing costs, and improving data quality across various industries. By automating data management processes, these systems free up valuable resources, allowing organizations to focus on strategic initiatives and innovation. As organizations continue to explore and adopt self-optimizing systems, they will be better positioned to leverage the opportunities presented by the digital age, ensuring that their data architectures remain competitive and capable of meeting future challenges.

AI-powered self-optimizing data systems represent a transformative approach to data management, offering significant benefits in terms of efficiency, scalability, and reliability. By leveraging AI algorithms to autonomously monitor and optimize data processes, these systems enhance performance, reduce operational costs, and improve data quality. While challenges remain in terms of accuracy, privacy, and transparency, the potential of self-optimizing systems to revolutionize data management is undeniable. As research and development in AI technologies continue to advance, self-optimizing systems will play an increasingly vital role in shaping the future of data architectures, ensuring that they are robust, efficient, and capable of meeting the demands of a rapidly changing world.

Conclusion

The exploration of future trends and emerging technologies in AI data architecture presented in this chapter underscores the transformative impact of artificial intelligence on modern data management practices. As organizations navigate the complexities of increasing data volume and diversity, AI-driven solutions offer innovative approaches to enhance efficiency, scalability, and decision-making capabilities. The integration of technologies such as natural language processing interfaces, self-optimizing systems, and data synthesis and simulation has demonstrated significant potential in addressing current challenges while opening new avenues for innovation. AI-powered self-optimizing systems, in particular, have shown remarkable promise in autonomously enhancing performance and optimizing data processes across various industries, including telecommunications, finance, and healthcare. These systems reduce operational costs and improve data quality, freeing resources for strategic initiatives and fostering innovation. Similarly, advancements in data synthesis and simulation methodologies provide robust tools for overcoming data scarcity and privacy concerns, ensuring the reliability and accuracy of AI models.

As AI technologies continue to evolve, their role in shaping the future of data architecture will become increasingly vital. The ongoing development of sophisticated AI algorithms and models will enhance the capabilities of data systems, enabling them to handle complex and dynamic environments more effectively. By embracing these advancements, organizations can ensure that their data architectures remain competitive, robust, and capable of meeting the demands of a rapidly changing world. This chapter's insights into emerging trends and technologies serve as a foundation for understanding and leveraging AI's transformative potential in the digital age.

Join our Discord space

Join our Discord workspace for latest updates, offers, tech happenings around the world, new releases, and sessions with the authors:

https://discord.bpbonline.com

Index

www.ingramcontent.com/pod-product-compliance
Lightning Source LLC
Chambersburg PA
CBHW061800210326
41599CB00034B/6826